THE FATHERS
OF THE CHURCH

A NEW TRANSLATION

VOLUME 11

THE FATHERS OF THE CHURCH

A NEW TRANSLATION

EDITORIAL BOARD

HERMIGILD DRESSLER, O.F.M.
Quincy College
Editorial Director

ROBERT P. RUSSELL, O.S.A.
Villanova University

THOMAS P. HALTON
The Catholic University of America

WILLIAM R. TONGUE
The Catholic University of America

SISTER M. JOSEPHINE BRENNAN, I.H.M.
Marywood College

FORMER EDITORIAL DIRECTORS

LUDWIG SCHOPP, ROY J. DEFERRARI, BERNARD M. PEEBLES

SAINT AUGUSTINE

COMMENTARY ON THE
LORD'S SERMON ON THE MOUNT
WITH
SEVENTEEN RELATED SERMONS

Translated by
DENIS J. KAVANAGH, O.S.A.

THE CATHOLIC UNIVERSITY OF AMERICA PRESS
Washington, D.C.

NIHIL OBSTAT:
JOHN M. A. FEARNS, S.T.D.
Censor Librorum

IMPRIMATUR:
✠ FRANCIS CARDINAL SPELLMAN
Archbishop of New York
January 26, 1951

The *nihil obstat* and *imprimatur* are official declarations that a book or pamphlet is free of doctrinal or moral error. No implication is contained therein that those who have granted the *nihil obstat* and *imprimatur* agree with the contents, opinions, or statements expressed.

Library of Congress Catalog Card No. 863-18827
ISBN 0-8132-1085-2
ISBN-13 978-0-8132-1085-8 (pbk.)

Copyright © 1951 by
THE CATHOLIC UNIVERSITY OF AMERICA PRESS
All rights reserved
Second Printing 1963
Third Printing 1977
Fourth Printing 1988
First short-run reprint 2001

CONTENTS

INTRODUCTION 3

COMMENTARY ON THE LORD'S SERMON ON THE MOUNT

    Book I 19

    Book II 109

RETRACTATIONS

    Book I: Chapter 19 201

SERMONS

    53. ON THE BEATITUDES 211

    54. HOW TO 'LET YOUR LIGHT SHINE BEFORE MEN' 227

    55. ON TAMING THE TONGUE 233

    56. ON THE LORD'S PRAYER 239

    60. ON ALMSGIVING 259

    61. ON ALMSGIVING 275

72. ON ALMSGIVING	287
94. THE SLOTHFUL SERVANT	293
109. THE ADVERSARY	295
346. ON LIFE'S PILGRIMAGE	301
4 (Denis). CHRIST: LAMB AND LION	307
5 (Denis). LIFE FROM DEATH	331
6 (Denis). THE HOLY EUCHARIST	321
7 (Denis). SONSHIP OR SERVITUDE	327
8 (Denis). ON BAPTISM	331
13 (Denis). CHRIST: THE GLORY OF MARTYRS	339
11 (Morin). ON THE BEATITUDES	357
INDEX	375

WRITINGS
OF
SAINT AUGUSTINE

VOLUME 3

INTRODUCTION

HE COMMENTARY presented in translation in this volume is one of fourteen works composed by St. Augustine[1] during the period of four or five years which elapsed between the dates of his ordination to the priesthood in 391 and his elevation to the episcopate in 395 or 396.[2] He himself tells us that he composed this work within the years 393-394, but he gives no information regarding any special circumstances which may have occasioned its composition.[3] His purpose in composing it may have been to give a more elaborate and complete treatment to a whole section of the Gospel which he had already expounded piecemeal in several of his earliest sermons in the cathedral at Hippo. For, as he expressly states in another work,[4] he believed that an oral discourse ought not ordinarily deal with difficult or complicated questions, but that all such questions ought to be fully discussed in a written treatise. He may therefore have intended this *Commentary* to serve as the complement

---

1 Of St. Augustine it is especially true that his works cannot be fully appreciated without an intimate knowledge of his character and the circumstances which influenced its formation. Hence, the reader is referred to the Foreword to Vol. 5 of this series.
2 Cf. *Retractations* 1.14-27. It used to be generally accepted that Augustine's consecration took place in the year 395 (Dom Germain Morin, in *Revue Bénédictine* [1928] 366). A. Casamassa, O. S. A., assigns that event to the year 396, and advances very convincing reasons in favor of that contention (*Enciclopedia italiana*, s. v. Agostino, Aurelio).
3 *Retractations* 1.19.
4 *De doctrina Christiana* 4.9.23.

to his earliest sermons. At any rate, it is rightly regarded as 'a product of Augustine's preaching during the years of his priesthood.'[5]

In exegesis, as in other departments of sacred science, St. Augustine is unexcelled in versatile originality. Through rare power of intuition, he gains a spiritual insight which scholarship alone would not enable him to obtain. Of course, he has notable limitations, for he had had no formal training in exegetical discipline or Biblical scholarship; and at no time in his life did his Biblical apparatus approach that of an Origen or a Jerome. But, just as his early entanglement in Manichaeism occasioned the development of his critical acumen in evaluating philosophic theories, so also did it furnish occasion for the development of that spiritual acumen which is so discernible in his exegetical works.

From his devout Christian mother he undoubtedly acquired at least some vague notion of the Scriptures during his childhood years at Tagaste, although the *Discipline of the Secret* would in those days forbid her giving him any systematic instruction in Christian doctrine.[6] At any rate, in his nineteenth year—when he first resolved to devote himself exclusively to a search for truth—he decided to seek it in the sacred Scriptures. Disdaining their simple style and finding himself unable to understand their content, he put them aside as unworthy of his further attention. As an 'auditor' among the Manichaeans for the following nine years, he became even more disdainful of the Scriptures; he could neither accept the childish interpretations which the Manichaeans offered nor discover anything but absurdity in the corrupt texts which they used. All this resulted in a state of mind which Augustine clearly reveals in the pages of his *Confes-*

---

5 A. Cassamassa, *loc. cit.*
6 See below, 2.2.7, n. 7; Sermon 6 (Den), n. 6.

sions, but which even such a keen analyst as Augustine himself cannot fully describe or explain. Even when he had severed his association with the Manichaeans, he still believed that their objections to the Scriptures were unanswerable, yet he yearned to discuss those objections with some learned Christian, for he remembered that a certain Elpidius had confounded the Manichaeans at Carthage.[7]

This was his state of mind with regard to the Scriptures when he first heard St. Ambrose preach in the cathedral at Milan. Overcoming the prejudice which he had fostered for about twelve years, he again took up a study of the Scriptures, for he was now anxious to investigate the claims of any system except Manichaeism and the false philosophic systems which he had alternately embraced and rejected during the fitful course of his distressing odyssey in search of truth. By this time he had put aside the pride which had led him to despise the Bible because of its unadorned style. Meanwhile, however, he had imbibed false notions which rendered him unable to understand its meaning, because he was now unable to conceive the notion of a spiritual being. In other words, he was unable to conceive the notion of a being in actual existence without dimensions in space. At this juncture, however, he sought and received prudent guidance in his approach to the study of the Scriptures, and, following this guidance, he first read the Latin translation of certain Neo-Platonic works.[8] This study led him to the process of

---

7 *Confessions* 3.4-6; 4.1.1.; 5.11.21; *Enarr. in ps.* 146.13.
8 *Confessions* 7.9.13. In this passage of the *Confessions,* Augustine says that he read 'certain books of the Platonists,' but elsewhere in the same work (8.2.5), he refers to them as 'certain books of the Platonists which Victorinus ... had translated into Latin.' Since Victorinus had translated the works of Plotinus and Porphyry, we conclude that Augustine is referring to the writings of those Neo-Platonists. This is in keeping with his use of the term; in the *City of God* (8.12), he expressly names Plotinus, Iamblichus, and Porphyry as eminent Platonists.

introspection, and, by reflecting on his own mind and its operations, he was finally able to grasp the notion of spiritual being. Having thus overcome what used to seem to him an unsurmountable obstacle, he rejoiced to find that he could now discern the spiritual meaning of certain scriptural texts which he had considered absurd when the Manichaeans were interpreting them in the literal sense. In this he was immeasurably aided by following the method which he saw St. Ambrose employing in his sermons at the cathedral. It is chiefly to this Ambrosian influence that we are to ascribe Augustine's lifelong tendency toward the symbolic interpretation of the Scriptures. 'And I used to rejoice to hear Ambrose, in his sermons to the people, frequently repeating the text, *The letter kills, but the spirit gives life,* and most earnestly commending it as a guiding principle; for when he had removed the mystical veil, he would reveal the spiritual meaning of those passages which seemed to teach falsehood when they were interpreted literally.'[9]

While his deception by the Manichaeans thus served as the occasion for his acquiring familiarity with the Scriptures and a certain competency in interpreting them, it did not furnish him with the technical training which scholarly exegesis requires. At the time of his ordination he had no mastery of any other language than Latin, although he was able to converse in Punic, his mother's native tongue.[10] It is true that in adolescence he was compelled to read the Greek classics in the school at Tagaste; but the compulsion engendered in him a strong dislike for that language, and we may safely assume that he afterwards retained no particular in-

---

9 *Confessions* 6.4.6.
10 In one of his sermons (167.3.4), he says: 'There is a well known Punic proverb, which I shall give you in Latin because not all of you understand the Punic.'

terest in it. In his early thirties, when he was avidly reading the Neo-Platonists, he was not reading those works in the original Greek, but in a Latin translation.[11] In his exegetical works, however, he reveals such a competency in Greek that we must conclude that at some time after his conversion—perhaps immediately after his ordination to the priesthood[12] —he took up the study of that language. In no small measure, it was this knowledge that enabled him to correct so many faulty expressions in the pre-Vulgate Latin versions of the Scriptures.[13] His own confidence with regard to his knowledge of Greek is revealed in the following passage from one of his letters to St. Jerome: 'We therefore give thanks to God for that work of yours in which you have translated the Gospel from the Greek; for, on the whole, there is scarcely any discrepancy when we compare it with the Greek Scripture.'[14] This confidence with regard to his knowledge of Greek is in sharp contrast with his diffidence regarding his knowledge of Hebrew, a language which he said he did not know.[15] However, his familiarity with the Punic gave him a certain advantage with regard to Hebrew. Sometimes, he availed himself of this advantage in his efforts to interpret Hebrew words or expressions: 'The *Anointed* is called the *Messias*. In Greek, the Anointed is called the Christ. In Hebrew, He is called the Messias; for, in the Punic tongue, the word, *messe*, has the same meaning as the word, *anoint*. The Hebrew, the Punic, and the Syriac are cognate and

---

11 *Confessions* 7.9.13.
12 *Epist.* 21.3.6.
13 Cf. De Bruyne, 'Saint Augustin reviseur de la Bible,' in *Miscellanea Agostiniana* (Rome 1931) 2 521-606.
14 *Epist.* 71.4.6.
15 *Epist.* 101.4. For examples of this confidence and this diffidence, cf. *Locut. in Pentateuchum, passim.*

similar.'[16] At other times, he sought the desired information from someone who was competent in Hebrew, as when he consulted 'a certain Hebrew' or the works of 'a certain learned Syrian Christian.'[17]

Although textual criticism was not Augustine's forte as an exegete, he did not wholly neglect that province of exegesis. As a result of his long association with the Manichaeans, he realized the danger arising from the use of corrupt texts and faulty translations of the Scriptures. He was, therefore, extremely cautious with regard to the numerous Latin versions which were current in his day. He regarded the *Itala* as the most faithful of all those versions, but he maintained that all Latin versions—the *Itala* included—ought to be verified by a comparison with the Greek texts. He believed that the most reliable Greek texts were those that were preserved in the churches which were distinguished for diligence and learning. With regard to the Old Testament, he ascribed pre-eminent authority to the Septuagint, because the Apostles were said to have used it and because it had received such universal acceptance in the Church. Furthermore, he believed that God had provided the Septuagint version for the instruction of the Gentiles in the same manner in which He had provided the Hebrew text for the instruction of the Hebrews, and that the Holy Spirit had inspired the Septuagint translators to deviate at times from the Hebrew text in order to express the truth in the manner in which God willed it to be expressed to the Gentiles.[18]

Like many of his contemporaries, he accepted from his pre-

---

16 *In Joan. evangel. tr.* 16.27. 'Messias, a word which—like many or nearly all Hebrew words—sounds like Punic.' (*Contra litt. Petil.* 2.104.239). Cf. H. J. Vogels, 'Die heilige Schrift bei Augustinus,' in Grabmann-Mausbach, *Aurelius Augustinus* (Cologne 1930) 414f.
17 Cf. below. 1.9.23; *De Gen. ad litt.* 1.18.36.
18 *De doctrina Christiana* 2.15.22; *De civitate Dei* 18.43.

decessors the account of the origin of the Septuagint version as attributed to the Pseudo-Aristeas, and repeated by Flavius Josephus and Philo of Alexandria. Unlike St. Jerome, he did not positively reject the added legend that each of the seventy-two Hebrew scholars was confined to a solitary cell and precluded from all communication with the others during the course of the translation, that each one of them made a complete translation of all the Hebrew books of the Old Testament without conferring or consulting with any of the others, and that all those independent translations were found to agree with one another word for word. However, he never made that legend the basis of any of his opinions or contentions, and he made ample allowance for the possibility of its falsity. 'But if (as we are told, and as many trustworthy men assert) those seventy interpreters made the translation while they were confined in solitary cells... On the other hand, if they so engaged in consultation that their version became one through general discussion and common judgment, not even then would it be fitting or proper for any one man, however skillful, to hope to improve what so many learned elders have agreed on.'[19] His own quotations from the Old Testament are taken either from the *Itala* or from some very similar African versions; in comparison with the Vulgate, they conform more closely with a direct translation from the Septuagint.[20]

In the work in which he expressly devotes himself to the treatment of exegesis in its twofold aspect, 'the method of discovering that which ought to be known, and the method of imparting that which has been learned,'[21] he devotes the

---

19 *De doctrina Christiana* 2.15.22; cf. *De civ. Dei* 18.42, where he explicitly states that there were seventy-two translators.
20 Cf. P. Capelle, 'Le texte du Psautier latin en Afrique' (*Collect. bibl. lat.* 4, Rome 1913). In the present translation, minor variations are ignored; attention is directed to those that are notable.
21 *De doctrina Christiana* 1.1.1.

fourth book to the treatment of rhetoric and sacred oratory. Throughout the other three books of the work, he deals minutely with the knowledge and disposition requisite for an understanding of the Scriptures. Among the necessary or useful attainments for an exegete, he lists a knowledge of Hebrew and Greek, natural history and astronomy, music and numeration, history, logic and philosophy.[22] Confessing his own deficiency in some of those requirements, he expresses the wish that some capable scholar would compile a dictionary of the Bible which would contain an explanation of 'the places, animals, plants, precious stones, metals, and other kinds of things mentioned in the Scripture.'[23]

Far more illuminating as to his own personality and far more illustrative of his reverent attitude toward the Scriptures is the disposition which he requires in the earnest exegete. 'In the holy Scriptures the God-fearing man makes a diligent search for a knowledge of God's will. When he has become so meek through piety that he is averse to strife, so equipped with a knowledge of languages that he will not be hindered by unfamiliar words and expressions, so versed in the relationships of things that he will be able to understand the nature and significance of figurative expressions, and when he has also the advantage of a text which skillful and diligent emendation has rendered accurate, then let him undertake the task of discussing and interpreting ambiguous expressions in the Scriptures.'[24] It is true that this description of his ideal exegete is found in a work which he had not yet composed when he was writing the present *Commentary,* but it is plain that he was conforming with this ideal while he was writing the *Commentary.* Throughout the whole work,

---

22 *Id.* 2.11.16; 16.24; 29.45; 16.26.25; 28.42; 31.48; 50.60.
23 *Ibid.* 39.59; cf. *De utilitate credendi* 3.5.
24 *Ibid.* 3.1.1.

he stands revealed as a God-fearing man engaged in a diligent search of the Scripture for a knowledge of God's will. 'He approaches the Scripture with the disposition of a child of God, rather than with the attitude of a scholar.'[25]

For furnishing examples of St. Augustine's lofty range of thought, venturesome originality, and profound speculation, this *Commentary* does not compare with his celebrated works *On Genesis,* and *On the Trinity.* But, in the judgment of competent critics, it is the most exact of his exegetical works.[26] In tone and content, it re-echoes and complements his homilies and sermons, for it differs from them in exactly the manner and degree in which St. Augustine himself believed that a written treatise ought to differ from oral discourses on the same subject.[27] This fact adds plausibility to the assumption that he wrote it expressly as a complement to his early sermons at Hippo. And for this reason, it has been deemed advisable to include in this volume a translation of some of the sermons of St. Augustine, in order to present to the reader two complementary forms of that author's exegesis:[28] the written treatise and the oral discourse. It is not to be assumed, however, that the sermons chosen for inclusion in this volume are the very sermons which St. Augustine had preached before he wrote the Commentary, for it is only in rare instances that the exact date of any of his sermons can be accurately determined. In fact, those earliest sermons of his may not have been preserved in their original form.

---

25 Maurice Pontet, *L'exégèse de S. Augustin* (Paris 1944) 152.
26 'Le plus exacts de ses livres d'exégèse'—Richard Simon, *Histoire critique du Nouveau Testament;* quoted by Pontet, *op. cit.* 230.
27 See note. 4.
28 On Augustine's theory and practice of preaching, cf. Sister M. Inviolata Barry, *St. Augustine, the Orator* (Washington 1940) ; A Kunzeman, O.S.A., 'Augustinus Predigttätigkeit'; Grabman-Mausbach, *Aurelius Augustinus* (Köln 1930) 155-168; R. E. Regan, O.S.A., 'St. Augustine the Preacher,' *Tagastan* (Washington 1946) 62-80.

At any rate, St. Augustine would have had good reason for wishing to revise them, because he had been constrained to preach them at a time when he was convinced that he was as yet unprepared to do so.

In the Africa of Augustine's day, the office of preaching was reserved to the bishop, but in the churches of the East, priests used to preach, even in the presence of the bishop. Valerius, a Greek, was Bishop of Hippo in 391. He lacked a ready command of the language used by the people of his diocese; Latin was for him a foreign tongue. Familiar with the practice in the Eastern churches, he introduced it into his diocese, and commissioned Augustine to preach regularly in the cathedral immediately after his ordination to the priesthood.[29] But Augustine feared to assume the office, because he was convinced that he was as yet unprepared to discharge that duty. He accordingly asked to be allowed to postpone the discharge of this duty for a brief period, 'for instance, until Easter,' in order to prepare himself for it by prayer and a study of the Scriptures. With reference to the new duties imposed upon him, he writes in his letter of petition to the bishop: 'But neither in boyhood nor in the early years of manhood did I learn what is the proper mode of discharging these duties; and at the very time when I was beginning to learn it, I was constrained on account of my sins (for I know not what else to think) to accept the second place at the helm when as yet I knew not how to handle an oar ... My duty is to study with diligence all the remedies which the Scriptures contain for such a case as mine, and to devote myself to prayer and reading in order that my mind may acquire the health and vigor necessary for labors so responsible. This I have not yet done, because I have not had time; for I was

---

29 Saint Possidius, *Sancti Augustini vita* cap. 5.

INTRODUCTION 13

ordained at the very time when we were thinking of a season, free from cares, in which we could devote ourselves to the study of the Scriptures ... I implore you by your charity and affection to have pity on me and to grant me as much time as I have asked for the purpose I have mentioned.'[30]

Even if we assume that this request was granted by the bishop, we may nevertheless assume, also, that the period of time allowed for Augustine's preparation was too short to enable him to prepare sermons which would win his own approval after he had acquired some experience in preaching. Of his sermons in general, he himself says: 'My own sermon nearly always displeases me,'[31] and also: 'I confess that I endeavor to be one of those who write by progressing, and who progress by writing.'[32] We may, therefore, well suppose that, when he had acquired a certain proficiency in preaching, he would wish to revise the sermons which he had preached in the meantime. This supposition is strengthened by the fact that in none of his extant sermons is there any reference to his inexperience as a preacher; for, in view of his many expressions of regret regarding his defects as a preacher, it is very likely that in his earliest sermons he made some reference to his inexperience.

Hence, the sermons included in this volume are not presented as those which Augustine expanded into the *Commentary*. Ten of them have been chosen because they expound the same texts of Scripture which are treated in the Commentary, and thus afford the reader an opportunity to compare Augustine's written treatise with his oral discourses. We believe the other seven sermons have a special interest arising from the twofold fact that they were never included in any

---
30 *Epist.* 21.3.6.
31 *De catechizandis rudibus* 2.
32 *Epist.* 143.2.

edition of the complete works of St. Augustine and that they have not hitherto appeared in an English translation.

The latest edition of the complete works of St. Augustine[33] contains 363 sermons and twenty-two fragments which are listed as certainly authentic. In addition, it contains thirty-three sermons which are qualified as doubtfully authentic, and 313 sermons which are designated as spurious. Since then, various libraries have yielded at least 640 additional manuscript sermons which were attributed to St. Augustine and which—rightly or wrongly—were severally accepted as authentic by eminent scholars. From the year 1792, when twenty-five of those sermons were published at Vienna, to the year 1930, when thirteen of them were published in various periodicals, they have been published in various separate collections. The smallest of those collections contained two sermons; the largest, 249. The noted scholar, Dom Germain Morin, submitted all these sermons to the most rigorous critical tests, in order to determine their genuineness, and he pronounced 138 of them to be authentic. These authenticated sermons were published in one collection in the *Miscellanea Agostiniana* (Rome 1930) and constitute the entire first volume of that publication. From that collection, seven sermons have been chosen for translation and inclusion here.

St. Augustine's pre-eminence as a model for sermon-writers in the Middle Ages is clearly indicated by the fact that more than 500 extant medieval sermons are so closely modeled on his sermons as to mislead eminent scholars into the belief that he was really their author.[34] If these additional sermons had indeed been composed by St. Augustine, that fact would merely show that he was the author of an almost incredible

---
33 The Maurist edition, 1683.
34 *Miscellanea Agostiniana* (Rome 1930) 1 vii-ix.

number of sermons. If these, indeed, were the only medieval sermons that had been modeled on those of St. Augustine, they would still show that he was extensively imitated by sacred orators in the Middle Ages. But, when we bear in mind that, as a rule, only relatively few sermons are preserved, and that only those which imitated Augustine so closely as to deceive eminent scholars are counted in the more than 500, then we can merely imagine the extent of his influence on sacred oratory during the Middle Ages. In the words of Bishop Shahan, Augustine's writings formed the reservoir which 'fed richly for a thousand years the piety and the preaching of priest and monk and saint.'[35] Windelband says that in the realm of philosophy, Augustine was 'the real teacher of the Middle Ages.'[36] It is not equally true to say that he was also the universal model for preachers in the Middle Ages?

---

[35] *Catholic World* (1930) 580.
[36] *Lehrbuch der Geschichte der Philosophie* (5th ed., Tübingen 1910) 220.

SAINT AUGUSTINE

Commentary on the Lord's

SERMON ON THE MOUNT

Translated
by
Denis J. Kavanagh, O. S. A., S. T. D.
Augustinian College
Washington, D.C.

Imprimi potest:

JOSEPH M. DOUGHERTY, O.S.A.
Prior Provincialis

THOMAS F. ROLAND, O.S.A.
Censor Librorum

February 26, 1951

BOOK I

Chapter 1 (Matt. 5.1-3)

IF ANYONE piously and earnestly ponders the Discourse which Our Lord Jesus Christ delivered on the Mount —as we read in the Gospel according to Matthew[1]— I believe that he will find therein, with regard to good morals, the perfect standard of the Christian life. We do not venture to make this statement rashly; we infer it from the very words of the Lord Himself. Indeed, that Discourse is brought to a conclusion in such a manner that it evidently contains all the precepts which pertain to the formation of such a life, for the Lord brings it to a close with the following words: 'Everyone therefore who hears these words of mine and acts according to them, I shall liken him to a wise man who built his house on a rock: the rain fell, the floods came, the winds blew and beat against that house; but it did not fall, for it had its foundation on a rock. And everyone who hears these words of mine, and does not act according to them, I shall liken him to a foolish man who built his house on sand: the rain fell, the floods came, the winds blew and beat a-

---

[1] The Sermon on the Mount, as recorded in Matthew 5-7. In this translation, based on the third Benedictine Edition (Venice 1807), the portions of the Sermon that are to be treated in each chapter will be cited within parentheses at the head of that chapter, and—without further citation—they will be italicized whenever they occur within the body of the chapter itself. Other Scriptural texts will be cited, but not italicized.

gainst that house; and it fell, and great was its ruin.'² Therefore—since He did not say merely 'Who hears my words,' but said, furthermore, 'Who hears these words of mine'—He has, I believe, made it sufficiently clear that the words which He spoke on the Mount give such complete instruction for the conduct of those who wish to live in accordance with them that those men are rightly compared to one who builds upon a rock. I have made this observation so that it may be clear that this Discourse is thoroughly composed of all the precepts by which the Christian life is formed. But there will be a more diligent treatment of this topic in its proper place.

(2) This Discourse begins as follows: *'And when he had seen the great crowds, he went up the mountain. And when he was seated, his disciples drew near to him. And opening his mouth, he taught them, saying, . . .'* If inquiry is made as to what the mountain signifies, it is rightly understood to signify the higher precepts of justice, for the precepts that had been given to the Jews were lower. Yet, through His holy prophets and servants and in accordance with a most orderly arrangement of circumstances, the same God gave the lower precepts to a people whom it behooved to be bound by fear; through His Son, He gave the higher precepts to a people whom it befitted to be set free by charity. When lesser things are given to a weaker people and greater things are given to a stronger, they are given by Him who alone knows how to proffer to the human race a medicine adapted to its circumstances. Nor is it any wonder that the same God who has made heaven and earth gives higher precepts for the sake of the kingdom of heaven and lower precepts for the sake of the earthly kingdom. Therefore, through the Prophet,

---

2 Matt. 7.27.

it is said with regard to this justice which is higher: 'Thy justice is as the mountains of God.'[3] And this rightly signifies that it is taught on the mountain by the One Master who alone is fit to teach such sublime thoughts. And He is seated while teaching, as befits the dignity of the office of teacher. And His disciples drew near to Him—so that they might be physically nearer to hear His words, since they were approaching Him in spirit to fulfill His precepts. *'And opening his mouth, he taught them, saying, . . .'* With regard to the redundant phrase, *'and opening his mouth,'* perhaps even this brief suspense indicates that the Discourse will be rather long; or perhaps there is some significance in the fact that He who in the Old Law used to open the mouths of the Prophets is now said to have opened His own mouth.

(3) What, therefore, does He say? *'Blessed are the poor in spirit, for theirs is the kingdom of heaven.'* Concerning the striving after temporal things, we read what is written: 'All is vanity and presumption of spirit.'[4] Now, presumption of spirit means arrogance and pride. Moreover, the proud are commonly said to have high spirits—and rightly so, because the wind also is called a spirit. Accordingly it is written: 'Fire, hail, snow, ice, spirits of tempest.'[5] And who does not know that the proud are said to be puffed up, as if bloating with wind? Hence, also, that saying of the Apostle: 'Knowledge puffs up, but charity edifies.'[6] Here, therefore, the poor in spirit are rightly understood as the humble and the God-fearing—that is to say, those who do not have a bloated spirit. And it would be entirely unfitting for blessedness to take its beginning from any other source, since it is to reach the sum-

---
3 Ps. 35.7.
4 Eccle. 1.14; a slight variant from the Vulgate. Cf. Introduction, note 20.
5 Ps. 148.8.
6 1 Cor. 8.1.

mit of wisdom, for 'the beginning of wisdom is the fear of the Lord,'[7] and on the other hand, pride is described as 'the beginning of all sin.'[8] Let the proud, therefore, strive after the kingdoms of the earth, and love them. But, *'Blessed are the poor in spirit, for theirs is the kingdom of heaven.'*

Chapter 2 (Matt. 5.4-9)

(4) *'Blessed are the meek, for they shall inherit the land.'* This, I believe, is the land of which it is said in the Psalm: 'Thou art my hope, my portion in the land of the living.'[1] For it denotes a certain firmness and stability of a perpetual inheritance, where, through its love for the good, the soul finds rest as in its proper place, just as the body finds rest on the land; where the soul is nourished by its proper food, just as the body is nourished from the land. For the saints this is, indeed, life and rest. The meek are those who submit to iniquities and do not resist evil, but overcome evil with good.[2] Let the haughty, therefore, quarrel and contend for earthly and temporal things. But, *'Blessed are the meek, for they shall inherit the land'*—the land from which they cannot be expelled.

(5) *'Blessed are they that mourn, for they shall be comforted.'* Mourning is grief over the loss of things that are highly prized. Those who have been converted to God are losing the things which in this world they used to embrace as precious things, for they find no delight in the things which they used to enjoy. They are torn with grief until a love for eternal things is begotten in them. They shall be com-

---
7 Eccli. 1.16; Ps. 110.10.
8 Eccli. 10.15.

---
1 Ps. 141.6.
2 Cf. Rom. 12.21.

forted, therefore, by the Holy Spirit—who on this account especially is called the Paraclete, that is, the Comforter—so that, when they have lost temporal happiness, they may fully enjoy the eternal.

(6) *'Blessed are they who hunger and thirst for justice, for they shall be satisfied.'* He calls them lovers of the true and unchangeable goodness. Therefore, they shall be satisfied with that food of which the Lord Himself says: 'My food is to do the will of my Father'[3]—and this is justice. And they shall be satisfied with that water, of which, as the same Lord says: 'Whosoever shall drink, it shall become in him a fountain of water springing up unto life everlasting.'[4]

(7) *'Blessed are the merciful, for they shall obtain mercy.'* He calls those blessed who come to the aid of the miserable, because their reward is so great that they shall be freed from misery.

(8) *'Blessed are the pure of heart, for they shall see God.'* How foolish, then, are those who try to find God through the use of their bodily eyes! It is through the heart that God is seen, and in another passage it is written: 'Seek Him in simplicity of heart.'[5] A simple heart is a heart that is pure; and, just as the light which surrounds us cannot be seen except through eyes that are clear, so neither is God seen unless that through which He can be seen is pure.

(9) *'Blessed are the peacemakers, for they shall be called the children of God.'* Where there is no contention, there is perfect peace. And, because nothing can contend against God, the children of God are peacemakers; for, of course, children ought to have a likeness to their father. And those who calm their passions and subject them to reason, that is, subject

---
3 John 4.34.
4 John 4.14.
5 Wisd. 1.1.

them to mind and spirit, and who keep their carnal lusts under control—those engender peace within themselves and become a kingdom of God. [They become a kingdom] in which all things are so well ordered that everything in man which is common to us and to the beasts is spontaneously governed by that which is chief and pre-eminent in man, namely, mind and reason; and that this same pre-eminent faculty of man is itself subject to a still higher power, which is Truth Itself, the only begotten Son of God. Man is unable to rule over the lower things unless he in turn submits to the rule of a higher being. And this is the peace which is promised 'on earth to men of good will.'[6] This is the life of a man of consummate and perfect wisdom. The prince of this world, who rules over the perverse and disorderly, has been cast out of a thoroughly pacified and orderly kingdom of this kind. When this peace has been established and strengthened within a man, then he who has been cast out —no matter what persecutions he may stir up from without— increases the glory which is according to God. He does not weaken anything in the edifice, but, by the fact that his devices are of no avail, he makes known what great internal stability has been established. Therefore, the next is, *'Blessed are they who suffer persecution for justice' sake, for theirs is the kingdom of heaven.'*

Chapter 3 (Matt. 5.10)

(10) Each of those eight pronouncements is a maxim. For, confining the rest of the Discourse to those who were then present, He addresses them, saying: 'Blessed will you be when men speak evil of you and persecute you.'[1] But He gave a

---
6 Luke 2.14.

---
1 Matt. 5.11.

universal application to the foregoing maxims. He did not say: 'Blessed are you, poor in spirit; for yours is the kingdom of heaven; He said: 'for theirs is the Kingdom of heaven.' And neither did He say: 'Blessed are you who are meek, for you will possess the land'; He said: 'because they will possess the land.' And so with regard to the other maxims up to the eighth, where He says: *'Blessed are they who suffer presecution for justice' sake, for theirs is the kingdom of heaven.'* At this point, He at once begins to direct His words to those who were present, although the previous pronouncements pertained also to His assembled audience, and although what was said later and seems to be addressed especially to those who were present pertains also to those who were not present or to those of later ages. Hence, the very number of maxims is worthy of careful consideration; for the first mentioned source of blessedness is humility: 'Blessed are the poor in spirit'; that is to say: Blessed are those who are not puffed up while the soul is submitting to divine authority, fearful that it may be on the way to punishments after this life, even though it may deem itself blessed in this life. Now it takes up the study of the divine Scriptures. Here it must act with the meekness of piety, lest it become so bold as to censure whatever seems absurd to the uninstructed, and become indocile through obstinacy in disputing. From this study it begins to see by what worldly fetters it is being held because of sins and the way of the flesh. In this third stage there is understanding; therefore, there is mourning, since the supreme good is being lost because of a clinging to goods that are lowest. In the fourth stage there is labor, because the mind is eagerly striving to extricate itself from the things in which it is entangled by a baneful pleasantness; great fortitude is needed, because whatever is possessed with delight is not relinquished without sorrow. But in the fifth stage a means of escape is offered to those who are persevering in labor; no one is capable of extricating himself from the entanglements of such great miseries unless he is aided by one who is more powerful. The counsel is reasonable, therefore, that whoever wishes to be aided by some one more powerful should give aid to one who is weaker where he himself happens to be less weak. Therefore, 'Blessed are the merciful, for they shall obtain mercy.'[2] In the sixth stage there is purity of heart; by a blessed consciousness of good deeds the pure heart is able to contemplate the supreme good, which cannot be discerned except by a pure and serene intellect. Finally, the seventh maxim is wisdom itself: it is the contemplation of truth, making the whole man peaceful, and taking on the likeness of God. It is summed up in this way: 'Blessed are the peacemakers, for they shall be called the children of God.'[3] The eighth maxim returns, as it were, to the beginning: it presents and approves something consummate and perfect. Thus, the kingdom of heaven is named both in the first maxim and in the eighth. In the first: 'Blessed are the poor in spirit, for theirs is the kingdom of heaven.' And as though in answer to the question: 'Who shall separate us from the love of Christ? Shall tribulation, or distress, or persecution, or hunger, or nakedness, or danger, or the sword'[4]—as though in answer to this question, He says: *'Blessed are they who suffer persecution for justice' sake, for theirs is the kingdom of heaven.'* Therefore, there are seven maxims which constitute perfection, for the eighth starts anew, as it were, from the very beginning: it clarifies and approves what is already complete. Thus, all the other grades of perfection are accomplished through these seven.[5]

---

2 Matt. 5.7.
3 Matt. 5.9.
4 Rom. 8.35.
5 St. Augustine enumerates the beatitudes, not by reason of the classes

Chapter 4 (Matt. 5.3-9)

(11) It seems to me, therefore, that the sevenfold operation of the Holy Spirit, of which Isaias speaks,[1] coincides with these stages and maxims. However, the order is different. In Isaias, the enumeration begins from the higher, while here it begins from the lower; in the former, it starts from wisdom and ends at the fear of God. But, 'the fear of the Lord is the beginning of wisdom.'[2] Therefore, if we ascend step by step, as it were, while we enumerate, the first grade is the love of God; the second is piety; the third is knowledge; the fourth is fortitude; the fifth is counsel; the sixth is understanding; the seventh is wisdom. The fear of God coincides with the humble, of whom it is here said: *'Blessed are the poor in spirit.'* That is to say: Blessed are those who are not puffed up, not proud—those to whom the Apostle says: 'Be not high-minded, but fear.'[3] That is, be not exalted. Piety coincides with the meek, for, if a man piously searches the Sacred Scripture and does not reprehend what as yet he does not understand, he honors the Sacred Scripture and, consequently, he does not resist it. This is meekness. Therefore, it is said at this point: *'Blessed are the meek.'* Knowledge coincides with those who mourn. The mourners are those who, having learned from the Scriptures, already know by what evils they are being

---

of persons to whom they are promised, but by reason of the distinct blessings that are promised. Since the same blessing is promised in the first pronouncement and in the eighth, he enumerates only seven beatitudes. He finds an analogy between this number of beatitudes and the seven gifts of the Holy Ghost, as well as the seven petitions in the Lord's Prayer (Cf. 2.11.38; 2.25.87). St. Ambrose, however, says that Matthew enumerates eight beatitudes, while Luke enumerates only four, but that the meaning is the same in both enumerations *Expos. in Luc.* 5.6.

1 Isa. 11.2.
2 Eccli. 1.16.
3 Rom. 11.20.

withheld, namely, those evils which they had mistakenly sought as good and useful things. Now it is said of them: *'Blessed are those who mourn.'* Fortitude coincides with those who hunger and thirst, for they labor while they are desiring to rejoice in things that are truly good, and they are longing to turn their love away from earthly and corporeal things. Of them it is said here: *'Blessed are they who hunger and thirst for justice' sake.'* Counsel coincides with the merciful, for the only remedy for escaping such great evils is to forgive as we wish to be forgiven and to aid others when we can, just as we wish to be aided by others when our own powers are insufficient. Of them it is written here: *'Blessed are the merciful.'* Understanding coincides with the pure of heart: it coincides with those of that cleansed eye, so to speak, by which that can be discerned which the corporeal eye has not seen, which the ear has not heard, and which has not entered into the heart of man.[4] Of them it is said here: *'Blessed are the pure of heart.'* Wisdom coincides with the peacemakers, for with peacemakers all things are in proper order, and no passion is in rebellion against reason, but everything is in submission to man's spirit because that spirit is obedient to God.[5] Here it is said of them: *'Blessed are the peacemakers.'*

(12) But the same reward—which is the kingdom of heaven—has received various names in proportion to those several degrees of perfection. Very fittingly, the kingdom of heaven has been placed first, for it is the perfect and supreme wisdom of the rational soul. Therefore, it has been announced in this way: *'Blessed are the poor in spirit, for theirs is the kingdom'*—as though the saying were: 'The fear of the Lord is the beginning of wisdom.'[6] To the meek—as to chil-

---
4 Isa. 64.4; 1 Cor. 2.9.
5 See *Retractations* 1.19.1.
6 Eccli. 1.16; Ps. 110.10; Prov. 9.10.

dren piously seeking a father's bequest—an inheritance is assigned: *'Blessed are the meek, for they shall inherit the land.'* To the mourners—as to those who know what they have lost, and in what miseries they are immersed—comfort is imparted: *'Blessed are they who mourn, for they shall be comforted.'* To the hungry and thirsty—as to men laboring and stoutly striving for salvation and, therefore, in need of refection—food unto fullness is offered: *'Blessed are they who hunger and thirst for justice' sake, for they shall be satisfied.'* To the merciful—as to those who so follow the true and righteous counsel that what they bestow on those who are weaker is bestowed on themselves by someone more powerful—mercy is rendered: *'Blessed are the merciful, for they shall obtain mercy.'* To the pure of heart—as to those who keep the eye cleansed for discerning eternal realities—the power to see God is awarded: *'Blessed are the pure of heart, for they shall see God.'* To the peacemakers—as to those who are perfected in wisdom, and conformed to the image of God through regeneration unto the new man—likeness to God is imparted: *'Blessed are the peacemakers, for they shall be called the children of God.'* And all these grades of perfection can be attained even in this present life, as we believe them to have been fully attained in the case of the Apostles.[7] But, as to that complete change into the angelic form which is promised after this present life—that change cannot be expounded through the medium of any kind of words. Therefore: *'Blessed are they who suffer persecution for justice' sake, for theirs is the kingdom of heaven.'* Perhaps this eighth maxim—which returns to the beginning, and designates the perfect man—is signified both by the circumcision on the eighth day in the Old Testament and by the Lord's Resurrection after the Sabbath (which is indeed both the eighth day and the first), and by the observance of the octave feasts which we celebrate

---

7 See *Retract.* 1.19.2.

on the occasion of the regeneration of the new man.[8] It may also be signified by the very word, Pentecost,[9] for, if what may be called an eighth unit is added to the product of seven times seven (which is forty-nine), a kind of return to the beginning is made on the day when the Holy Spirit was sent. For, by Him we are led to the kingdom of heaven, and receive an inheritance, and are comforted and fed and obtain mercy and are cleansed and rendered peaceful. When we are thus rendered perfect, we inwardly sustain all the afflictions brought upon us on account of truth and justice.

Chapter 5 (Matt. 5.11-12)

(13) *'Blessed shall you be when men reproach you, and persecute you, and speaking falsely, say all manner of evil against you on account of me. Rejoice and exult, because your reward is great in heaven.'* Whoever in the Christian household seeks after the delights of this world and the wealth of temporal things, let him bear in mind that our bliss is within us, as is said by the mouth of the Prophet with regard to the soul of the Church: 'All the beauty of the king's

---

8 The feasts of Easter and Pentecost; see below, Sermon 6 (Den), n. 6. The newly baptized ceased to be called 'competents' and began to be called 'infants.' Garbed in their white robes, they assembled in the church each day throughout the following week. Several of Augustine's sermons were delivered on those occasions. With regard to those two octaves, he says: 'Ecclesiastical custom has confirmed the practice . . . of making the eight days of the neophytes distinct from all other days' (*Epist.* 55.16.32. Cf. *Sermons* 228.1; 260.1).

9 *Pentēcostē* [*hēmera*] means the fiftieth day. Like nearly all the Church Fathers and other Christian writers from Irenaeus to Venerable Bede, Augustine attached a mystical signification to numbers, as recorded in the Scripture. His exegetical works abound in mystical interpretations. (See above, 1.4.11; see below, 1.11.30; 1.19.61; 2.25.87. Cf. Van Lierde, *Doctrina Sancti Augustini* [Würzburg 1935] *passim*) While he speaks of 'particular numbers which the divine Scriptures especially commends, such as seven, ten, twelve, and so forth, he expressly rejects the claim of the Donatist, Tichonius, that there are certain mystical rules which clarify all the obscurities of the Scriptures. (*De doct. christ.* 3.30.43; 3. 35. 51.)

daughter is within';¹ for reproaches and persecutions and detractions are promised from without. From these things, however, there is a great reward in heaven—a reward which is felt in the heart of those sufferers who are able to say: 'We glory in tribulations, knowing that tribulation works out endurance; and endurance, trial; and trial, hope. And hope does not confound, because the love of God is diffused in our hearts by the Holy Spirit who has been given to us.'² Now, the profitable thing is, not suffering those evils, but bearing them with equanimity and cheerfulness for the sake of Christ. Many heretics suffer many such evils while they are deceiving souls through the Christian name. But they are excluded from that reward, precisely because the pronouncement is not merely: 'Blessed are they who suffer persecution,' for there is the added phrase, namely, 'for justice' sake.' Justice cannot be where there is not sound faith, for justice lives by faith.³ And let the schismatics not hope for any part of that reward, because it is likewise true that where there is not love there cannot be justice, for 'love does no evil to a neighbor.'⁴ If they had love, they would not rend asunder the body of Christ, 'which is the Church.'⁵

(14) It may be asked how the expression, 'When men speak ill of you,' differs from the saying, 'They will speak all manner of evil against you,' for 'to speak ill' is the same as 'to speak evil.'⁶ But, when an evil word is insultingly uttered

---
1 Ps. 44.14.
2 Rom. 5.3-5.
3 Hab. 2.4; Rom 1.17.
4 Rom. 13.10.
5 Col. 1.24. In his writings against the Donatists, Augustine gives elaborate treatment to his twofold theme—the unity of the Church, as the body of Christ, and the lack of charity, as the reason for schism. 'Why do you [Donatists] wish to destroy the body of Christ? He is one. Why do you wish to make His people two? . . . The body of Christ was left unbroken at the hands of His persecutors, but the body is not left unbroken at the hands of Christians.' (*Enarr. in ps.* 33.7).
6 '*Maledicere*' and '*malum dicere.*'

in the presence of him against whom it is spoken—as they said to Our Lord: 'Do we not speak the truth, that thou art a Samaritan and hast a devil?'[7]—it is not hurled in the same manner as when the reputation of an absent man is injured —as the case in which it is likewise written of Our Lord: 'Some were saying, "He is a prophet"; but others were saying, "No, but he is seducing the populace."'[8] But, to persecute is to attack by force or to seize by stratagem, as was done by the man who betrayed Our Lord and by those who crucified Him. The statement is not made in such general terms as to promise you a blessing whenever 'they will speak all manner of evil against you.' It is restricted by the phrases, 'speaking falsely,' and, 'on account of me,' and I believe that this restriction is made in order to forestall those who would glory in persecution and ignominy, and who would claim that Christ is with them just because evils are being imputed to them even when such evils are being rightfully ascribed to their error. And if at times many false charges are hurled at them—a thing which frequently happens through the temerity of men—they nevertheless do not suffer those evils on account of Christ; for no one is a follower of Christ unless he is called a Christian in accordance with the true faith and Catholic discipline.

(15) *'Rejoice,'* He says, *'and exult, because your reward is great in heaven.'* I believe it is not the upper regions of this visible world that are mentioned here, for our reward—which is bound to be constant and eternal—cannot rest on changeable and temporal things. But I think that the expression, *'in heaven,'* is the same in meaning as the expression, 'in the spiritual firmament'—where sempiternal justice resides. For, in contrast with this firmament, an unrighteous person

---

7 John 8.48.
8 John 7.12.

is called 'earth.' To man in the state of sin it was said: 'Earth thou art, and to the earth shalt thou go.'[9] And of this heaven the Apostle says: 'Our conversation is in heaven.'[10] Accordingly, they already experience this reward who rejoice in spiritual things, but it will be absolutely perfect when this mortal body will have put on immortality.[11] *'For so did they persecute,'* says He, *'the Prophets who were before you.'* Here, he mentioned persecution in general—persecution through maledictions and persecution through slander. And He gave exhortation through an apposite illustration. For, persecution is the usual lot of those who proclaim the truth; yet the Prophets of old did not—through fear of persecution—desist from preaching the truth.

Chapter 6 (Matt. 5.13-15)

(16) *'You are the salt of the earth.'* This very properly comes next, for it points out that we are to regard as foolish those men who—while either striving after an abundance of temporal goods or fearing a scarcity of them—lose the eternal blessings which men can neither give nor take away. *'But if salt becomes insipid, with what shall it be salted?'* In other words, if through fear of persecution you lose the kingdom of heaven, how, then, will there be any men through whom your wavering may be removed? God has chosen you, in order to remove, through you, the wavering from the rest of men; through you the peoples are to be, as it were, preserved from corruption. Therefore, insipid salt *'is of no use but to be thrown out and trodden underfoot by men.'* Consequently, the one who is trodden underfoot by men is not the man who suffers persecution, but the man who becomes foolish by fearing

---
9 Gen. 3.19.
10 Phil. 3.20.
11 1 Cor. 15.53.

persecution. No one can be trodden underfoot unless he is underneath, and a man is not underneath if his heart is fixed in heaven, even though he may be enduring many bodily evils on earth.

(17) *'You are the light of the world.'* In the same sense in which He called them the salt of the earth in the foregoing sentence, He now calls them the light of the world. In the foregoing sentence we are to understand, not this earth which we tread with corporeal feet, but the men who dwell on the earth, and especially those who are sinners, for the salting and searing of whose putrid sores the Lord has sent apostolic salt. In this present sentence we are to undertand that the term, *'world,'* does not denote the earth and the sky, but that it denotes the men who are in the world or those who love the world—men for whose enlightenment the Apostles have been sent. *'A city set on a mountain cannot be hidden.'* This means a city that is established on pre-eminent justice. And this is signified by the very Mount on which the Lord is delivering the Discourse. *'Neither do men light a lamp and set it under the measure.'* What are we to think of this? Are we to think that the phrase, *'under the measure,'* is employed in such a way that only the hiding of a lamp is to be understood?—just as if He were to say: 'No one lights a lamp and hides it?' Or does the word, *'measure,'* have such a meaning that the setting of a lamp under the measure signifies the attaching of greater importance to the needs of the body than to the preaching of truth, so that everyone would refrain from preaching the truth as long as he feared that he might suffer some disquietude with regard to corporal and temporal affairs? The word, *'measure,'* is aptly used for two reasons. In the first place, it may signify a measured recompense, since everyone receives back what he has accomplished in

the body. The Apostle says: 'So that each man may receive what he has won in the body.'[1] And as if in reference to this bodily measure, it is said in another passage: 'For in what measure you will have measured, in that same it shall be again measured to you.'[2] Secondly, it is aptly used with reference to temporal goods, for, since they are accomplished in a body, they have their beginning and duration in a certain measure of days. Perhaps the word, *'measure,'* signifies this kind of measure. But eternal and spiritual things are encompassed by no such limitation, 'for not by measure does God give the spirit.'[3] Therefore, a man sets a lamp under the measure, if through temporal gains he darkens and conceals the light of truth. *'But on the lamp-stand.'* Now, a man sets it on a lamp stand if he subordinates the body to the service of God in such a way that the preaching of the truth will be above and the bodily ministration will be beneath, but so that the light which is above will shine also through the bodily ministration, in order that it may be presented to disciples through bodily ministrations, namely, through voice and tongue and the other operations of the body in good works. Consequently, the Apostle is setting a lamp on the lamp stand when he says: 'I so fight as not beating the air; but I chastise my body and bring it into subjection, lest perhaps, while preaching to others, I myself be found rejected.'[4] And as to the Lord's saying, *'that it may shine to all who are in the house,'* I think that the word, *'house,'* signifies the habitation of men, the world itself, for He says above: *'You are the light of the world.'* However, if anyone wishes to understand the word, *'house,'* as meaning the Church, that is not absurd.

---

1 2 Cor. 5.10.
2 Matt. 7.2.
3 John 3.34; *Retract.* 1.19.3.
4 1 Cor. 9.26 f.

Chapter 7 (Matt. 5.16)

(18) He says: *'Let your light so shine before men that they may see your good works and give glory to your Father, Who is in heaven.'* If He said merely, *'Let your light so shine before men that they may see your good works,'* He would seem to have set up human praise as the purpose of those good works—the praise that is sought by hypocrites and by those who solicit honors and strive after glory most vain. The very opposite of this is expressed in the saying, 'If I were still trying to please men, I should not be the servant of Christ.'[1] And it is said through the Prophet: 'They who please men have been confounded, because God has esteemed them as nought.'[2] And it is also said: 'God has broken the bones of those who please men.'[3] And the Apostle says furthermore: 'Let us not become desirous of vain glory,'[4] and: 'Let a man test himself, and thus he will have glory in himself, and not in comparison with another.'[5] For this reason the Lord did not say merely: *'That they may see your good works'*; He added: *'And that they may give glory to your Father, Who is in heaven.'* Hence, the mere fact of pleasing men through good works does not now constitute the reason why a man should please men. He ought to direct this to the glory of God; consequently, he ought to please men in order that God may be glorified in him. For, when men bestow praise, they ought to render honor to God, not to a man. The Lord shows this in the case of the man who was brought to Him. For, according to the Gospel narrative,[6] the crowds being in admiration of His power when the paralytic had been healed,

---

1 Gal. 1.10.
2 Ps. 52.6.
3 *Ibid.*
4 Gal. 5.26.
5 Gal. 6.4.
6 Matt. 9.8.

'were struck with fear, and gave glory to God, Who had given such power to men.' His follower, the Apostle Paul, says: 'But they had heard only that he who formerly persecuted us, now preaches the faith which once he ravaged. And they glorified God in me.'[7]

(19) Then, after He had exhorted His hearers to prepare themselves to suffer all things for the sake of truth and justice and not to hide the good gift they were about to receive, but to learn it with such good disposition that they would teach it to the others, while aiming their good work toward the glory of God, and not toward praise for themselves—then He begins to instruct them and to show them what they should teach. And, just as if they were saying by way of inquiry: 'Behold, we are willing both to suffer all things for thy name's sake, and not to hide thy teaching. But what is this very thing which you forbid to be hidden, and for which you command that all things be suffered? Are you going to mention other things in opposition to what is written in the Law?'—He answers, *'No.'* For He says: *'Do not think that I have come to destroy the Law or the Prophets. I have not come to destroy, but to fulfill.'*

Chapter 8 (Matt. 5.17-19)

(20) This sentence admits of a twofold meaning, and it must receive a corresponding twofold treatment. For, by saying that He has not come to destroy the Law, but to fulfill it, He says either that He is going to make it complete by adding what it lacks or that He is going to observe it by doing what it contains.[1] Let us, therefore, first consider my first

---

7 Gal. 1.23f.

---

1 The Latin word, *'implere,'* means both to make complete and to observe or fulfill.

supposition. He does not destroy what He has found in the Law when He supplies what it lacked; on the contrary, He strengthens it by giving it completeness. Therefore, He goes on to say: *'Amen, I say to you, till heaven and earth pass away, not one iota or one tittle shall pass from the Law till all things have been accomplished.'* For, when one is observing what has been added for the sake of completeness, he is all the more surely observing what has been previously established as the foundation. And, when the Lord says, *'Not one iota or one tittle shall pass from the Law,'* His words cannot be understood as being anything else than a vehement expression of perfect observance.[2] That perfect observance is exemplified by letters of the alphabet. Now, because the *'iota'* is formed by a single stroke, it is the smallest of those letters, and the *'tittle'* is merely a small part of it, placed on top. By these words, He indicates that every slightest detail in the Law is being fulfilled in practice. Then He continues: *'Therefore, whoever breaks one of these least commandments, and so teaches men, shall be called least in the kingdom of heaven.'*[3] The least commandments are therefore signified by the *'one iota'* and the *'one tittle.'* Hence, *'whoever breaks and so teaches'* (that is to say: whoever teaches accordingly as he breaks, and not in accordance with what he finds and reads), *'shall be called least in the kingdom of heaven.'* Therefore, perhaps he will not be in the kingdom of heaven, where none but the great can be. *'But whoever observes them and teaches them'* (which means: whoever does not break them, and teaches accordingly, that is, in accordance with his not breaking them) *'shall be called great in the kingdom of heaven.'* Of course, it follows that whoever will be called great in the kingdom of heaven will be in the kingdom of heaven,

---

2 See *Retract.* 1.19.3.
3 See *Retract.* 1.19.4.

where the great are admitted. And the next sentence refers to this.

Chapter 9 (Matt. 5.20-22)

(21) *'For I say to you that unless your justice exceeds that of the Scribes and Pharisees, you shall not enter the kingdom of heaven.'* This means that you shall not enter the kingdom of heaven unless you fulfill not only those least commandments of the Law—which are merely rudimentary prescriptions with regard to a man's moral development—but also those which will be added by Me; for I have come, not to destroy the Law, but to fulfill it. In the preceding sentence, however, when He was speaking about those least commandments, He said that whoever breaks one of them and teaches in accordance with his violation is called least in the kingdom of heaven, but that whoever observes them and teaches accordingly is called great and will therefore be in the kingdom of heaven because he is great. Now you ask me: What need is there of any addition to the least precepts of the Law if everyone who observes them and teaches accordingly can thereby be in the kingdom of heaven because he is great? That pronouncement, *'But whoever observes them and teaches them shall be called great in the kingdom of heaven,'* is to be understood in this sense, namely: Not according to the measure of those least commandments, but in accordance with those which I am about to proclaim. And what are those commandments? That your justice, says He, exceed that of the Scribes and Pharisees; for, *unless it exceeds, you shall not enter the kingdom of heaven.* Therefore, he will be called least who breaks those least commandments and teaches accordingly. But he who observes

them and teaches accordingly is not thereby to be considered great and fit for the kingdom of heaven. Yet he is not so very little as the man who breaks them. In order to be great and to be fit for that kingdom, a man is bound to do and to teach as Christ is now teaching, so that his justice may exceed the justice of the Scribes and Pharisees. The justice of the Pharisees is that they shall not kill; the justice of those who are to enter the kingdom of God is that they shall not become angry without cause. Not to kill is, therefore, the least commandment, and whoever breaks it will be called least in the kingdom of heaven. But the man who so fulfills it as not to kill is not that once a great man and fit for the kingdom of heaven. Nevertheless, he has risen to a certain degree, and he will be a perfect observer if he does not even become angry without cause. If he succeeds in doing this, he will be much farther removed from committing murder. Therefore, he who teaches us not to be angry does not destroy the law which forbids us to kill. On the contrary, he implements it so that we may preserve our sinlessness outwardly so long as we do not kill, and safeguard it in the heart so long as we do not become angry.

(22) Then He says: *'You have heard that it was said to the ancients, "Thou shalt not kill"; and that whoever shall murder shall be liable to judgment. But I say to you that everyone who is angry with his brother without cause,*[1] *shall be liable to judgment; and whoever says to his brother, "Raca" shall be liable to the council; and whoever says, "Thou fool!" shall be liable to the Gehenna of fire.'*[2] What is the difference between being liable to judgment, liable to

---
1 See *Retract.* 1.19.4.
2 Augustine's conclusion that there are various Gehennas (see below, 1.9.24), shows that he is speaking of the 'Gehenna of fire,' rather than 'the fire of Gehenna.' (Cf. Mark 9. 46; *Enarr. in ps.* 68.3.)

the council, and liable to the Gehenna of fire? This final liability denotes the most serious predicament, and it reminds us of certain advances made from the lesser transgressions while the Gehenna of fire was being reached. If it is less serious to be liable to judgment than to the council, and likewise less serious to be liable to the council than to the Gehenna of fire, we must therefore understand that there is less guilt in being needlessly angry with a brother than in saying, 'Raca,' and that there is still less guilt in saying, 'Raca,' than in saying 'Thou fool!' For the accusation itself would not have degrees unless the sins also were enumerated by gradations.

(23) One obscure word, however, has been used in this passage: while the other words are of common usage in our language, the word, 'Raca,' is neither Greek nor Latin. Nevertheless, not a few interpreters have been inclined to derive the interpretation of this word from the Greek. They believe that the word, 'Raca,' denotes a ragged fellow, because the the Greek word for rag is *'racos.'* Yet, if they were asked what a ragged fellow is called in Greek, they would not say that he is called *'Raca.'* Furthermore—instead of using a word which is not Latin in any respect and which is not used in Greek—the Latin translator could have used [the Latin word for] ragged fellow where he used the word, *'Raca.'* More probable, therefore, is the answer I received from a certain Hebrew when I asked him about this. He said that it is a word of no signification whatever, that it merely expresses the feelings of an impatient man.[3] Interjections are what grammarians call those particles of discourse which express the feelings of an aroused mental state, as when 'alas' is uttered by one in sorrow, or 'bah' by one in anger. Such words are peculiar to certain languages, and are not easily

---

[3] Authors generally agree that *'Raca'* implies extreme contempt; cf. F. Zorell, *Lexicon Graecum Novi Testamenti* (2nd ed., Paris 1931).

translated into another. This was the reason that compelled both the Greek and the Latin translators to set down the word itself, since they were unable to find any way of translating it.

(24) In those sins there is, therefore, such a gradation that at first a man becomes angry and holds that passion harbored in his heart. Now, if that very passion extorts from the angry man a word which is indeed meaningless, but which by its very utterance gives evidence of his perturbation of mind, and by which an injury is done to the man with whom he is angry —this is certainly a greater sin than if the rising anger were repressed in silence. If there be heard from the angry man not only an exclamation, but also a word by which he designates and denotes a definite reproach to him against whom it is pronounced, who can doubt that this is a greater sin than if a mere word of indignation were uttered? In the first case there is, therefore, one sin: anger alone; in the second case there are two sins: anger and the exclamation that betokens anger; in the third case there are three sins: anger, and the angry exclamation, and an expression of definite reproach in the exclamation itself. Now, notice the three degrees of liability: that of the judgment, that of the council, and that of the Gehenna of fire. For, at the judgment, there is still an opportunity for defense; but—even though there is usually a trial at the council, yet because the very distinction compels us to admit that there is some kind of difference here —it seems to be the council's function to pronounce the sentence at a time when the accused is no longer on trial as to his guilt or innocence, but when the judges hold joint consultation as to the punishment that may be rightly inflicted on a man whose guilt is already determined. But the Gehenna of fire, unlike the judgment, does not consider the condemnation as uncertain, and, unlike the council, has no

uncertainty about the punishment of the culprit. In the Gehenna of fire, both the conviction and the penalty of the accused are beyond all doubt. Certain gradations are evident, therefore, both in the sins and in the liability. But who can say how they will be invisibly registered as regards the punishment of souls? Consequently, we must understand what great difference there is between the justice of the Pharisees and the greater justice which leads to the kingdom of heaven. For, although it is a more grievous sin to kill than to utter a verbal reproach, killing makes a man liable to the judgment in the former justice, but anger—which is the least of those three sins—makes a man liable to judgment in the latter justice. In the former justice, men used to pass judgment on the question of murder, but in the latter justice, all things are remitted to the divine judgment, where the end of those condemned is the Gehenna of fire. If in the greater justice a reproach is punished by the Gehenna of fire, then, if anyone says that murder is punished by a greater penalty, he thereby compels us to understand that there are various Gehennas.

(25) In these three pronouncements we must certainly understand something which is not expressly mentioned. However, the first contains all the necessary words: no additional words have to be supplied. In that pronouncement He says: *'Whoever is unreasonably angry with his brother, shall be liable to judgment.'* But, when He says in the second pronouncement, *'And whoever says, "Raca," to his brother,* the word, *'unreasonably,'* is to be understood. With that word understood, the conclusion follows, namely, *'shall be liable to the council.'* Moreover, when He says in the third pronouncement, *'Whoever says, "Thou fool!"'* two unexpressed phrases are to be understood, namely, 'to a brother' and 'without cause.' Hence it is that the Apostle is justified in

calling the Galatians fools while he is also calling them brothers:[4] he is justified for the precise reason that he is not doing it without cause. And it is evident that the word, *'brother,'* is to be understood in this passage, for there is a later pronouncement regarding the manner in which an enemy also is to be treated in accordance with the greater justice.

Chapter 10 (Matt. 5.23-24)

(26) Then He continues: *'Therefore, if thou art offering thy gift at the altar, and there rememberest that thy brother has anything against thee, leave thy gift there before the altar, and go away: first be reconciled to thy brother, and then come and offer thy gift.'* This pronouncement is joined to the preceding by the kind of conjunction that calls for a logical antecedent: He does not say, *'But if thou are offering thy gift'*; He says, *'Therefore, if thou art offering thy gift.'* This logical connection makes it abundantly clear that the previous pronouncement refers to a brother. For, if it is wrong to be unreasonably angry with a brother, or to say, 'Raca' or 'Thou fool!' it is far worse to harbor something in the mind so that indignation is turned into hatred. This is the import of what is said elsewhere, namely, 'Do not let the sun go down upon your anger.'[1] Therefore, when we are about to bring a gift to the altar, if we remember that a brother has anything against us, we are commanded to leave the gift before the altar and to go and be reconciled to the brother, and then to come and offer the gift. If this should be taken in the literal sense, perhaps one would believe that we ought to act in this way if the brother is pre-

---

4 Gal. 3.1; 1.11.

---

1 Eph. 4.26.

sent, for it cannot be put off any longer, since you are commanded to leave your gift before the altar. So, if any such thought comes to mind with reference to an absent brother or—as could happen—even with reference to a brother who is in residence beyond the sea, it would be absurd to believe that the gift is to be left before the altar until you can offer it to God after you have traversed lands and seas. In view of all this, we are compelled to have recourse to the inner spiritual meaning, so that the saying may be understood without being absurd.

(27) In the spiritual sense, therefore, we may understand faith as an altar in the inner temple of God, of which the visible altar is a symbol. Whatever gift we offer to God—be it prophecy, or doctrine, or prayer, or a hymn, or a psalm, or whatever other spiritual gifts of this kind may come to mind—cannot be acceptable to God unless it be held up by sincere faith and be firmly and immovably fixed on it, so that our words may be pure and undefiled. Many heretics have uttered blasphemies instead of praise: not having an altar, that is, the true faith, they are laden, as it were, with earthly imaginings, and it is as though they were casting their offering on the ground. And one must have a wholesome intention while making an offering, for to offer any such gift in our heart is to offer it in the inner temple of God. The Apostle says: 'For the temple of God is holy, and you are this temple,'[2] and: 'That Christ may dwell through faith in the inner man in your hearts.'[3] Therefore, when we are about to offer any such gift in our heart, we must proceed to a reconciliation with a brother if it occurs to our mind that he has anything against us, that is, if we have injured him in any way. For then he has something against us, just as we have something

---
2 1 Cor. 3.17.
3 Eph. 3.17.

against him if he has injured us. But, in the latter case, there is no need to proceed to a reconciliation. You would not ask forgiveness from one who has injured you; you would simply forgive him, just as you would wish to be forgiven by the Lord for any offense you may have committed. We must proceed to a reconciliation, therefore, when we become aware that we have perhaps in some way offended a brother. But the advance is to be made, not on bodily feet, but by the affections of the mind, so that with humble disposition you may prostrate yourself before your brother, and with loving affection have recourse to him in the presence of Him to whom you are about to offer your gift. Even if the brother be present, you will be able in this way to appease him with unfeigned desire and to regain his friendship by begging forgiveness, if you first do it in the presence of God—hastening to Him, not by the sluggish motion of the body, but by the swift affection of love. And then, coming—that is, redirecting the intention to what you had begun to do—offer the gift.

(28) Who is it that so behaves as not to be angry with a brother, without cause?[4] or not to say, 'Raca,' without cause? or not to call him a fool, without cause? All this is done through sheerest pride. Or who is it that implores forgiveness with suppliant heart—which is the only remedy—if perchance he has transgressed in any of these? Who, indeed, except whoever is not puffed up with the spirit of empty boasting? Therefore: 'Blessed are the poor in spirit, for theirs is the kingdom of heaven.'[5] Now, let us see at once what follows.

Chapter 11 (Matt. 5.25-26)

(29) *'Be benevolent towards thy adversary quickly,'* says

---
4 See *Retract.* 1.19.4.
5 Matt. 5.3.

He, *'whilst thou art with him on the way; lest thy adversary deliver thee to the judge, and the judge deliver thee to the officer, and thou be cast into prison. Amen I say to thee, thou wilt not come out from it until thou hast paid the last farthing.'* I understand who the judge is, for 'the Father does not judge any man, but He has given all judgment to the Son.'[1] I understand who the officer is, for [the Evangelist] says: 'Angels ministered unto him';[2] and we believe that He will come with His angels to judge the living and the dead.[3] I understand what the prison is, namely, the punishment of darkness which He elsewhere calls the exterior darkness.[4] Therefore, I believe that the joy of the divine rewards is within the mind itself, or that it is even more inward—if such a thing can be conceived. Of this joy it is said to the well-deserving servant: 'Enter thou into the joy of thy master'[5]—just as in our civil tribunals the man who is committed to prison is sent out from the courtroom or the courthouse.

(30) But, with regard to paying the last farthing,[6] the expression can be quite reasonably understood as the equivalent of saying that nothing is left unpunished—just as in ordinary parlance we use the expression, 'To the very dregs,' when we wish to declare that something is so completely consumed that nothing is left. Or it can be understood in the sense that earthly sins could be designated by the last fourth; for the earth is found to be the fourth and the last part of the distinct elements of this world—provided that you begin from the heavens, count the air second, the water third, and

---
1 John 5.22.
2 Matt. 4.11.
3 Matt. 13.49.
4 Matt. 8.12; 22.13; 25.30.
5 Matt. 25.23.
6 Literally, 'the last fourth.

the earth fourth. For this reason the expression, *'Until thou hast paid the last farthing,'* can be rightly understood as meaning, 'Until you have expiated earthly sins'; for the sinner has also heard the expression, 'Earth thou art, and to the earth thou shalt go.'[7] But, as to the expression, *'Until thou hast paid,'* I wonder if it signifies that which is called everlasting punishment. For how can that debt be paid where there is afforded no opportunity for repenting and living more uprightly? Therefore, the expression, *'Until thou hast paid,'* has been used here in the same sense, perhaps, as in the passage wherein it has been said: 'Sit at my right hand, until I place all thy enemies under thy feet.'[8] Of course, He will not cease to sit at the right hand when the enemies will have been placed under His feet. Or is it like that expression of the Apostle, 'For He must reign, until He has put all his enemies under His feet.[9] Certainly, He will not cease to reign after they have been put under His feet. Therefore, just as it is understood that He will reign forever, when it is said that 'He must reign until He has put His enemies under His feet,' because they will be forever under His feet, so also can it be understood here that the man of whom it is said, *'Thou wilt not come out from it until thou hast paid the last farthing,'* will never come out; he is endlessly paying the last farthing while he is suffering everlasting punishment for earthly sins. However, I would not assert this with such assurance as to seem to have precluded a more diligent treatment of the punishment of sins, in order to determine the sense in which the Scriptures call it an eternal punishment. At any rate, it is better to escape it than to learn its nature.

(31) Let us now see who this adversary is toward whom

---

7 Gen. 3.19.
8 Ps. 109.1.
9 1 Cor. 15.25.

we are ordered to be benevolent quickly while we are with him on the way. He is either the Devil, or a man, or the flesh, or God, or the commandment of God. Now, I do not see how we could be ordered to be benevolent toward the Devil, for that would mean to be of one heart or of one mind with him. (Because the Greek word, *eúnoon,* is used, some have translated it as *concordant;* others, *consentient.*) Surely, we are not ordered to show benevolence toward the Devil, for where there is benevolence there is friendship—and no one would say that friendship with the Devil is to be sought after. It is not to our advantage to be of one heart with him, for we have declared war on him by renouncing him once for all,[10] and when he is vanquished we shall receive a crown. And it ill behooves us to be of one mind with him, for, if we had never consented with him, those miseries of ours would never have befallen us. As to whether the adversary is a man, it is true that we are commanded to have peace with all men insofar as it depends on us.[11] Nevertheless, although benevolence and concord and consent can certainly be seen in the notion of peace, I am unable to believe that we shall be delivered to the judge by a man, for I understand that the judge is Christ, and—as the Apostle says—all men are to be led to His tribunal.[12] Now, how can we be delivered to the judge by one who is likewise to be led to the judge? And if everyone who has injured a man is to be handed over to the judge—even though the injured man does not hand him over—it is much more reasonable to believe that the culprit is handed over by the very law against which he acted when he was injuring the man. This is all the more evident by the fact that, if he has injured a man by killing him, there will then be no opportunity for him to come to an agreement; he is no longer

---
10 In the ceremony of baptism.
11 Rom. 12.19.
12 Rom. 14.10; 2 Cor. 5.10.

with him on the way, that is, in this life. Yet, he will not on that account remain unhealed by repenting and by having recourse—with the sacrifice of a contrite heart[13]—to the mercy of Him who forgives the sins of those who are converted to Him, and who rejoices more over one repentant sinner than over ninety-nine just men.[14] And much less do I see how we could be ordered to be well disposed toward the flesh or to be of one heart or of one mind with it. Rather, it is sinners who love their own flesh and are of one heart and of one mind with it. But what of those who bring it unto subjection?[15] They do not consent to it: they force it to consent to them.

(32) Perhaps, then, we are commanded to be of one mind with God and to be rightly disposed toward Him, so that we may be reconciled with Him. For, by committing sin, we have turned away from Him so completely that He can be called our adversary. And He is rightly called an adversary of those who resist Him, for 'He resists the proud, but gives grace to the humble.'[16] Furthermore, 'Pride is the beginning of all sin'[17] and: 'The beginning of man's pride is to fall away from God.[18] And the Apostle says: 'For if when we were enemies we were reconciled to God by the death of His Son, much more, having been reconciled, shall we be saved by his life.'[19] (From the mere fact that even former enemies are being reconciled to God, it can be seen that there is no such thing as an evil nature in hostility toward Him.)[20] On this journey,

---

13 Ps. 50.18.
14 Luke 15.7.
15 1 Cor. 9.27.
16 James 4.6; Matt. 23.12; Prov. 3.34.
17 Eccli. 10.15.
18 Eccli. 10.14.
19 Rom. 5.10.
20 A reference to Manichaeism (See below, 2.24.79, n. 2). 'The Manichaeans profess that evil is co-eternal with God, that this evil is a substance and a kind of foreign nature which cannot be changed into good, either by itself or by the good God' (*Contra Julianum opus imperf.* 5.25).

therefore—that is, during the course of this life—whoever will not have been reconciled with God will be handed over by Him to the judge, for 'the Father does not judge any man, but He has given all judgment to the Son.'[21] But, all the other opinions which we have discussed in this section are just as logical. In fact, there is one thing which creates a difficulty with regard to this interpretation. If in this passage God is to be understood as the adversary of the impious—the adversary with whom we are ordered to be quickly reconciled —how can it be rightly said that we are with Him on a journey? Or, perhaps, we are with Him even in this life because He is everywhere, for the Psalmist says: 'If I ascend into heaven, Thou art there; if I descend into hell, Thou art present. If I straighten my wings and dwell in the uttermost part of the sea, even there shall Thy hand lead me and Thy right hand shall hold me.'[22] Or, if it is not correct to say that the impious are with God, even though God is nowhere not present (for it would be correct to say that the blind are without light, although the light is diffused all around their eyes), then the only remaining alternative is to take it that the present adversary is the commandment of God. For, to those who would commit sin, what else is so adverse as the commandment of God? And that commandment is the Law of God, and the divine Scripture, which has been given to us to be with us on the journey for the duration of this life. Of course, we ought to be in agreement with it quickly and not to contradict it, lest it hand us over to the judge, for no one knows when he may depart from this life. Who is it that is in agreement with the divine Scripture? Only the man who is imbued with piety while he is reading

---
21 John 5.22.
22 Ps. 138.8-10. Varies from the Vulgate; see Introduction, note 20.

it or hearing it read, and who ascribes to it the highest authority, so that his seeing it to be in opposition with his own sins does not make him hate what he understands, but, on the contrary, makes him cherish the rebuke he is receiving, and makes him rejoice over the fact that no forbearance will be shown to his maladies until they are healed; and so that the seemingly obscure or absurd does not arouse him to disputes and wranglings, but, rather, makes him pray for understanding, and makes him remember that—notwithstanding obscurity or seeming contradiction—good will and reverence must be shown to such great authority. Who is it that behaves in this manner? Only the man who comes with meekness and filial affection to the opening and reading of his father's last will and testament. It is certainly not the haughty man—the man who comes with a threat of litigation. Therefore: *'Blessed are the meek, for they shall inherit the land.'* Let us now consider what follows.

Chapter 12 (Matt. 5.27-28)

(33) *'You have heard that it was said to the ancients, "Thou shalt not commit adultery." But I say to you that whosoever looks at a woman to lust after her, has already committed adultery with her in his heart.'* Therefore, the lesser justice is not to commit adultery by carnal intercourse; the greater justice of the kingdom of God is not to commit adultery in the heart. Whoever does not commit adultery in his heart guards much more securely against committing adultery in the flesh. Accordingly, He who has given this precept has confirmed the former precept, for He did not come to destroy the Law, but to fulfill it. And of course we must bear in mind that He did not say: 'Whosoever lusts after a woman,'

---

23 Matt. 5.4.

but that He said: *'Whosoever looks at a woman to lust after her.'* That means whosoever fixes his attention on her with the aim and intention of lusting after her. This is not the same as to experience a sensation of carnal pleasure, but it is the giving of such full consent that the aroused desire for it is not repressed, but would be satisfied if opportunity presented itself.

(34) For, there are three steps toward the complete commission of a sin: suggestion, pleasure, and consent. The suggestion is made either through the memory or through the bodily senses—when we are seeing or hearing or smelling or tasting or touching something. If we take pleasure in the enjoyment of this, it must be repressed if the pleasure is sinful. For example, if the craving of the palate is aroused at the sight of viands while we are observing the law of fasting, it arises only through pleasure; we do not consent to it, we repress it by the law of reason, to which it is subject. But, if consent is given, then a sin is fully committed in the heart, and it is known to God, even though it be not made known to men through the medium of any act. Therefore, these three successive stages are such as if the suggestion were made by a serpent, that is to say, it is made by a slimy and sinuous motion, namely, a transient action of the body. For, if any such images hover within the soul, they have been drawn from without, that is, from the body. And if, in addition to those five senses, any occult operation of a body comes into contact with the soul, it, too, is transient and moving quickly; therefore, the more occultly it glides into contact with thought, so much the more rightly is it compared with a serpent. Therefore, as I was beginning to say, these three successive stages may be likened to the action that is described in Genesis.[1] For the suggestion, as well as a

---

[1] Gen. 3.

kind of persuasion, is made as though by a serpent; the pleasure is in the carnal desire, as though in Eve; and the consent is in the reason, as though in the man [Adam]. And if a man passes through these three stages, he is, as it were, cast out from Paradise; that is to say, he is expelled from the most blessed light of justice and is cast unto death. And this is most strictly in accordance with justice, for persuasion is not compulsion. While all natures are beautiful in their proper orders and gradations, yet from the higher natures —and the rational mind is one of these—there ought to be no falling down to the lower. No one is forced to do this; consequently, if any one does it, he is punished by the just law of God, because he does not commit this sin unwillingly. Before the habit is acquired, either there is no pleasure whatever or it is so slight that it is scarcely present. But when it is illicit, to consent to it is a grave sin, and whenever anyone consents to it, he commits a sin in his heart. If he then goes so far as to perform the corresponding act, the craving seems to be satisfied and extinguished, but a more intense pleasure is enkindled when the suggestion is repeated afterwards. This pleasure, however, is far less than that which has turned into a habit by continuous acts, for it is very difficult to overcome this habit. Nevertheless, under the leadership of Christ and with His aid, everyone will overcome this habit if he does not debase himself and shrink from the Christian warfare. And in this way, man is subjected to Christ, and the woman is subjected to man—in accordance with the pristine peace and order.[2]

---

2 Cf. 1 Cor. 11.3. 'Not by nature, but because of sin, woman was rightly subjected to man. Unless this order is observed, nature will deteriorate and sin will increase.' (*De Gen. ad litt.* 11.37.50; cf. *De Gen contra Manich.* 2.11.15; *Enarr. in ps.* 143.6; *Conf.* 13.32.47)

(35) Therefore, just as sin is reached through the three successive stages of suggestion, pleasure, and consent, so also there are three distinct degrees of the same sin, accordingly as it is in the heart, in a deed, or in a habit. These three degrees of sin are, as it were, three types of death. The first—when consent in the heart is given to lust—is as though typifying death within the home; the second—when assent becomes deed—typifies the dead man just carried outside the door; the third—when, by the weight of a bad habit, the mind is pressed down as by a mound of earth—typifies the dead body rotting in the grave. Now, every reader of the Gospel is aware of the fact that the Lord restored life to these three types of dead men; perhaps he ponders over the distinctive significance of the Lord's very words when He was restoring life. For in one case He says: 'Girl, arise'[3]; in another case He says: 'Young man, I say to thee, arise'[4]; in still another case He groaned in spirit, and wept, and wept again, and afterwards cried with a loud voice: 'Lazarus, come forth.'[5]

(36) Therefore, by the name of such adulterers as are mentioned under this head we are to understand every kind of carnal and lustful concupiscence. Indeed, since the Scriptures so constantly give to idolatry the name of fornication,[6] and since the Apostle Paul calls avarice idolatry,[7] who can doubt that every evil consupiscence may be rightly called fornication? For, when the soul disregards the higher law by which it is governed, and prostitutes itself as though for a price, then it corrupts itself through base delight in lower

---
3 Mark 5.42. Cf. *Sermo* 128.12.14.
4 Luke 7.14.
5 John 11.33-44.
6 Ezech. 16.20f.
7 Col. 3.5; Eph. 5.5.

natures. Wherefore, whoever perceives that—because of a sinful habit which will continue to drag him into captivity as long as it remains unchecked—the craving of the flesh is in rebellion against his upright will, let him do his utmost to remind himself of the kind of peace he has lost by committing sin. Let him exclaim: 'Unhappy man that I am! Who will deliver me from the body of this death? The grace of God through Jesus Christ.'[8] While he is thus exclaiming that he is unhappy, he is mournfully beseeching the aid of the Comforter, and the awareness of his own wretchedness is no small approach to blessedness. Therefore: 'Blessed are they that mourn, for they shall be comforted.'[9]

Chapter 13 (Matt. 5.29-30)

(37) He now continues, and says: *'So if thy right eye scandalize thee, pluck it out and cast it from thee; for it is better for thee that one of thy members should perish than that thy whole body should go into Gehenna.'* Here there is need of great fortitude, so that bodily members may be amputated, for, whatever the word, *eye,* may signify, it is undoubtedly the kind of object that is ardently loved. Indeed, the expression, 'I love him as I love my own eyes, or even more than I love my own eyes,' is commonly used by those who wish to give vehement expression of their love. And the addition of the word, 'right,' serves perhaps to increase the intensity of love, for men have a greater fear of losing the right eye, notwithstanding the fact that the two bodily eyes are conjointly directed for seeing and that one eye can see as well as the other if both are directed. So the meaning may be this: Whatever you love so much as to prize it as highly

---
8 Rom. 7.24.
9 Matt. 5.5.

as your own right eye, pluck it out and cast it from you if it is a stumbling block for you, that is, if it is a hindrance to you with regard to true blessedness. For, rather than that your whole body should go into Gehenna, it is better for you to lose one of those things which you love as intensely as if they belonged to you, like bodily members.

(38) But because He straightway speaks about the right hand and uses a similar expression, He compels us to make a more diligent inquiry as to what He meant by the eye. For He says: *'If thy right hand scandalize thee, cut it off and cast it from thee; for it is better for thee that one of thy members should be lost than that thy whole body should go into Gehenna.'* In this connection, I can think of no more fitting example than that of a very dearly beloved friend, for that which we ardently love is certainly that which we may rightly call a member. And we may rightly call this member a counsellor, for he is, as it were, an eye that shows the way. Because he is on the right side, we may rightly call him a counsellor in divine matters. In this way, a friend on the left side is indeed a counsellor, but a counsellor in earthly matters, which pertain to the needs of the body. However, it would be superfluous to talk about him insofar as he may be an occasion of sin, since not even the friend on the right side is to be spared. But a counsellor in divine matters is actually a stumbling block, if, under the guise of religion and doctrine, he is trying to lead us into some pernicious heresy. Let the right hand, therefore, be understood as a beloved helper and minister in divine works. For, just as contemplation is properly represented by the word, *'eye,'* so action is rightly represented by the word, *'hand.'* In this way, the left hand signifies the works that are necessary for this life and body.

Chapter 14 (Matt. 5.31-32)

(39) *'It was said, moreover, "Whoever puts away his wife, let him give her a written notice of dismissal."'* This is the lesser justice of the Pharisees, and there is no opposition to it in the Lord's saying: *'But I say to you that everyone who puts away his wife, save on account of fornication, causes her to commit adultery; and whoever marries her that is loosed from her husband, commits adultery.'* By commanding that a written notice of dismissal be given, He did not thereby command that the wife be put away. But in order that a careful consideration of the written notice might moderate the rash anger of the man who is casting out his wife, He said: *'Whoever puts her away, let him give her a written notice of dismissal.'* So, by seeking a delay of the dismissal of the wife, He made it known that He did not wish a marriage to be dissolved—insofar as He could make this known to obdurate men. And when the Lord Himself was questioned about this on another occasion, He gave the following reply: 'Moses did this on account of your harshness.'[1] No matter how harsh might be the man who wishes to put away his wife, he would be readily placated after he had reflected on the fact that she could securely marry another when the written notice of dismissal had been given. Therefore, in order to confirm the fact that a wife is not to be put away without grave reason, the Lord made no other exception than the case of fornication. And He commands that all the other annoyances—if perchance any arise—be steadfastly borne for the sake of conjugal fidelity and chastity. Moreover, he applies the name of adulterer to a man who marries a woman who has been loosed from her husband. The Apostle Paul shows how long this prohibition continues; he says that it is to be observed as

---
1 Matt. 19.8.

long as her husband is alive, but he permits her to marry when her husband is dead.² The same Apostle certainly upheld this law. In this case he is not publishing his own counsel, as he does in many of his admonitions; he is announcing the precept of the Lord, who commands it, for he writes: 'But with reference to those who are in wedlock, not I, but the Lord commands the wife not to depart from the husband; and if she departs, to remain unmarried or to be reconciled with her husband. And let not a husband put away his wife.'³ And I believe that by a similar ordinance the husband is not to marry another woman if he puts away his wife, or that he is to become reconciled with her, for it may happen that he has put her away on account of the kind of fornication which the Lord meant when He laid down the condition. Of course, if she is not allowed to marry during the lifetime of the husband from whom she has departed, and he is not allowed to marry another woman during the lifetime of the wife whom he has put away, it is all the more sinful for them to commit unchaste acts with anyone whatever. At any rate, husbands and wives are to be regarded as more truly happy if, by mutual consent, they are able to abstain from all carnal intercourse with each other. Whether they do this only after they have procreated children, or whether they are foregoing the joy of earthly offspring, they are not disobeying that precept of the Lord which forbids the dismissal of a wife—for a husband does not put away his wife if he lives with her according to the spirit, but not according to the flesh. In fact, there is then an observance of that which is spoken through the Apostle: 'It remains that those who have wives be as of they had none.'⁴

---

2 Rom. 7.2.
3 1 Cor. 7.10-11.
4 1 Cor. 7.29.

Chapter 15 (Matt. 5. 31-32)

(40) On another occasion, however, the Lord Himself says: 'Whoever comes to me, and does not hate his father and mother, and wife and children, and brothers and sisters, and even his own soul,[1] cannot be my disciple.'[2] As a rule, this is more perturbing to the mind of neophytes, who are nevertheless eager to begin at once to live in accordance with the precepts of Christ. To those who do not fully grasp its meaning, it would seem contradictory that on one occasion He forbids the dismissal of a wife except on account of fornication, while on another occasion He says that no man can be his disciple unless he hates his wife. If he were speaking about carnal intercourse, he would not make the same stipulation with regard to a father and a mother and brothers. Yet, how true it is that 'the kingdom of heaven suffers violence, and they that use violence take it by force'![3] And how much violence is truly needed so that a man may indeed love his enemies and hate his father and mother and children and brothers! Yet, He who is calling men to the kingdom of heaven is enjoining both these duties. Under His leadership, it is easy to show how these precepts are not in mutual opposition, but it is hard to observe them even when they are thoroughly understood. And yet, even that is very easy—with His help. The eternal kingdom to which He has deigned to call His disciples, whom He also called brothers, does not, indeed, have temporal relationships of this kind, for 'there is neither Jew nor Greek, neither male nor female, neither slave nor freeman, but Christ is all things and in all.'[4] And the Lord Himself says:

---

1 See below, 1.15.42.
2 Luke 14.26.
3 Matt. 11.12.
4 Gal. 3.28; Col. 3.11.

'For in the resurrection they will neither be married nor marry, but will be as the angels of God in heaven.'[5] Therefore, whoever wishes to prepare himself now for the life of that kingdom, must hate, not men themselves, but those temporal relationships through which the present life is sustained, that is, the transitory life which begins at birth and ends with death. For, whoever does not hate this necessity, does not yet love that other life in which there will be no condition of birth and death—the condition which renders marriages natural on earth.

(41) Now, suppose that I put the question to some man who is truly Christian, and has a wife. Even though he be still procreating offspring by her, suppose that I ask him whether he would wish to have a wife when he is in that kingdom. Because that man is mindful of God's promises and of that life wherein this corruptible body will put on incorruption and this mortal body will put on immortality,[6] and because he is already uplifted by great love or, at any rate, by a certain degree of love—because of all this, he will swear that most decidedly he has no such wish. Suppose that I then ask him whether he would like to have his wife with him in that kingdom when—after the resurrection—they will have received that angelic transformation which is promised to the saints. In this case, he would reply that he is just as keenly desirous of this as he is averse to the other. From this it is evident that in the same woman a good Christian loves the being that God has created, and that he wishes her to be transformed and renewed, while he hates the corruptible and mortal relationship and marital intercourse. In other

---

5 Matt. 22.30.
6 1 Cor. 15.53.

words, it is evident that he loves her insofar as she is a human being, but that he hates her under the aspect of wifehood. And he also loves an enemy, not insofar as he is an enemy, but insofar as he is a human being; he loves him in such a way that he wishes for him the same good fortune that he wishes for himself. This means that he wishes him to be corrected of his faults, to become a new man, and thus to enter the kingdom of heaven. This is also the meaning with regard to a father and a mother and the other bonds of blood. It means that in them we are to hate what befalls the human race through the occurrences of birth and death,[7] but that we are to love what can be brought with us into those realms where no one says, 'my father,' but where everyone addresses the one God as 'our Father'[8]; where no one says, 'my mother,' but where everyone greets that Jerusalem as 'our Mother'[9]; where no one says, 'my brother,' but where everyone refers to everyone else as 'our brother'; and where, when we shall have been led back into unity, there will be a marriage—a marriage, as it were, of one spouse[10]—with Him who has set us free from the prostitution of this world by the shedding of His own blood.[11] Consequently, the disciple of Christ must hate the things that are transitory in those persons whom he wishes to come with him to the things that endure; the more he loves those persons, so much the more must he hate those things.

(42) A Christian, therefore, can live in harmony with a wife, for, whether he is satisfying the yearnings of the flesh

---

7 See *Retract.* 1.19.5.
8 Matt. 6.9.
9 Cf. Gal. 4.26.
10 Cf. 2 Cor. 11.2; Eph. 5.22f.
11 Cf. Col. 1.20; 1 Peter 1.18; 1 John 1.7; Apoc. 5.9.

with her (the Apostle mentions this as a favor, not as a command),[11] or whether he is procreating offspring with her (indeed, this can be highly praiseworthy), or whether—having no carnal intercourse with her—he is affording her the companionship of a brother, that is, having a wife as if not having her (in the marriage of Christians this is most excellent and sublime)—at all events, he can live with her in such harmony that in her he loves the hope of eternal blessedness, even though he hates in her everything that goes by the name of relationship in time. Certainly, we hate that which we assuredly hope will come to an end some day, for example, the very life of this present world. Indeed, if we did not hate it because it is temporal, we would not be desirous of the life to come, which is not subject to time. Accordingly, the word, *'soul,'* which was used in the sentence, 'Whoever does not hate even his own soul cannot be my disciple'—that word was used there to denote this present life. For this present life has need of that corruptible food of which the Lord says: 'Is not the soul more than the food?'[12] It denotes this present life, for which victuals are necessary. And as to His saying that He will lay down His soul for His sheep,[13] of course He means that He will lay down His life, for He is declaring that He will die for us.

Chapter 16 (Matt. 5.31-32)

(43) Since the Lord permits that a wife be put away on account of fornication,[1] another question arises as to

---

11 1 Cor. 7.6.
12 Matt. 6.25.
13 John 10.15.

---

1 See *Retract.* 1.19.6.

how the word, *'fornication,'* is to be understood in this context; whether it is to be taken in the sense in which everybody understands it, or in the sense in which the Scriptures usually employ it. In the first case, it would be understood to denote the kind of fornication that is committed in unchaste acts; in the other case, as we have already noted,[2] it would be understood as denoting every sinful corruption—such as idolatry or avarice—and, consequently, every transgression of the Law through sinful desire. Lest we make any rash statement, let us consult the Apostle. He says: 'To those who are in wedlock, not I, but the Lord commands that a wife is not to depart from her husband, and if she departs, that she is to remain unmarried or be reconciled with her husband.'[3] Of course, it may happen that she departs because of what the Lord allows as a reason for departing. But, if a wife is allowed to put away her husband on account of some other reason than fornication, while a husband is not thus allowed to put away his wife, then what answer shall we give with regard to what he says afterwards: 'And let not a husband put away his wife'? Why did he not add the clause, 'except on account of fornication,' as the Lord permits? Only because he intends a like rule to be understood, namely, that if a husband puts away his wife (and this is permitted on account of fornication), he is to remain without a wife or be reconciled with the wife that he put away. Certainly, it would not be wrong for a husband to be reconciled with that celebrated woman to whom—after no one had dared to cast a stone at her—the Lord said: 'Go, and see that thou sin no more.'[4] And when He says, 'It is not allowed to put away a wife except on account of fornication,' He certainly obliges a husband

---

2 See above, 1.12.36.
3 1 Cor. 7.10-11.
4 John 8.11.

to keep his wife if there is no case of fornication, but He does not oblige him to put her away if there is such a case; He merely permits him to do that. Likewise is it said: 'Let not a wife be allowed to marry another man unless her husband is dead.'[5] So, if she marries before the death of her husband, she is guilty; if she does not marry after his death, she is not guilty, for she is not commanded to marry—she is allowed to do so. In this law of marriage, therefore, if the rule as to both husband and wife is so similar that the same Apostle has not only mentioned it with regard to the wife, but has not even remained silent about it with regard to the husband (for, with reference to her, he says: 'Not the wife, but the husband, has authority over her body'; and with reference to him, he says: 'The husband likewise has not, but the wife has, authority over his body'[6])—therefore, if the rule is the same, we must understand that a wife is not allowed to put away her husband except for the same reason for which a husband is allowed to put away his wife, that is, fornication.

(44) We must therefore consider what meaning we ought to attach to the word, *'fornication.'* And as we had begun to do, we must consult the Apostle, for he next says: 'But I, not the Lord, say to you.' We must at once see who are those others: heretofore he was speaking in the name of the Lord to those who are in wedlock, but now he is speaking in his own name to the others. Perhaps he is speaking to those who are not in wedlock. This, however, is not the correct inference, for he continues in this manner: 'If any brother has an unbelieving wife and she consents to live with him, let him not put her away.'[7] Therefore, even now he is speaking to those who are in wedlock. What, then, is the implication of

---

5 Cf. 1 Cor. 7.39.
6 Cf. 1 Cor. 7.4.
7 Cf. 1 Cor. 7.12.

his calling them 'the others'? It can mean only that at first he was speaking to those who were so united in wedlock that they were both equally in the Christian faith, and that he is now speaking to the others, that is, to those who are so united in wedlock that one of them is an unbeliever. And what does he say to them? 'If any brother has an unbelieving wife and she consents to live with him, let him not put her away. And if any woman has an unbelieving husband and he consents to live with her, let her not put away her husband.' Now, if he gives this in his own name as an admonition and not as a command in the name of Christ, there is the consequent advantage that, if someone fails to observe it, he does not thereby become a transgressor of a commandment. Likewise, with regard to virgins, he shortly afterwards says that he has no commandment of the Lord, but that he is giving advice. And he commends virginity in such manner that he who desires the advice may take it, but that a man is not adjudged as having violated a commandment if he does not take it. A command is one thing; an admonition, another; a permission differs from both. A wife is commanded not to depart from her husband, and, if she departs, to remain unmarried or to be reconciled with her husband. Because this is a command, she is not to go against it. But, if a believing husband has an unbelieving wife who consents to live with him, he is advised not to put her away. Therefore, he is also allowed to put her away, because there is no commandment of the Lord against his putting her away: there is only the advice of the Apostle. A virgin is likewise advised not to marry. If she marries, of course she will not be following the advice, but neither will she be acting against a commandment. Permission is given when the saying is: 'But I say this by way of concession, not by way of commandment.'[8]

---
8 1 Cor. 7.6.

Now, if it is allowed to put away an unbelieving spouse—even though it may be better not to do so—and if, on the other hand, according to the commandment of the Lord it is not allowed to put away a spouse except on account of fornication, then even unbelief itself is fornication.[9]

(45) Apostle, then what do you say? At any rate, you say that a believing husband should not put away an unbelieving wife who consents to live with him. 'Yes,' he replies. But in view of the fact that the Lord also gives this commandment, namely, that a husband should not put away his wife except on account of fornication, why do you now say: 'I, not the Lord, am saying it'? Precisely because the idolatry which unbelievers follow is fornication—and the same is true of every other pernicious superstition. Yes, the Lord permitted that a wife be put away on account of fornication, and, because He permitted it without commanding it, He furnished occasion for the Apostle's advising that even when a husband would like to put away an unbelieving wife, he should keep her, so that perchance she could thus become a believer. 'For,' says he, 'the unbelieving husband is sanctified in the wife; and the unbelieving wife is sanctified in a brother.'[10] It had already come to pass, I suppose, that some wives were coming to the faith through believing husbands and that some husbands were coming to the faith through believing wives. And, without mentioning names, he exhorted through these examples in order to strengthen his admonition. He now continues: 'Otherwise your children would be unclean; but, as it is, they are holy.' For

---
9 Augustine is not now expounding the Pauline Privilege. He is speaking of the separation of husband and wife, not of the remarriage of either during the lifetime of the other (See below, 1.16.48). In another work, written some seven years later, he says: 'The marriage bond is not dissolved except on the death of the husband or the wife' (*De bono conjug.* 24.32).
10 1 Cor. 7.14.

there were now Christian children who had been sanctified either through the influence of one of the parents or with the consent of both. This would not have come to pass if the marriage had been dissolved when one of the spouses became a believer, and if the unbelief of a spouse were not so far tolerated as to furnish him or her an opportunity for becoming a believer. This, then, is the advice of one to whom I believe it had been said: 'If thou dost spend anything over and above, I shall repay thee when I return.'[11]

(46) Furthermore, if unbelief is fornication, and if idolatry is unbelief, and if covetousness is idolatry, then there can be no doubt that covetousness is fornication. Now, if covetousness is fornication, how can anyone rightly dissociate any kind of sinful lusts from the category of fornication? Hence, it is seen that a husband can guiltlessly put away his wife and that a wife can guiltlessly put away her husband, on account of sinful lusts, and that these lusts are not only those that are committed in unchaste actions with others' wives or husbands, but absolutely all sinful lusts whatsoever that cause a soul to deviate from the law of God and to be perniciously and basely corrupted while it is abusing the body. For the Lord makes fornication an exception, and, as has been already observed, we are compelled to understand this fornication as generic and all-embracing.

(47) But, when the Lord said, *'except on account of fornication,'* He did not specify the kind of fornication. He did not say whether it is the fornication of the husband or that of the wife. For, not only is it permitted to put away a wife who commits fornication, but, if any husband puts away his wife

---

11 Luke 10.35. Just as the innkeeper was given two denarii and was authorized to spend more if he deemed it advisable to do so, St. Paul was commissioned to preach all that the Lord had prescribed and to add to it by way of counsel. In this way, his counsel has divine approval.

because he is forced by her to commit fornication, he certainly puts her away on account of fornication. For instance, if some wife is forcing her husband to offer sacrifice to idols, then if he puts her away, he puts her away certainly on account of fornication—not her fornication alone, but his own as well. He puts her away on account of her fornication, because she is committing it, and on account of his own fornication, so that he may not commit it. But, if the husband also is guilty of committing fornication, there is nothing more unjust than that he put away his wife on account of fornication. Indeed, this saying occurs: 'For wherein thou judgest another, thou dost condemn thyself; for thou dost the very things thou judgest.'[12] Hence, whenever a husband wishes to put away his wife on account of fornication, he himself ought first to be guiltless of fornication. And I would say this likewise with regard to a wife.

(48) But as to His saying, *'Whoever marries a woman that has been divorced from her husband, commits adultery,'* it may be asked whether adultery is committed not only by the man who marries, but also by the woman he marries, for she is commanded to remain unmarried or to be reconciled with her husband. However, the Apostle's words are: 'But if she departs from her husband,'[13] and it is a matter of great import whether she is putting away her husband or is herself being put away. If she puts away her husband and marries another man, she seems to have deserted her former husband through a desire to change husbands, and this is certainly an adulterous intention. But, if she is willing to remain with her husband and is nevertheless put away by him, then—according to the Lord's pronouncement—the man who marries her commits adultery. It is uncertain whether she also is to

---
12 Rom. 2.1.
13 1 Cor. 7.11.

be held guilty of the same sin, yet—since both the man and the woman have carnal intercourse by mutual consent—it would be far more difficult to discover how one of them could be an adulterer while the other is not. Furthermore, because a man commits adultery by marrying a woman who has been divorced from her husband—even though she has not put away her husband, but has herself been put away—she makes him commit adultery, for the Lord forbids this marriage no less strongly [than marriage to a woman who has put away her husband]. Hence, the conclusion is that —whether she has put away her husband or has herself been put away—she is obliged to remain unmarried or to be reconciled with her husband.[14]

(49) There is also a question as to whether a husband can be guiltless of fornication if, with his wife's permission—because she is either sterile or unwilling to submit to intercourse—he takes to himself another woman who is neither another man's wife nor a wife separated from her husband.[15] Of course, an example is found in the history of the Old Testament,[16] but in our day we have the higher precepts which the human race has reached after the earlier stage. And those earlier precepts are to be examined, not for the purpose of adopting their moral standards, but in order to set forth the distinct eras of the dispensation of Divine Providence, which has furnished aid to the human race in most orderly fashion.[17] However, as the Apostle says, 'Not the wife, but the

---

14 See above, 1.16.44, n. 9.
15 'In past ages this was lawful, but I would not rashly assert that it would be lawful now' (*De bono conjug.* 15.17).
16 Cf. Gen. 16.
17 At one time, Augustine enumerates three such 'eras' of divine dispensation: an era preceding the Law, the era of the Law, and the Christian era (*Sermo* 72.3). At another time, he enumerates four: (a) from Abraham to David, (b) thence to the Babylonian captivity, (c) thence to the coming of Christ, (d) thence to the end of the world

husband, has authority over her body; and likewise the husband has not authority over his body, but the wife has it.'[18] Can this go so far as to mean that, with his wife's permission —since she has authority over his body—a husband may have carnal intercourse with another woman who is neither another man's wife nor a wife separated from her husband? But this is not the true meaning. Otherwise, it would follow that a wife also would be allowed to do the same—a conclusion which would be repugnant to the universal moral sense.

(50) Nevertheless, some cases can occur in which even a wife may seem to be obliged to do this for the sake of the husband himself, provided that he consents. Such is the case that is reported to have occurred at Antioch about fifty years ago, during the reign of Constantius and the governorship of Acyndinus, who was also a consul. This governor became greatly enraged for some reason or other while demanding payment from a man who owed a pound of gold to the public treasury. This is usually a dangerous thing in the case of such officials, for their every whim is lawful—or rather, is thought to be lawful. With asseverations and oaths he threatened that the debtor would be put to death unless he had paid the aforesaid gold on a certain day which he, Acyndinus, had determined. The dreaded day began to hover close and to draw near while the man was being held under harsh duress, being still unable to rid himself of the debt. It happened that he had a wife who was very beautiful, but without any money with

---

(*Contra Adimant.* 7.2). Again, he names two preceding eras: one, from Adam to Noe, and another from Noe to Abraham (*De catech. rudibus* 22.39). Finally, he mentions a seventh era, namely, the reign of the just with Christ after His second coming (*De. Gen. contra Manich.* 1.23.35). In refuting the Manichaeans' contention that such differences involve contradictions, Augustine cited Luke 9.3 and 22.36 as an instance of contrary commands even in the New Testament, which the Manichaeans professed to revere (*Contra Faustum* 22.77).
18 1 Cor. 7.1.

which to come to her husband's aid. There was a certain wealthy man who had become impassioned by this woman's beauty, and had learned that her husband was placed in such great jeopardy. He sent her a message, and promised to give her a pound of gold if she would consent to have carnal intercourse with him for one night. Bearing in mind that it was her husband, and not she herself, who had authority over her body, she submitted the case to him and told him that she was willing to do this for his sake, provided that he wished thus to save his life in exchange for something which could be regarded as his own because her chastity belonged entirely to him as her husband, who therefore had dominion over her body. He thanked her and told her to comply; for, because her motive was entirely devoid of any lustful desire and was based exclusively on her great love for him and because he himself was consenting to her act and even ordering it, he did not even surmise that her act would be adulterous. The wife went to the mansion of the rich man and submitted to his lustful desires. But she yielded her body to her husband only, although he was now desirous of using it in order to save his life, and not in the usual manner of marital intercourse. She received the gold, but the giver took it back surreptitiously and substituted a similar appearing package of clay. The woman discovered this when she had returned to her own home. Then—with the same marital love that had impelled her to do what she had done— she rushes forth to proclaim publicly that she had done it. She implores the governor. She confesses everything. She shows how great a fraud she has suffered. And now the governor —as if pronouncing sentence on someone else—at first declares himself guilty because all this had happened as the result of his threats; then he orders that from the possessions of Acyndinus a pound of gold be paid to the state treasury, and that the woman be put into possession of the land from which she had received the clay instead of gold. From this incident, I offer no argument for either side. Let each one judge of it as he will, for the story is not taken from divine authorities. However, what that wife did at her husband's bidding becomes less repulsive to human feelings when the whole incident is explained: we do not experience the same loathing as we did at first, when the question was proposed without any example. In this chapter of the Gospel, however, there is nothing that ought to be more seriously pondered than the fact that fornication is so great an evil that, even though a husband and his wife are bound together by so strong a bond, an exception is made in the case of fornication: it is the only cause for their separation. And we have already discoursed on the kind of fornication this may be.[19]

Chapter 17 (Matt. 5.33-37)

(51) He says: '*Again, you have heard that it was said to the ancients, "Thou shalt not swear falsely, but fulfill thy oath to the Lord." But I say to you not to swear at all: neither by heaven, for it is the throne of God; nor by the earth, for it is the footstool of his feet; nor by Jerusalem, for it is the city of the great King. Neither do thou swear by thy head, for thou canst not make one hair white or black. But let your speech be, "Yes, yes"; "No, no." And whatever is over and above this, is from evil.*' Not to swear falsely is the justice of the Pharisees. That justice is confirmed by him who forbids every kind of swearing. And this is the justice of the kingdom of heaven. For, just as a man cannot speak a falsehood if

---
19 See above, 1.16.43-47.

he does not speak at all, so neither can he swear falsely if he does not swear at all. But, inasmuch as a man is swearing if he is calling God as his witness, this passage must be carefully considered in order that the Apostle may not seem to have acted against this precept of the Lord, for he often swore in this manner. For instance, he says: 'But as to what I am writing to you, behold, before God, I do not lie';[1] and again: 'The God and Father of our Lord Jesus Christ, Who is blessed forevermore, knows that I do not lie.'[2] And the following also is similar: 'For God is my witness, Whom I serve in my spirit in the gospel of His Son, how unceasingly I always make mention of you in my prayers.'[3] Or perhaps someone may say that no one really swears unless he uses the word 'by' in connection with that by which he swears, and, therefore, that the Apostle did not really swear by saying: 'God is my witness,' because he did not say: 'By God.' It would be ridiculous to hold this opinion. Nevertheless, lest anyone—because of dullards or the contentious—should think that it makes any difference, let him remember that the Apostle has sworn also in this manner; for he says: 'I die daily, by your glory.'[4] And let no one think this expression is used in such a way as to mean: 'Your glory makes me die every day.' (Just as we say: 'By that man's teaching, he has become learned,' that is to say: 'By means of that man's teaching, it has come to pass that he is thoroughly taught'.) The Greek text determines the meaning, and in that text the expression is: *'Nē tēn kaūchésin hymetéran,'* an expression that is not used except by one who is taking an oath.[5] The Lord's prohibition of swearing is to

---
[1] Gal. 1.20.
[2] 2 Cor. 11.31.
[3] Rom. 1.9.
[4] 1 Cor. 15.31.
[5] Regarding St. Augustine's competency in Greek and his confidence in the Greek texts, see Introduction, nn. 14,15.

be understood, therefore, as meaning that no one is to desire an oath as if it were something good, lest—through a habit engendered by the constant repetition of swearing—he gradually descend to false swearing. Accordingly, let a man restrain himself as much as he can, since he understands that swearing is not to be counted among the things that are good, but as one of the things that are necessary. Let him make use of it only through necessity. In other words, let him not use it except when he sees that, unless men are assured by an oath, they are averse to believing what it is to their benefit to believe. This is the import of the saying, *'But let your speech be, "Yes, yes"; "No, no."'* This is good, and desirable. But, *'whatever is over and above, is from evil.'* In other words, if you are forced to take an oath, remember that the necessity for it arises from the infirmity of those whom you are trying to persuade with regard to something. And of course this is the evil from which we make daily supplication to be delivered, when we say, 'Deliver us from evil.'[6] Consequently, He did not say, 'Whatever is over and above, is evil.' For you do no evil when you make good use of an oath which, although it is not a good thing, is nevertheless necessary for the purpose of persuading someone to believe what you are trying to induce him to believe for a good purpose. But He said that it is 'from evil,' that is, from the evil of the man whose infirmity forces you take an oath. But, no one, unless he has actually experienced it,[7] knows how difficult it is to overcome the

---

6 Matt. 6.13.
7 Augustine had had that personal experience. Elsewhere, he says: 'I, too, have sworn indiscriminately. I had that most abominable habit... From the time when I began to serve God, and saw what great evil there is in false swearing, I have been exceedingly fearful, and I have curbed that most obstinate habit. When curbed, it is restrained; when restrained, it grows weak; weakening, it dies, and a good habit succeeds the bad' (*Serm.* 180.9.10).

habit of swearing and to refrain from ever doing needlessly what necessity sometimes compels one to do.

(52) In view of the fact that it was said, *'But I say to you not to swear at all,'* one may inquire as to the reason for adding, *'Neither by heaven, for it is the throne of God.'* And the same is true with regard to the other particulars up to the expression, *'Neither by thy head.'* I suppose they were added because the Jews did not consider themselves bound by an oath if they had sworn by those things. For, because they had heard, 'Thou shalt fulfill thy oath to the Lord,'[8] they did not believe themselves obliged to fulfill an oath to the Lord if they had sworn by heaven or the earth, by Jerusalem or by the head. This had come to pass, not through any fault of the Lawgiver, but through their misunderstanding. Therefore—beginning from the throne of God, and continuing even to the white hair or the black—the Lord teaches that none of the things which God created is of such little value that anyone may decide to swear falsely by it, for all created things—from the highest to the lowest—are governed by Divine Providence. *'Neither by heaven,'* says He, *'for it is the throne of God; nor by the earth, for it is the footstool of His feet.'* This means that, when you swear by heaven or by the earth, you are not to think yourself not bound to fulfill your oath to the Lord, for you are shown to be swearing by Him whose throne is in heaven, and whose footstool is the earth. *'Nor by Jerusalem, for it is the city of the great King.'* This is a more apt expression than 'My city,' although He is certainly to be understood as having meant that, also. Therefore, because He is its Lord, whoever swears by Jerusalem is bound to fulfill his oath to the Lord. *'Neither do thou swear by thy head.'* Now, what could anyone believe to be more truly

---

8 Cf. Num. 30.3.

his own than his head? But how is it ours, since we have no power to make one hair white or black? Therefore, if anyone wishes to swear even by his own head, he is bound to fulfill his oath to God, who eminently contains all things and is present everywhere. And in this observation, the other forms of oath also are understood—forms which certainly cannot all be enumerated—such as that saying which we have quoted from the Apostle, 'I die daily, by your glory.' And to show that he was bound to fulfill this oath to the Lord, he added: 'Which I have in Christ Jesus.'

(53) But from the fact that heaven has been called the throne of God and the earth the footstool of His feet, we are not to think that God has bodily members placed in heaven and on earth, the way we are at rest when seated. (I make this observation for the sake of those who are as yet carnal.[9]) That seat signfies judgment, and, because in this whole body of the universe the heavens have the greatest splendor and the earth has the least, God is said to have His seat in heaven and to tread the earth with His feet. It is as though the divine power were more closely present to the transcendent beauty, but had arrayed the lesser beauty at the greatest distance and the lowest level. In the spiritual sense, however, heaven signifies holy lives, and earth signifies sinful lives. And the spiritual man is fittingly called the seat of God, for 'the spiritual man judges all things, but is himself judged by no man.'[10] And the sinner is rightly regarded as the footstool of His feet, for to him have been spoken the words, 'Earth thou art, and to the earth shalt thou return.'[10] Since he was unwilling to be within the Law, he is justly set among the lowest, and placed under the Law, for justice requites according to merit.

---

9 Cf. 1 Cor. 3.1.
10 1 Cor. 2.15.
11 Gen. 3.19.

Chapter 18 (Matt. 5.29-37)

(54) But, to epitomize even this brief summary. What, indeed, can be mentioned or imagined more laborious and toilsome than the struggle in which the mind of a believer is exercising all its active powers in overcoming a vicious habit?[1] To sum it up: Let the believer cut off members that are impeding the kingdom of heaven, and let him not be crushed with sorrow. In conjugal fidelity, let him endure all things which, howsoever burdensome, do not involve the sin of moral depravity, namely, fornication. For instance, if a man should happen to have a wife who is either sterile or deformed in body or weak in bodily members, a wife who is either blind or deaf or lame or afflicted with any other ailment, a wife who is wasted by diseases and sufferings and infirmities or by the most horrible affliction that can be imagined, with the sole exception of fornication—let that man endure all this for the sake of fidelity and companionship. Let no believing husband put away such a wife. Moreover, let no believer marry a woman who is separated from her husband, even though she be a beautiful woman, healthy, wealthy, and capable of bearing him children. Since it is not lawful for him to do this, let him know that it is much more unlawful for him to assent to any other illicit carnal intercourse. And let him shun fornication so thoroughly that he will avoid every sort of base corruption. Let him speak the truth; let him commend it, not with habitual swearing, but with upright conduct. Let him hasten to the citadel of the Christian warfare,[2] and from that citadel—as from a superior position—let him hurl the countless hosts of all the bad habits that are in rebellion against him. (A few of those

---
1 *Conf.* 8.5.10.
2 Cf. 2 Cor. 10.3-6.

habits have been mentioned, so that all of them may be understood.) But, who would venture to undertake such great labors unless he were so inflamed with love of justice that—like a man aflame with hunger and thirst—he would do violence to the kingdom of heaven? For in no other way can he have the fortitude to endure all the hardships which the lovers of this world consider laborious, arduous and extremely difficult—in order to sever bad habits. Therefore: 'Blessed are they who hunger and thirst after justice, for they shall be fully satisfied.'[3]

(55) But, when one is advancing through rough and rugged defiles, and is walled around with various temptations, and sees the cliffs of his past life rising on this side and on that, if he then experiences difficulty in those efforts, and fears that he will be unable to succeed in his endeavors, let him take counsel in order to gain aid. And what else is the counsel but that a man who is desirious of aid for his own infirmity should bear with the infirmity of others and relieve it insofar as he can? Let us, therefore, consider the precepts of mercy. There seems to be no difference between a merciful man and a meek man, of whom we have treated above. However, there is this difference between them, namely, that through piety the meek man does not contradict either the divine maxims that are advanced against his sins or the words of God which he does not yet understand; but he confers no benefit on him whom he neither contradicts nor resists. The merciful man, however, refrains from offering any resistance, lest he impede the correction of someone whom he might make worse by resisting.

---

3 Matt. 5-6.

Chapter 19 (Matt. 5.38-42)

(56) The Lord then continues, and says: *'You have heard that it was said, "An eye for an eye," and, "A tooth for a tooth." But I say to you not to resist an evildoer; but if someone strikes thee on the right cheek, turn to him the other also; and whoever wishes to go to law with thee and to take thy tunic, give up to him thy cloak as well; and whoever forces thee to go one mile, go with him another two. Give to him who asks of thee; and turn not away from him who would borrow from thee.'* Not to exceed due measure in inflicting punishment, lest the requital be greater than the injury—that is the lesser justice of the Pharisees. And it is a high degree of justice, for it would not be easy to find a man who, on receiving a fisticuff, would be content to give only one in return, and who, on hearing one word from a reviler, would be content to return one word exactly equivalent. On the contrary, either he exceeds moderation because he is angry, or he thinks that, with regard to one who has inflicted an injury on another, justice demands a penalty greater than the injury suffered by the innocent person. To a great extent, such a spirit is restrained by the Law, in which is written the directive, 'An eye for an eye' and 'A tooth for a tooth.'[1] Moderation is signified by these words, so that the penalty may not be greater than the injury. And this is the beginning of peace. But to have absolutely no wish for any such retribution—that is perfect peace.

(57) Through the maxim that the requittal must be equal to the injury, a transition has been made from the sheerest discord to the greatest concord—made gradually, in accordance with the orderly succession of eras.[2] And that maxim holds, as it were, a middle position between the first dictum

---
1 Exod. 21.24; Deut. 19.21.
2 See above, 1.17.49, n. 16.

—which is not within the Law—and the principle which the Lord prescribed for the perfecting of His followers; that is to say, it stands mid-way between the rule of inflicting a penalty greater than the injury committed, and the principle that no evil is to be returned for evil. Now, see what a great difference there is between a man who, without having suffered any injury, does evil to another with the intention of hurting and injuring him, and a man who returns no evil even when he himself has been injured. But, a man who never injures anyone who has not injured him, and yet either actually or by desire returns a greater injury when he himself has been injured—such a man has risen to some extent from the depth of injustice and has made some progress toward the summit of justice. And yet, that man is not observing the commandment of the Law that was given through Moses.[3] However, a man is showing some forgiveness if he retaliates with an injury that is exactly equivalent to the injury he has received, for a guilty man deserves a penalty that is not the exact equivalent of the injury which an innocent man has suffered from him. Therefore, this preparatory justice—which is not a severe justice, but a merciful one—has been brought to perfection by Him who came, not to destroy the Law, but to fulfill it. He has nevertheless left two degrees of perfection still to be understood, for He preferred to discourse on mercy at its very highest. So, we still have to consider the conduct of a man who indeed does not observe in all its fullness the precept of the kingdom of heaven. Such would be the man who so acts as to return, not as great an evil as he has received, but a lesser evil; for instance, he returns one fisticuff for two, or he cuts off an ear in retaliation for an eye

---
[3] Lev. 24.19-22.

that has been plucked out. Even if a man rises above this degree of perfection, and does not retaliate at all, he is, of course, coming closer to the Lord's precept, but he has not yet reached it. For, even if you return no evil for the evil you receive, the Lord seems to deem it insufficient unless you are ready to receive even further evil. Accordingly, He does not say: 'But I say to you not to return evil for evil,' although even that would be a great precept; He says: '*Not to resist evil.*' Hence, not only may you not retaliate for the evil inflicted upon you, but you may not even make any resistance against the infliction of further evil. And, in fact, this is what He expounds as a consequence: '*But if someone strikes thee on the right cheek, turn to him the other also.*' For He does not say: 'If someone strikes thee, do thou not strike'; He says: 'Arrange for him to strike thee again.' Experience shows that mercy demands this, for it is a most intimate experience of those who minister to little children and deranged persons whom they dearly love, and to whom they minister as they would minister to their own children or to any of their own most beloved friends afflicted with illness. They suffer much from those children or deranged persons; yet—until the infirmity of either childhood or illness will have ceased— they submit themselves to further suffering if the welfare of those persons requires it. As the Physician of souls,[4] therefore, what other instruction could the Lord give to those whom He was preparing to heal their fellow men, except the precept that they should bear with equanimity the infirmities of those for whose health they were to be ready to prescribe? All moral turpitude arises from a weakness of character, for

---

[4] 'The entire human race was sick, not with bodily diseases, but with sin. Over the whole earth, from the East to the West, lay the giant sick man. The All-powerful Physician came down to heal the sick giant' (*Sermon.* 87.11.13). See also *Enarr.* in ps. 34.20; 35.17; 98.3; 102.5; 109.3; 130.7; Serm. 80.1.4; 88.1.1; 174.5.6; 175.3.3; 176.8.9.

there is nothing more faultless than a man who is strengthened to perfection.[5]

(58) But we may inquire as to the significance of the *'right* cheek;[6] for this is the reading in the Greek texts (and they are the more trustworthy), while many of the Latin texts have just the word, *'cheek,'* and not the additional word, *'right.'* Now, the face is the feature by which everyone is recognized. And we read in the writings of the Apostle: 'For you suffer it if a man enslaves you, if a man devours you, if a man takes from you, if a man is arrogant, if a man slaps your face:'[7] Then, in order to explain what a slapping of the face means, he straightway adds: 'I speak according to dishonor.' It means contempt and disdain. The Apostle did not intend this to mean that they should not bear with those men. Rather, he meant that they should bear with him, since he loved them so much that he was willing to be expended for them.[8] However, the face cannot be designated as the right face and the left, but high rank can be either according to God or according to this world. Hence, it is as though the face were divided into the right cheek and the left, in order to signify that, whenever his being a Christian becomes an occasion of contempt in the case of any follower of Christ, he should be much more ready to be despised in his own person if he holds any of the honors of this world. Just as in the case of the Apostle himself, when in his person men were persecuting the Christian denomination; if he then remained silent regarding the dignity which he held in the world, he would not have turned the other cheek to those who were striking him on the right cheek. But by saying, 'I am a Roman

---

5 Cf. Rom. 1.11; 2 Thess. 3.3.
6 For further—and perfectly consistent—interpretations of 'the right' and 'the left', see *Enarr. in ps.* 108.8; 120.8; 136.15; 137.14; 143.18; *Serm.* 149.14.15; *Locut. in Gen.* 24.49; *in Deut.* 28.13.
7 2 Cor. 11.20.
8 Cf. 2 Cor. 12.15

citizen,'⁹ he was not unprepared to have them despise in his person the thing that he deemed of least value, when in his person they had despised a name so precious and salutary. Did he thereby endure in any less degree the chains which it was not lawful to place on Roman citizens? Or did he blame anyone for this injustice? Even though some people spared him on account of the title of Roman citizen, he did not on that account fail to offer them something to strike, for he yearned to correct by his own patience the perversity of those whom he saw to be honoring in his person the left portion rather than the right. The one thing to be considered is the spirit of kindness and clemency with which he acted toward those from whom he was suffering the injuries. Of course, those who do not understand him think that he uttered a reproach when he had been slapped by order of the high priest, for, with seeming insolence, he then said: 'God will strike thee, thou whitewashed wall.'¹⁰ But, those who understand him take this as a prophecy.¹¹ The 'whitewashed wall' stands for hypocrisy; it is pretense, veiled beneath the priestly dignity,¹² and under this title—as though beneath a white covering—it conceals, as it were, an inner slimy filthiness. But, when he was asked: 'Dost thou revile the high priest?' then he marvelously complied with the requirements of humility, for he replied, 'Brethren, I did not know that he was the high priest; for it is written, "Thou shalt not speak ill of a ruler of thy people." '¹³ The mildness of this prompt reply shows how calmly he had spoken what he seemed to have uttered in anger, for such a reply could not be given by those who are angered or perturbed. And

---

9 Acts 22.25.
10 Acts 23.3.
11 See below, 1.21.71f.
12 See below, 2.2.5; 2.19.64.
13 Acts 2.3.5; Exod. 22.28.

in the reply, 'I did not know that he was the high priest,' he spoke the truth to those who understand him. It is as though he were saying: 'I have come to know another High Priest, for whose name's sake I am suffering these injuries—a High Priest whom it is not lawful to revile, but whom you are reviling, because in me you hate nothing else than his name.' Thus, a man ought not to parade those prerogatives under a false pretense, but he should have his heart prepared for everything, so that he will be able to accord with that expression of the Prophet, 'My heart is ready, O God, my heart is ready.'[14] Of course, many persons have learned to offer the other cheek, but have not learned to love the man by whom they are struck. And yet, the Lord Himself—although He was certainly the first to fulfill the precepts of His own teaching—did not offer the other cheek to the servant of the high priest when that servant had struck Him on one cheek. On the contrary, He said: 'If I have spoken evil, reproach me with the evil; but if I have spoken well, why dost thou strike me?'[15] In His heart, however, He was not thereby unprepared; He was prepared not only to be struck on the other cheek for the salvation of all, but even to have His whole body nailed to a cross.

(59) Therefore, the very next sentence is rightly understood as a precept with regard to the preparation of the heart, and not with regard to the visible performance of the deed. *'And whoever wishes to go to law with thee and to take thy tunic, give up to him thy cloak as well.'* Now, it is not exclusively with regard to the tunic and the cloak that we are to observe the instruction given us with reference to those garments; we are to observe it also with respect to everything which we have any right to call our own in the

---
14 Ps. 56.8.
15 John 18.23.

realm of time. For, if this command is given with reference to something necessary, how much more does it behoove us to have no care for what is superfluous? However, those things which I have called 'our own' are to be confined to that category of goods to which the Lord Himself confines the injunction, when He says: *'If anyone wishes to go to law with thee and to take thy tunic.'* Consequently, let those goods be understood as the things which can be the object of a lawsuit against us, for the purpose of having them pass from our ownership to the ownership of the one who goes to law with us, or the one on whose behalf the lawsuit is entered. Such goods would be clothing, a house, landed property, a beast of burden, and all kinds of property in general. But, it is very doubtful whether the injunction is to be understood as applying to slaves as well; for it does not befit a Christian to possess a slave in the same way as he would possess a horse or money, even though it may happen that a horse —and to far greater degree, an object of gold or silver—is valued at a higher price than a slave.[16] Moreover, if a slave is receiving from you, his master, a better moral training or a guidance more correct and better adapted to the worship of God than can be given him by the man who wishes to take him away, I doubt whether anyone would venture to say that this slave—like a garment—ought to receive no consideration. For, as subsequent pronouncements reveal,[17] a man

---

16 Augustine recognized slavery as an evil resulting from sin, and, in the Roman Empire, originating from defeat in war. 'Either iniquity or advesity has made man a slave to man' (*In Heptateuch. ad Gen.* 46.32). He did not accept the Roman concept of a slave as a mere chattel. His concept of slavery was derived from the Mosaic Law, which prescribed humane treatment of slaves, and was refined by the Christian teaching on charity and universal brotherhood. (Cf. *De civ. Dei* 19.15-16; *Enarr. in ps.* 124.7; *De moribus ecclesiae* 1.30.63; *Sermo* 21.6-7).

17 See below. 1.21.69.

ought to love a man as he loves himself, because the Lord of all commands him to love even his enemies.

(60) Of course, we must bear in mind that every tunic is a garment, but that not every garment is a tunic. Therefore, the word, *'garment,'* has a broader signification than the word, *'tunic.'* Consequently, I think that with regard to the saying, *'And whoever wishes to go to law with thee and to take thy tunic, give up to him thy cloak as well,'* it is as though one were to say: 'Whoever wishes to take your tunic, give up to him whatever other clothing you have.' Hence, many translators have used the word, *'pallium,'* to render the meaning of the Greek word, *'himátion,'* which has been employed.

(61) *'And,'* says He, *'whoever forces thee to go one mile, go with him another two.'* Of course, this does not mean that you should actually walk, but rather that you should be disposed in mind to do so. In the history of Christianity (and there is authority in that history), you will not find that any such thing has been done by the saints. Neither will you find that it was done by the Lord Himself, notwithstanding the fact that—in the human nature which He has deigned to assume—He was furnishing us with an example of how to live. But you can find that in nearly all places they were serenely prepared to suffer whatever unjust measures might be taken against them. Are we, therefore, to think that the expression, *'Go with him another two,'* was used just as an example? Or did He mean fulfillment to the third degree, since the number, *'three,'* is a symbol of perfection?[18]— so that when anyone is fulfilling this precept, he might bear in mind that he is fulfilling the perfect justice by mercifully

---

18 See above, 1.4.12, n. 9. For other examples of similar interpretations of the number, 'three', see *Sermo* 252.10; *Epist.* 55.11.20; *In Joan. evang.* tr. 27.10; *Enarr. in ps.* 59.2; *Enarr. in ps.* 86.4; *De civ. Dei* 20.5.3.

sustaining the infirmities of those whom he wishes to see restored to health? According to this view, it can be seen that the Lord gradually intimated these precepts by three examples. The first of those examples is *'If anyone strikes thee on the right cheek'*; the second, *'If anyone wishes to take away thy tunic'*; and the third, *'If anyone forces thee to go a mile.'* In the third example a double is added to a single and the number, three, is thus reached. If this number does not here signify perfection, as has been said, then let it be understood as follows: namely, that when the Lord was giving precepts, He began with something rather easy to endure and that He then advanced gradually until He reached another burden which is twice as difficult. At first, He ordered that the other cheek be offered whenever the right cheek has been struck. This means that you ought to be ready still to endure something that is less than what you have already suffered. For, no matter what the *'right cheek'* may signify, it is certainly more highly prized than what the left cheek symbolizes; when a man has suffered an injury with respect to something very highly prized, it is a less hardship for him to bear with an injury regarding something less highly prized. The next precept of the Lord is that the cloak also be given to the man who wishes to take away the tunic. Now, the cloak is of the same value as the tunic, or of little more value, but certainly not twice as valuable. Thirdly, with regard to the mile to which He says that two more are to be added, He commands you to refrain from resisting further injury even though it be twice as great. Hence, He indicates that if anyone wishes to be unjust to you, he is to be endured with equanimity whether he wishes to be unjust in a lesser degree than he has been, or in the same degree, or in a greater degree.

Chapter 20 (Matt. 5.39-42)

(62) And I see at once that no kind of injury has been overlooked in these categories of the three examples, for all the wrongs from which we suffer reproach are divided into two categories: namely, the wrong that can be repaired and the wrong that cannot be repaired. The compensation of revenge is sought usually in the case of a wrong that cannot be repaired. Yet, of what advantage is the fact that you hit back when you have been hit? Is the bodily injury repaired in any way by this? A spirit that is puffed up needs such poultices, but they afford no solace to a healthy and steadfast mind. On the contrary, such a mind deems it better that another's infirmity be mercifully sustained rather than that its own infirmity—but such a mind has no infirmity—be mitigated by another's punishment.

(63) A punishment that is designed for the purpose of correction is not hereby forbidden; for that very punishment is an exercise of mercy, and is not incompatible with the firm resolve by which we are ready to suffer even further injuries from a man whose amendment we desire. But no one is fit for the task of inflicting such punishment unless—by the greatness of his love—he has overcome the hate by which those who seek to avenge themselves are usually enraged. For instance, there is no reason to fear that parents will seem to hate their little child when they chastise him as an offender, so that he may not continue to offend. And the perfection of love—by an imitation of the very love of God the Father—is clearly proposed to us in the following words, for they read: 'Love your enemies, do good to those who hate you, and pray for those who persecute you.'[1] Yet, through the Prophet it is said of God Himself: 'For the Lord chastises

---
1 Matt. 5.44.

whom He loves, and He scourges everyone whom He receives as a son.'[2] And the Lord says: 'The servant who does not know his master's will, and does things deserving of stripes, will be beaten with few stripes; but the servant who knows his master's will, and does things deserving of stripes, will be beaten with many stripes.'[3] Hence, the only requisite is that the punishment be inflicted by one who really is endued with authority, and that he inflict the punishment as affectionately as a father would punish his little child, because, in view of its youth, the father cannot as yet hate his child. Hence, a very appropriate moral is adduced, in order to make it sufficiently clear that love for an offender may demand his punishment, rather than a condonation of his offense. The moral is that, when a man inflicts a penalty, his intention ought to be to make the offender happy by a correction, rather than unhappy by a punishment; and that, if necessity demands it—whether he possesses or lacks the authority to restrain the offender—he ought to be ready at all events to tolerate calmly even further injuries done to him by a man whose correction he is seeking to bring about.

(64) Nevertheless, noble and saintly men inflicted death as a punishment for many sins, although they knew well that no one ought to fear the death which separates soul and body. But they were acting in conformity with the sentiment of those who do fear it, so that the living would be struck with salutary fear. Those who were put to death did not suffer the injury from death itself; rather, they were suffering injury from sin, and it might have become worse if they had continued to live. This authority was not exercised rashly by those to whom God had committed it. It was not through rashness that Elias inflicted death on many persons, whether he inflicted it by his own hand or by invoking fire from

---
2 Prov. 3.12; cf. Heb. 12.6.
3 Luke 12.47-8.

heaven.⁴ And other great and godly men did it, also—not rashly, but with the same desire of consulting human welfare. And the Lord did not reprehend the example of Elias when His disciples had cited it. (For they did cite the example of that holy Prophet by naming what had been done by him, so that the Lord might empower them also to bring fire from heaven to consume those who were refusing the hospitality He was seeking.) But He reprehended the unenlightenment of the disciples themselves with regard to the righting of a wrong, when He saw that they were hatefully seeking vengeance, and not lovingly desiring correction.⁵ They were ignorant in that regard, because they were as yet untaught. Accordingly, such punishments were not entirely lacking even after He had taught them the meaning of loving one's neighbor as one's self, and after they had been infused with the Holy Spirit, whom—as He had promised⁶—He sent down on them on the completion of ten whole days after His Ascension.⁷ However, such punishments were then much less frequent than in the Old Testament; under the Old Law men were ruled like servants and restrained by fear, while in the New Dispensation they were treated like sons and were being most fully nourished by love. Yet—as we read in the Acts of the Apostles⁸—Ananias and his wife fell dead at the words of the Apostle Peter. And they were not restored to life; they were buried.

(65) If the heretics who impugn the Old Testament refuse to accept the testimony of this book,⁹ let them attend to the

---
4 3 Kings 18.40; 4 Kings 1.10.
5 Cf. Luke 9.51-56.
6 John 15.26.
7 Acts 2.1-4.
8 Acts 5.1-10.
9 A reference to 'the Manichaeans, whose error does not consist in a wrong interpretation of the writings of the Old Testament, but who blaspheme by rejecting and detesting them' (*De Gen. ad litt.* 8.2.5). For, 'some of the Manichaeans repudiate the canonical book which

words of the Apostle Paul, for they, as well as we, read his writings. Let them hear what he has to say about a certain sinner whom he had delivered over to Satan for the destruction of the flesh, 'so that his soul may be saved.'[10] Even if they refuse to admit that the sinner's death is denoted by these words—for, perhaps, the meaning is indefinite—let them at least acknowledge that some kind of punishment was inflicted by the Apostle through Satan. The added clause, 'so that his soul may be saved,' makes it plain that he acted through love, and not through hatred. Or in those books to which *they* certainly attribute great authority, let them note what we are saying, for in those books it is written that the Apostle Thomas, having first commended the man's soul to salvation in the life to come, imprecated the most atrocious punishment of death on a certain man by whom he had been slapped. After that man had been killed by a lion, a dog brought his hand—now severed from the rest of the body—to a table where the Apostle was dining with others.[11] We are not obliged to believe that written account, for it is not found in the Catholic canon. But, through some kind of blindness which I cannot understand, those men not only read it but even approve it as a wholly genuine and truthful narrative, while they rage most bitterly against the corporal punishments that are to be found in the Old Testament, although they know absolutely nothing about the purpose of those punishments or the condition of the times in which they used to be inflicted.

(66) With regard to the class of injuries that can be expiated by punishment, the Christian mind will observe so

---

is called *The Acts of the Apostles'* (*Epist.* 237.2). Cf. *De Gen. contra Manich.* 1.1.2; 1.22.23; 2.25.38; *De utilitate credendi* 2.4; *De dono persever.* 11.26; *Sermo* 1.1.1; *Epist.* 236.2.
10 1 Cor. 5.5.
11 *The Acts of St. Thomas,* an apocryphal work which scholars assign

much moderation that it will not become incensed unto hatred when an injury is received. On the contrary, it will be so moved by compassion for the weakness of the offender that it will be prepared to bear with even greater injuries, and it will not neglect any corrective remedies that it may be able to apply through counsel, influence or authority. As to the injuries that can be completely repaired—they belong to another class. There are two species of this class: one species has reference to money; the other, to personal service. In the case of the tunic and the cloak, we have an example of the first; in the case of the forced journey of one mile and two additional miles, we have an example of the other. A cloak can be given back; the man whom you have aided can aid you if needs be. Or, perhaps we ought to understand their diverse implications in this sense, namely, that what is first supposed with reference to the smitten cheek signifies every injury that is inflicted by the wicked, and inflicted in such a way that no reparation can be made except through punishment; that what is then proposed with reference to the garment signifies every injury for which amends can be made without punishment (and perhaps this is the reason for the extra clause, *'if anyone wishes to go to law with thee,'* for, if something is taken away by process of law, it is not regarded as taken away by the kind of violence that deserves punishment); and that the third example is a combination of the other two—signifying both the injury for which amends can be made through punishment and the injury that can be repaired without punishment. For, whoever exacts a service to which he has no right, if he exacts it by force and

---

to the beginning of the third century (Cf. Harnack, *Chronologie* 2.172; Pick, *The Apocryphal Acts of Paul, Peter, and Thomas*, Chicago, 1909). On at least two other occasions, Augustine cites the same instance and develops the same argument (Cf. *Contra Faustum* 22.79; *Contra Adimant.* 17.2).

not by judicial decree, can be made to suffer a penalty for his wickedness and to repay the service if the injured person demands it. An example of such conduct is presented in the instance of one who wrongly forces a man to travel, or who unlawfully exacts a personal service from one who is unwilling to render it. So, in all the above-mentioned kinds of injury, the Lord teaches that it behooves a Christian mind to be most patient, most merciful, and most ready to endure even greater injuries.

(67) The mere fact of your refraining from inflicting an injury is not enough, for you must also bestow benefits insofar as you are able. He therefore supplements this, and says: *'To everyone who asks of thee, give; and from him who would borrow of thee, do not turn away.'* When He says: *'Give to everyone who asks,'* He does not say: 'Give him everything he asks'; for he means that you are to give in accordance with propriety and justice. But, what if a man should ask you for money with which he intends to try to impose hardship on an innocent person? And what if he should even ask for lewdness? Well—without going into details, for the examples are countless—you are to give whatever will not be injurious to you or to someone else, insofar as that can be humanly foreseen or conjectured. And to the man whom you justly refuse, you ought to point out the justice of your refusal, so that you will not send him away empty. In this way, you will give to everyone who asks, although you will not always give him what he asks; at times you will give something better, for you will give a correction to the man who is making unjust requests.

(68) And as to His maxim, *'From him who would borrow of thee, do not turn away,'* we are to understand this also with reference to the heart, for God loves a cheerful giver.[12]

---

12 2 Cor. 9.7.

Even if the receiver himself is not going to make repayment, everyone borrows whenever he receives, for whenever a man bestows a benefit, he lends at interest, because God makes a greater recompense to the merciful. Or if it seems incorrect to regard as a borrower anyone except a recipient who is expected to make repayment, then we should understand that the Lord included those two general ways of doing a favor. For, either we benevolently donate what we give to another, or we lend it to someone who intends to return it. And men who are willing to make a donation because a divine reward has been promised are generally disinclined to give anything that is sought as a loan—as though they would receive nothing from God, because the recipient is going to pay back what was given him. Toward this kind of welldoing, therefore, Divine Authority rightly exhorts us, when He says: *'From him who would borrow of thee, do not turn away.'* For, this is the same as to say: 'Do not think that a petitioner who would repay you is beyond the reach of your benevolence, and that the money you lend him will bring you no reward. Do not think that God will make you no recompense, because the borrower will repay you.' Since you are lending it by God's command, it cannot be fruitless in the eyes of Him who commands this.

Chapter 21 (Matt. 5.43-48)

(69) Then He continues, and says: *'You have heard that it was said, "Thou shalt love thy neighbor, and shalt hate thy enemy." But I say to you, love your enemies, do good to those who hate you, and pray for those who persecute you,*[1]

---

1 Augustine is following a direct translation from Greek texts which, unlike the Vulgate, does not contain the words, 'and calumniate'. Cf. Introduction, note 18.

so that you may be children of your Father Who is in heaven, Who makes His sun to rise on the good and on the evil, and sends rain on the just and the unjust. For if you love those who love you, what reward shall you have? Do not even the publicans do that? And if you salute your brethren only, what are you doing more than others? Do not even the Gentiles do that? Be you therefore perfect, even as your Father Who is in heaven is perfect.' Who could fulfill those precepts here mentioned, unless he had that very love with which we are commanded to love even our enemies and persecutors? But the fulfillment of mercy—by which the greatest possible aid is given to one in distress—cannot be extended beyond the love of an enemy. Accordingly, it is summed up in this way: *'Be you therefore perfect, even as your Father Who is in heaven is perfect.'* This is to be understood in the sense that God is perfect as God, and that a soul should be perfect as a soul.

(70) But, many persons hate those by whom they are loved, just as dissolute sons hate their parents when they repress those sons' debauchery. Hence, it may be seen that there is some degree of perfection in the justice of the Pharisees, which is the justice of the Old Law, for, even though a man still hates his enemy, he has risen somewhat if he loves his neighbor. But, under the dominion of Him who came to fulfill the Law, and not to destroy it,[2] a man will bring his generosity and kindness to full perfection if he extends them so far as to love even an enemy. Although the former degree is at least a slight advance, it is still so slight that it does not distinguish one from the publicans. Even though *'Thou*

---
2 Matt. 5.17.

shalt hate thy enemy' is written in the Law,³ it is to be understood as a concession to the weak, not as a command to the righteous.

(71) At this juncture, a question arises which allows of no dissembling whatever. To those who give only a haphazard and heedless attention to the Scriptures, many other Biblical passages seem to be in opposition to the precept whereby the Lord exhorts us to love our enemies, to do good to those who hate us, and to pray for those who persecute us, for in the writings of the Prophets one finds many imprecations against enemies, and these are believed to be curses. For instance, this expression, 'Let their table become as a snare,'⁴ as well as the other imprecations that are uttered in that passage. And—in addition to the other maledictions which, either earlier or later in the same Psalm, are uttered by the Prophet against the person of Judas—there is this expression, 'May his children be fatherless, and his wife a widow.'⁵ The Scriptures contain many other expressions which may seem to

---

3 '*Thou shalt hate thy enemy*' had become part of the Jewish teaching, for our Lord cites it in Matt. 5.43. But it was not written in the Mosaic Law. On this point, Knabenbauer writes: 'Very many rightly believe that Jewish teachers had derived it as an inference from various passages of the Law.' Having cited Exod. 17.14; 23.22; Lev. 19.18; Num. 25.17; Deut. 7.2; 23.6; 23.19; 25.19, the same author continues: 'They could also have been led to draw this inference from various passages of the psalms in which curses and reproaches are uttered against the enemies of God and of the people' (*Comment. in Quatuor S. Evang.* [Paris 1892] 241). Lagrange remarks: 'The difficulty is to find the second part [of Matt. 5.43] in the Law. Chrysostom, Jerome and Augustine were probably aware of this difficulty, but they made no observation on it. . . . In accordance with the usage in the schools (Fiebig, *Altjüdische Gleichnisse*, p. 35, note 1), a citation is often followed by an explanatory note, without anything to distinguish the one from the other' (*Evangile selon Saint Matthieu* [Paris 1927] 114)
4 Ps. 68.23.
5 Ps. 108.9.

be contrary to this precept of the Lord, and to the Apostle's precept whereby he says: 'Bless and do not curse.'[6] Furthermore, it is written of the Lord that He cursed the cities which did not receive His word,[7] and the same Apostle, speaking of a certain man, said this about him: 'The Lord will render to him according to his deeds.'[8]

(72) Those instances, however, are easily explained. In the first place, the Prophet employed a form of imprecation in announcing what was to happen, and he uttered the imprecation, not through wishful desire, but through the spirit of foresight. The Lord and the Apostle acted in similar fashion, although we find in their words, not their wish, but their prediction. So, when the Lord says: 'Woe to thee, Capharnaum,'[9] His meaning is nothing else than that some evil is about to befall it as a punishment for unbelief. The Lord did not hatefully wish this to happen, but by His divinity He saw that it would happen. And the Apostle does not say: 'May the Lord render to him according to his deeds'; he says: 'The Lord will render . . .' These are the words of a man who is hurling inprecations. And in like manner, because he saw that the hypocrisy of the Jews was about to be destroyed, he said what we have already mentioned:[10] 'God will strike thee, thou whitewashed wall.' The Prophets usually foretell coming events under the semblance of a man uttering imprecations, just as they often employed the past tense to announce events that were to happen; for instance: 'Why have the Gentiles raged, and the people devised vain things?'[11] Although he was not mentioning this as something already

---

6 Rom. 12.14.
7 Matt. 11.21; Luke 10.13.
8 2 Tim. 4.4.
9 A misquotation. Cf. Matt. 11.21-23; Luke 10.13-15.
10 See 1.19.58; Acts 23.3.
11 Ps. 2.1.

come to pass, but was viewing it in the future, he nevertheless did not say: 'Why will the Gentiles rage, and the people devise vain things?'[12] Of the same character is the following: 'They parted my garments amongst them, and upon my vesture they cast lots.'[13] In this passage he did not say: 'They will part my garments amongst them, and upon my vesture they will cast lots.' Nevertheless, no one cavils at those words except someone who does not perceive that these various figures of speech do not in any degree detract from the real truth, but that they greatly affect our emotions.

Chapter 22 (Matt. 5.44)

(73) But the following words of the Apostle John make this question more troublesome. He says: 'If anyone knows that his brother is committing a sin that is not unto death, he shall beseech; and the Lord will give life to him who is committing a sin not unto death. For there is a sin unto death. I do not say that anyone should beseech as to that.'[1] Even though the Lord commands us to pray for our very persecutors, this passage clearly shows that there are some brethren for whom we are not commanded to pray. And this difficulty cannot be solved unless we acknowledge that there are some sins among the brethren which are more grievous than persecution by enemies, for by many instances from

---
12 An example of Augustine's absolute faith in the Septuagint (See Introduction, note 18). That version and its literal Latin translations merely transcribe the tenses from the Hebrew, and give a faulty expression of the original sense. In both instances here cited by Augustine, the latest Latin translation uses the present tense. (Cf. *Psalterium Breviarii Romani*, Rome, 1945; Bea, 'The New Psalter: Its Origin and Spirit,' *Catholic Biblical Quarterly* 8 [1946] 17ff.)
13 Ps. 21.19.

1 1 John 5.16.

the divine Scriptures it can be proved that Christians are designated by the word brethren. The most obvious example is furnished by the Apostle's use of the word, *'brother,'* in that sense: 'For the unbelieving husband is sanctified in the wife, and the unbelieving wife is sanctified in the brother.'[2] He did not use the additional word, *'our';* he thought that word was plainly understood whenever he used the name of brother in order to designate a Christian who had an unbelieving wife. Accordingly, he says shortly afterwards: 'But if the unbeliever departs, let him depart; for a brother or sister is not under bondage in such cases.' Therefore, I suppose that a brother's sin is a sin unto death, if he assails the brotherhood after he has come to the knowledge of God through the grace of Our Lord Jesus Christ, and is inflamed by the fire of envy against the very grace by which he was reconciled to God.[3] And a sin is a sin not unto death whenever one does not withdraw his love from a brother, but—through some weakness of character—fails to perform the required duties of the brotherhood. Wherefore, even on the Cross, the Lord says: 'Father, forgive them, for they do not know what they are doing.'[4] For they had not entered the fellowship of the holy brotherhood, since they had not as yet become partakers of the grace of the Holy Spirit. And in the Acts of the Apostles, blessed Stephen prays for those by whom he is being stoned,[5] because they had not as yet believed in Christ and were not contending against that universal grace. And the Apostle Paul, I suppose, does not pray for Alexander, precisely because that man was already a brother and had sinned unto death; that is to say, he had sinned by assailing

---

2 1 Cor. 7.12-15.
3 See *Retract.* 1.19.7.
4 Luke 23.34.
5 Acts 7.60.

the brotherhood through envy. He beseeches forgiveness for those who had not ceased their love, but had succumbed through fear. Hence, he says: 'Alexander, the coppersmith, has done me much harm; the Lord will render to him according to his deeds. Do you also avoid him, for he has vehemently opposed our words.' Then he continues, saying with reference to those for whom he is praying: 'At my first defense no one came to my support, but all forsook me; may it not be imputed to them.'[6]

(74) This distinction with regard to sins marks the difference between Judas the betrayer and Peter the denier. But, of course, it does imply that a repentant sinner is not to be forgiven; for, in that case, we would be in opposition with the Lord's precept that forgiveness be always granted to a brother who asks a brother to forgive him.[7] But the infamy of the sin of Judas was so great that he could not submit to the humiliation of beseeching forgiveness, even though his consciousness of guilt forced him to acknowledge his sin and to proclaim it. For, although he said: 'I have sinned, for I have betrayed innocent blood,'[8] he nevertheless despaired and had recourse to the halter, rather than humble himself and ask for pardon. Wherefore, it is very important for us to know what kind of repentance obtains forgiveness from the Lord. There are many who confess—much more readily than Judas did—that they have sinned. They become so incensed with themselves that they feel vehement sorrow for having sinned. Yet, they do not put away their pride in order to render their hearts humble and contrite, and thus to implore forgiveness. We cannot but believe that those men have already reached the

---

6 1 Tim. 4.14-16.
7 Cf. Matt. 18.21f.; Luke 17.3f.
8 Matt. 27.4.

same state of mind [as Judas] regarding their condemnation because of the enormity of their sin.

(75) Maliciously and enviously to assail brotherly love after having received the grace of the Holy Spirit—perhaps this is the sin against the Holy Spirit, the sin which the Lord says will not be forgiven either in this world or in the world to come.[9] Hence, one may ask whether the Jews sinned against the Holy Spirit when they said that the Lord was casting out devils by Beelzebub, the prince of devils.[10] It may be asked whether we are to understand this as spoken against the Lord himself (for elsewhere He says of Himself: 'But if they have called the master of the house Beelzebub, how much more those of his household!'),[11] or whether—although as yet they were not Christians—they are nevertheless to be regarded as having sinned against the Holy Spirit because of the very depth of their envy; for, in their ingratitude in the face of such good works, they had spoken out of great envy. But this cannot be inferred from the Lord's words, even though He says in the same passage: 'And whoever speaks an evil word against the Son of Man, it will be forgiven him; but whoever speaks a word against the Holy Spirit, it will not be forgiven him either in this world or in the world to come.'[12] It still seems possible to believe that He was giving them an admonition to the effect that they should accede to

---

9 Matt. 12.32. Augustine was always diffident regarding the interpretation of this text. 'In the entire holy Scripture, there is, perhaps, no weightier and more difficult question' (*Sermo* 71.5.8). 'Since this sin is not defined, there can be many different opinions concerning it. I think it is the forsaking until death of the faith which works through charity' (*De corrept. et gratia* 12.35). 'This sin is a hardness of heart which continues to the end of life, and through which a man refuses to receive forgiveness of sins in the unity of the body of Christ, which the Holy Spirit enlivens' (*Epist.* 185.11.49).
10 Matt. 12.24.
11 Matt. 10.25.
12 Matt. 12.32.

grace, and that, when they had received the grace, they should not repeat the sin they had now committed. For, on this occasion, they had spoken an evil word against the Son of Man, and this can be forgiven them if they be converted, and believe in Him, and receive the Holy Spirit. But, after they have received the Holy Spirit, if they then choose to be envious of the brotherhood and to resist the grace which they have received, it will not be forgiven them either in this world or in the world to come. For, if He believed them so condemned that no hope was left for them, He would not still think them capable of profiting by the following admonition, which He gave them by saying: 'Either make the tree good and its fruit good, or make the tree bad and its fruit bad.'[13]

(76) And now, lest our want of proficiency should make it appear that the divine Scripture is self-contradictory (something that cannot happen) with regard to loving our enemies, doing good to those who hate us, and praying for those who persecute us,[14] let that precept be so accepted as to have it understood that we are not commanded to pray for certain sins of the brethren themselves. There are some men whom we are not to pray *for*. Are there also men whom we are to pray *against?* That is not quite clear. For there is a universal command, 'Bless, and do not curse,' and, 'To no man render evil for evil';[15] and you do not pray against a man when you do not pray for him at all, because you regard his punishment as certain, and his salvation as utterly hopeless. And it is certainly not through hatred that you do not pray for him, but through conviction that it would avail you nothing, and through an averseness toward having your prayer rejected by

---
13 Matt. 12.33.
14 See above, 1.21.69.
15 Rom. 12.14-17; cf. 1 Peter 3.9.

the highest tribunal of justice. But what shall we say with regard to those against whom we have learned that petitions were made by holy men? For those petitions were not made for the amendment of those persons—since in that case, the petitions would have been made for them, rather than against them—but for their final condemnation. Those holy men were not speaking as the Prophet spoke against the Lord's betrayer, for—as we have said[16]—his prayer was a prediction of future events, and not an expressed wish for punishment. They were not speaking as the Apostle spoke against Alexander, for on that point sufficient comment has also been made.[17] They were praying in the manner in which—as we read in the Apocalypse of John—the martyrs were praying to be avenged,[18] although the famous proto-martyr prayed for the forgiveness of those who were stoning him.[19]

(77) There is no reason to be disturbed on this account, for who would venture to say whether those white-robed martyrs—when they were praying to be avenged—were praying against the persons of men or against the reign of sin. Of course, the true avenging of martyrs, the avenging that is at once replete with mercy and with justice, is precisely the destruction of the reign of sin, under whose dominion they have suffered so much, and for whose overthrow the Apostle is striving when he says: 'Therefore, do not let sin reign in your mortal body.'[20] Now, the reign of sin is overthrown and destroyed, partly by such an amendment on the part of men that the flesh is made subject to the spirit, and partly by the condemnation of those who are persevering in sin, in order that they may be so justly restrained that they cannot be

---
16 See above, 1.21.72.
17 See above, 1.22.73.
18 Apoc. 6.10.
19 Acts 7.59.
20 Rom. 6.12.

troublesome to the just, who reign with Christ. Take the example of the Apostle Paul. In his own person, does he not seem to you to be making atonement to Stephen the Martyr, when he says: 'I do not fight as one beating the air, but I chastise my body and bring it unto subjection.'[21] In his own person he was certainly laying prostrate and subduing and restraining the already vanquished body with which he had been persecuting Stephen and the other Christian martyrs. Therefore, who can prove that the holy martyrs were not praying for this kind of avenging by the Lord on their behalf? In seeking self-vindication, they may possibly have been praying for the end of that kind of world in which they had endured so many forms of martyrdom. And, when men are praying for this, they are praying even for their enemies who are corrigible, but they are not praying against those who choose to be incorrigible. Even when God punishes these latter, He is not hatefully inflicting torture; He is most justly maintaining order. Without the least wavering, therefore, let us love our enemies, do good to those who hate us, and pray for those who persecute us.

Chapter 23 (Matt. 5.45-48)

(78) With regard to what immediately follows, namely, *'That you may be children of your Father, Who is in heaven,'* it is to be understood in the sense in which John also speaks when he says: 'He gave them the power of becoming children of God.'[1] For, there is One who is the Son by nature, and He absolutely knows not sin. But, since we have received the power, we are made sons insofar as we fulfill the precepts

---

21 1 Cor. 9.26-27.

---

1 John 1.12.

that have been given by the Son. 'Adoption' is the term used by the Apostle to denote the character of our vocation to the eternal inheritance, in order to be joint heirs with Christ.² By spiritual regeneration we therefore become sons and are adopted into the kingdom of God, not as aliens, but as His creatures and offspring. In this way, there is one kind of benefit by which He gave us being, whereas previously we were nothing; and there is another benefit by which He adopted us, so that as sons we might enjoy eternal life with Him in proportion to our participation. Therefore, the Lord does not say: 'Do those things because you are children'; He says: 'Do those things so that you may be children.'

(79) Since He calls us to this through the only begotten Son Himself, He calls us to His own likeness, for, as the Lord at once adds: *'He makes His sun to rise on the good and on the evil, and sends rain on the just and the unjust.'* Now, if you would understand the expression, *'His sun,'* to mean not the sun which is visible to bodily eyes, but His wisdom, to which the following expressions refer—'She is the brightness of eternal light,'³ and also, 'The sun of justice is risen upon me,'⁴ as well as, 'But to you that fear the name of the Lord, the sun of justice shall arise'⁵—then you must also understand the rain as a watering by the teaching of truth, because that teaching has become manifest to the good and to the evil, and Christ has been preached to the good and to the evil. But, you may prefer to understand it as the sun which is manifest to the bodily eyes of beasts as well as men, and to understand the rain as the showers through which are produced the fruits that have been bestowed for the refection of the body. I

---
2 Rom. 8.17; Gal. 4.5.
3 Wisd. 7.26.
4 *'Ortus est sol justitiae'* is found, not in the Scripture, but in the Breviary; cf. Resp. VIII, Comm. Fest. B.V.M.
5 Mal. 4.2.

believe this to be surely the more probable meaning, since the other 'sun' does not rise except on the good and the holy, for this is the very thing that the unjust bewail in that book which is called the *Wisdom of Solomon*: 'And the sun [of understanding] has not risen upon us.'[6] And the spiritual rain refreshes only the good, for the bad are signified by that vine of which it is said, 'I will command my clouds not to rain upon it.'[7] But, whether you understand the word, *'sun,'* in the former sense or in the latter, it is the effect of the great goodness of God, and this goodness is prescribed as our model if we wish to be children of God. For, who would be so thankless as to be insensible of the large share of the comforts of this life which is supplied by that visible light and that material rain? We see that in this life the comfort is offered alike to the just and to those who are sinners. Moreover, He does not say: 'Who makes *the* sun to rise on the good and on the evil.' He called it *His* sun, that is, the sun which He has made and properly placed, who took something from nothing in making it, as is written in Genesis concerning all the luminaries;[8] for He can properly name as His own everything which He has created from nothing. Hence, we are thus admonished as to the liberality with which—in accordance with His precept—we ought to bestow on our enemies the things which we ourselves have not created, but have received from His bounty.

(80) But, who can be ready to endure injuries even from the weak—insofar as it is profitable to their salvation; to prefer to suffer even more injury from another, rather than to retaliate in equal measure; to give to everyone who asks something from him—to give what is asked, if he has it, and

---
6 Wisd. 5.6.
7 Isa. 5.6.
8 Gen. 1.16.

if it can be rightfully given, or to give good advice or show a kindly disposition; not to turn away from one who would borrow; to love enemies; to do good to those who hate him; and to pray for those who persecute him? Who, indeed, can be prepared for all this, but a man who is completely and perfectly merciful? And it is only by means of this counsel that misery can be avoided—with the aid of Him who says: 'I have desired mercy rather than sacrifice.'[9] Therefore: *'Blessed are the merciful, for mercy shall be shown them.'*[10]

I think it is now fitting that the reader, already fatigued by such a long discussion, should rest a while, and thus refresh himself for considering the remainder—in another book.

---
9 Osee 6.6.
10 Matt. 5.7.

BOOK II

On the latter part of the Lord's Sermon on the Mount, contained in the sixth and seventh chapters of Matthew.

AFTER MERCY, comes the cleansing of the heart. With a treatment of the former, the first book came to a close; with a treatment of the latter, this book takes its beginning. A cleansing of the heart is, as it were, a cleansing of that eye by which God is seen, and the solicitude for keeping it single ought to be great in proportion to the dignity of the reality that can be perceived by such an eye.[1] But, even when this eye has been cleansed in large measure, it is difficult to prevent the imperceptible ingress of certain kinds of grime—for instance, human praise—which are wont to attend even our upright actions. Not to live an upright life is certainly pernicious. But, to live an upright life and to have no desire for praise—what else is this but to run counter to the ways of men, which are all the more deplorable according as an upright human life falls short of pleasing? So, if those among whom you live fail to praise you for living an upright life, they are at fault; if they praise you, then you are in danger unless you keep your heart so simple[2] and clean that you will not perform your good works for the sake of human praise. If you have such a

---
1 See above, 1.2.8; cf. Matt. 6.22; Luke 11.54.
2 Cf. Acts 2.46; 2 Cor. 1.12.

heart, you will rejoice because they bestow their praise, and not because you receive it; for their praise of you shows that the good is pleasing to them, though you would lead an upright life even if no one were to praise you for it. Moreover, you know that the praise you are receiving is of advantage to those who are bestowing it, if they mean it, not as an honor to you in your work, but as an honor to God, whose most holy temple is every man who lives an upright life. Thus the saying of David is fulfilled: 'In the Lord shall my soul rejoice, let the meek hear and rejoice.'[3] It is characteristic of the clean eye to disregard the praise of men with regard to virtuous actions, and not to apply a human standard in measuring the good that one is doing. This means that a man is not to perform a good deed for the sole purpose of pleasing men. If his sole aim is the receiving of human praise, then he will be inclined to simulate the good, for, since men cannot gaze into the heart, they may praise even what is spurious. But whenever a man simulates goodness, he has a divided heart. Therefore, no one has a single heart— and this is the same as a clean heart—unless he rises above human praise while he is living an upright life, that is to say, unless his thoughts and his efforts to please are directed solely toward Him who alone is the discerner of conscience. Whatever proceeds from the purity of such a conscience is the more deserving of praise according as it is less desirous of the praise which men bestow.

Chapter 1 (Matt. 6.1)

(2) *'Take heed therefore,'* He says, *'not to practise your righteousness before men, in order to be seen by them.'* In other words: take heed not to live an upright life with such

---

3 Ps. 33.3.

an intention; take heed not to make it your aim to have men see you. *'Otherwise you shall have no reward with your Father, Who is in heaven.'* This means that you will have no reward if you live uprightly for the sole purpose of being seen by men. It does not mean that you will have no reward if it should happen that you are seen by men; for, in that case, how could anyone apply what was said at the beginning of this Sermon: 'You are the light of the world. A city set on a mountain cannot be hidden. Neither do men light a lamp and set it under the measure, but upon the lampstand, that it may shine to all who are in the house. Let your light so shine before men that they may see your good works'?[1] But He did not fix the purpose of good works in their being seen by men, for He added: 'So that they may give glory to your Father, Who is in heaven.' In the present instance, however, He does not add anything after He has said: *'Take heed not to practise your righteousness before men, in order to be seen by them.'* He does not add to it, because He is now reproving the fault of having the aim of righteousness fixed in this desire, that is, the fault of performing righteous deeds for the sole purpose of being seen by men. It is clear, therefore, that He has not forbidden us to practise righteousness in the presence of men, but that He has forbidden us to practise it in their presence for the purpose of being seen by them. This means that we are not to direct our intention toward that end, and make it our aim.

(3) For the Apostle also says: 'If I were still trying to please men, I should not be the servant of Christ.'[2] But elsewhere he says: 'Please all men in all things, even as in all things I also try to please all men.'[3] Those who do not

---
1 Matt. 5.16. See above, 1.7.18.
2 Gal. 1.10.
3 Cf. 1 Cor. 10.32f.; Rom. 15.2.

understand this saying of his consider it contrary to the other. But he said that he was not trying to please men, because he was doing good in order to please God, and not in order to please men; for, by the very act of trying to please men, he was trying to turn their hearts toward the love of God. Therefore, he could rightly say that he was not trying to please men, for, even in his efforts to please men, he was aiming to please God. Although the pleasing of men ought not to be sought as a reward for good works, he could consistently prescribe that we ought to please men, for—since no one can try to imitate a man who is not pleasing to him—a man could not please God unless he were to present himself as a model for imitation by those whose salvation he was seeking. Therefore, just as it would not be absurd for a man to say: 'In this effort by which I am seeking a ship, I am not seeking a ship: I am seeking my homeland,' so also might the Apostle aptly say: 'In this effort by which I am trying to please men, I am not trying to please men; I am trying to please God. To please men is not my aim, but I attend to it in order that I may be imitated by those whose salvation I am seeking.' Just as he says with regard to an offering that is being made for the saints: 'Not that I am eager for the gift, but I am eager for the profit.'[4] This is as though he were to say: 'As to the fact that I am seeking your gift, I am not seeking your gift; I am seeking your profit.' Their Godward advance could be clearly seen by the fact that they were willingly offering what was being asked of them for the sake of a mutual sharing of charity, and not for the sake of any pleasure from their gifts.

(4) And although He goes on to say: *'Otherwise you shall have no reward with your Father, Who is in heaven,'* He

---

4 Phil. 4.17.

points out nothing else than that it behooves us to guard against this tendency, lest we seek human praise as a reward for our good works, that is to say, lest we think that we are receiving a blessing through such praise.

Chapter 2 (Matt. 6.2-4)

(5) He says: *'Therefore when thou givest alms, do not sound a trumpet before thee, as the hypocrites do in the synagogues and streets, in order that they may receive glory from men.'* Do not seek to become renowned, He says, as the hypocrites wish to do. Of course, it is plain that what hypocrites flaunt before the eyes of men, they do not entertain in the heart as well, for hypocrites are pretenders. It is as though they were assuming a character, as is done on the stage. For instance, it is not really Agamemnon who plays the role of Agamemnon in a tragedy, and the same is true with regard to any other character in a story or drama that is being enacted; the player assumes that person's character, and he is called a hypocrite.[1] Likewise, in the Church or in any class of society, if a man seeks to appear to be what in reality he is not, he is a hypocrite, for he assumes the character of a righteous man. He does not sustain that character, because he regards human praise as his whole reward. Even pretenders can receive this reward as long as they are deceiving those to whom they appear righteous, and are receiving praise from them. But from God, the discerner of the heart, such men receive no recompense but the penalty of deceit, for they have, He says, 'received their reward' from men.[2] And with consummate justice it will be said to them:

---
1 The Greek word, *hupokrités,* means an interpreter, pretender, theatrical performer.
2 Matt. 6.3.

'Depart from me, you deceitful workers: you had my name, but you have not done my works.'³ Therefore, they who give alms for the sole purpose of receiving glory from men—they have received their reward. They have received it, not because they happen to receive glory from men, but—as we have already pointed out—because they give alms precisely in order to receive glory. Human praise ought not to be sought by the worker of righteousness. It ought to follow as a consequence of his righteous deeds, so that it may be profitable to those who can imitate what they are praising, not so that the recipient of their praise may regard their praise as of any advantage to himself.

(6) *'But when thou givest alms, let not thy left hand know what thy right hand is doing.'* If you think that the *'left hand'* designates the unbelievers, then a desire to please believers will seem to be blameless, although we are absolutely forbidden to make the profit and the aim of a good work rest on the praise of any class of men. And as regards the fact that you may be imitated by those who are pleased with your good works, those works are to be made manifest to the unbelievers as well as to those who have the faith, so that by praising our good works they may give honor to God and come to salvation. And if you think that the *'left hand'* signifies an enemy, so that an enemy is not to know when you are giving an alms, then why did the Lord Himself mercifully heal men when hostile Jews were standing around? Why did the Apostle Peter bring the wrath of enemies upon both himself and the other followers of Christ by healing the man on whose infirmity he took compassion at the Beautiful Gate?⁴ Furthermore, if it is wrong to let an enemy know that we are giving an alms, how shall we deal with that same enemy re-

---
3 Cf. Matt. 7.23.
4 Acts 3.2.

garding the fulfillment of the precept, 'If thy enemy is hungry, give him food; if he is thirsty, give him drink'?[5]

(7) There is still a third opinion, but it is so absurd and ridiculous that I would not even mention it if I had not seen that many are fettered by this error of the carnal-minded. It maintains that a wife is designated by the term, *left hand,* and that for the sake of domestic tranquillity—since wives are usually somewhat stingy in domestic affairs—the matter is to be kept hidden from wives when their husbands expend something on the needy. As though only men were Christians! And as though this precept were not given to women as well! From what 'left hand' would a wife then be bidden to conceal a work of mercy? Or would the husband be his wife's 'left hand'?—a statement that would be most absurd. Or, if it be thought they are mutually 'left hands' to each other, then their wedlock would not be a Christian marriage, since one of the parties would be opposed to the other's giving something as an alms from the family possession. For it is inevitable that when either of them wishes to give an alms in accordance with God's precept, the partner who objects is in opposition with God's precept, and must therefore be classed among the unbelievers. And with regard to unbelievers, the rule is that by a good mode of life and conduct a believing husband is to try to gain his wife to the faith, and the believing wife is to try to gain her husband.[6] So, they ought not to hide their good works from each other, for by those good works one is attracted to the other in such measure that one may be able to attract the other to the communion of the Christian faith. Moreover, deceit is surely not to be practised for obtaining God's favor. And even though some things are not to be revealed as long as the frailty of

---
5 Rom. 12.20; Prov. 25.21.
6 Cf. 1 Cor. 7.12-16.

the other spouse is unable to bear them without perturbation,[7] and even though this concealment does not involve any injustice or infraction of law, yet, a consideration of the whole chapter makes it clear that a wife is not the *'left hand'* mentioned here. And that same consideration will reveal the signification of what He calls the *'left hand.'*

(8) *'Take heed,'* says He, *'not to practise your righteousness before men, in order to be seen by them; otherwise you shall have no reward with your Father, Who is in heaven.'* Having now spoken about righteousness in general, He goes on to recount the particulars, for a deed that is performed through almsgiving is a particular act of righteousness. He indicates the connection by saying: *'Therefore, when thou givest alms, do not sound a trumpet before thee, as the hypocrites do in the synagogues and streets, in order that they may receive glory from men.'* This comes under the heading of what He had just said: *'Take heed not to practise your righteousness before men, in order to be seen by them.'* But His very next pronouncement, *'Amen I say to you, they have had their reward,'* is an application of His other pronouncement above, *'Otherwise you shall have no reward with your Father, Who is in heaven.'* At once He goes on to say: *'But when thou givest alms . . . .'* By saying: 'But when *thou* givest,' is He not saying: 'Not as *they* give'? Then, what is the command that He gives me? He says: *'But when thou givest alms, let not thy left hand know what thy right hand is doing.'* From this it follows that the hypocrites are acting in such a way that their left hand knows what their right hand is doing. Now, you are forbidden to do what has been reproved in

---

7 A reference to the *Discipline of the Secret* (*Disciplina arcani*), by which Christians were forbidden to reveal to unbelievers—even to catechumens—certain articles of faith, or to permit their presence at certain acts of worship. For Augustine's explanation of the reason for this prohibition, see *In Joann. evang.* tr. 96.3.

them. But, they are reproved because they act in such a way as to seek after the praise of men. Therefore, the most logical conclusion would seem to be that the *'left hand'* signifies precisely this same desire for praise, for the *'right hand'* signifies the intention of fulfilling the divine precepts. So, when a desire for the praise of men is associated with the good intention of one who gives alms, then it is that his left hand becomes aware of what his right hand is doing. Then, *'let not thy left hand know what thy right hand is doing.'* In other words, let no longing for human praise be commingled with your good intention when you are striving to fulfill the divine precept of almsgiving.

(9) *'So that thy alms may be in secret.'* What else does the expression, *'in secret,'* mean but a good intention? For, a good intention cannot be revealed to the eyes of men, and —since many men tell many lies—neither can it be made known by words. Then, if the right hand acts inwardly and in secret, the left hand embraces all outward things, that is, the visible and temporal. Let your alms, therefore, be within your own conscience, for in their conscience many persons give alms through a good intention, even though they have neither money nor anything else that could be bestowed on a needy person. On the other hand, many give alms outwardly without giving them inwardly, for—through a striving after honors or for the sake of some temporal object—they wish to appear merciful. In such persons as these, the left hand alone is to be regarded as active. And there are still other almsgivers, who hold, as it were, a middle position between those two classes. They are those who indeed give alms by virtue of an intention which is Godwards, but some yearning for praise or for some passing temporal possession nevertheless intrudes itself into this most upright intention. Since our Lord forbids the left hand even from meddling in the affairs of the right

hand, He all the more strongly forbids the left hand from working alone in us. This means that we are to take heed not only not to give alms through a mere desire for temporal things, but also not to give alms with our mind so distractedly on God that a seeking after extraneous advantages may become commingled or attached. We are concerned with a cleansing of the heart; unless the heart be single, it will not be clean. But how shall it be single if it is serving two masters and dimming its vision by an inclination toward mortal and transitory things, rather than brightening it by fixing it on the things that are eternal? Therefore, in all justice and truth, *'let thy alms be in secret; and thy Father, Who sees in secret, will reward thee.'* For, if you expect a reward from Him who alone is the discerner of conscience, then let conscience itself suffice for the gaining of your reward. Many Latin copies read this way: 'And thy Father, who sees in secret, will reward thee in public.' But in the Greek copies, which are older, we have not found the expression, 'in public'; we have therefore decided not to discuss it here.[8]

Chapter 3 (Matt. 6.5-8)

(10) *'And when you pray,'* He says, *'you shall not be like the hypocrites, who love to pray standing in the synagogues and at the street corners, in order that they may be seen by men.'* In this matter, also, the wrong does not consist in being seen by men; it consists in doing those things for the express purpose of being seen by men. But it is needless to repeat this observation each time. The one rule to be observed is the rule by which it has become known that what is to be feared or

---

8 Regarding Augustine's preference for the Greek texts, see Introduction, note 18. This is one of the several instances in which, as De Bruyne observes (*op. cit.* 594ff.), Augustine corrected pre-Vulgate Latin translations of the Scriptures.

shunned is the performing of those acts with such an intention that the pleasing of men is sought as a result from them; we need not fear the fact that men may actually become aware of them. And in this instance, the Lord repeats His own very words when He adds: *'Amen I say to you, they have had their reward.'* Hence, He shows that He forbids the seeking after the reward which fools enjoy when they are praised by men.

(11) *'But,'* says He, *'when you pray, go into your bedrooms.'* Now, what are these bedrooms but the very hearts that are signified also in the Psalm wherein it is said: 'The things you say in your hearts, be sorry for in your bedrooms.'[1] He then continues: *'And closing the doors, pray in secret to your Father.'* Our entering the rooms is not enough if the door be left open to the importunate, for external things rush brazenly in through this door, and lay hold on our inmost affections. And we have said that all temporal and visible things are on the outside; and through this door, that is, one of the senses, they enter our thoughts and—by a swarm of idle fancies—noisily disturb us while engaged in prayer. Therefore, the door must be closed; that is to say, the bodily sense must be resisted, so that the prayer of the spirit may be directed to the Father. For this prayer is formed in the depths of the heart, where a man prays in secret to the Father. *'And,'* says He, *'your Father, Who sees in secret, will reward you.'* It was fitting that this passage should end with a pronouncement of this kind. For, just as the preceding passage does not admonish us to give alms, but tells us what our intention ought to be when we are giving them, so, likewise, this passage does not admonish us to pray; it teaches us how to pray. This is due to the fact that He is now prescribing for a cleans-

---

1 Ps. 4.5.

ing of the heart, and nothing can cleanse the heart but a continuous and undivided striving for eternal life through no other motive than a pure love of wisdom.[2]

(12) *'But in praying,'* says He, *'do not multiply words, as the heathens do; for they think that in saying a great deal, they will be heard.'* Just as it is characteristic of hypocrites —whose reward is to please men—to display themselves for the purpose of being seen in prayer, so is it characteristic of the heathens—that is to say, the Gentiles—to think that in much talking they will be heard. In fact, all sorts of wordiness come from the Gentiles, who take pains to exercise the tongue rather than to cleanse the mind. And they endeavor to transfer this futile effort to the purpose of swaying God by entreaty, for they think that words can lead Him—like a human judge—to reach a decision. *'So do not be like them,'* says the one true Teacher,[3] *'for your Father knows what you need before you ask Him.'* Though many words are delivered in order to teach and instruct an ignorant man, what is the need of them with regard to Him who knows all things? To Him, all things that are speak by the very fact that they are, and show that they have been made. From His knowledge and wisdom the things that are to come are not hidden, since both the things that have passed away and the things that are to pass away are all present in that knowledge and wisdom, and therein are not passing away.

(13) Since the Lord himself is about to speak words—a few words indeed, but words nevertheless—in order to teach

---

2 'In the present life, wisdom is the true worship of the true God, so that He may be its unfailing reward in the life to come' (*Epist.* 155.2.5).
'The consummate and true wisdom, therefore, is in that first commandment: "Thou shalt love the Lord thy God with thy whole heart and with thy whole soul"' (*Epist.* 140.18.45).
3 Matt. 23.10.

us how to pray, it may be asked why there is any need for even those few words with regard to Him who knows all things before they come to pass, and who, as has been said, knows what is needful for us before we ask Him. In the first place, the answer is that in order to obtain our petitions from God we ought to plead our cause with Him, not by means of words, but by the truths which we cherish in our mind and by the application of thought, with pure love and single affection. Through the medium of words our Lord has taught us those very truths, so that, when those words are committed to memory, we may be mindful of those truths while we are engaged in prayer.

(14) And yet—whether prayer ought to be formed by words or by thoughts—one still may ask what is the need of any kind of prayer, since God already knows what is needful for us. Precisely because the very attention to prayer clears and cleanses our heart, and makes it more capable of receiving the divine gifts which are spiritually infused into us. For God graciously hears us, not on account of the repetition of our entreaties, but because He is always inclined to give us His light—not, indeed, a visible light, but the light which is intelligible and spiritual. However, as long as we have any inclination toward other things, that is, as long as we are seeking after the temporal things of darkness, we are not always ready to receive this light. Through prayer, therefore, it is brought about that the heart is turned toward Him who is always ready to give, provided that we are ready to accept whatever He may give. And in that change of heart there is a cleansing of the inner eye through the exclusion of the erstwhile longing for temporal things, and the gaze of the single heart is able to bear the single light divinely shining without any setting or motion. Not only is the single heart able to bear this light, but it is also able to abide in it. And

it is able to abide in it, not only without uneasiness, but even with ineffable joy. In this way, life is rendered truly and sincerely blessed.

Chapter 4 (Matt. 6.9-13)

(15) We must now consider what it is that we have been commanded to pray for—commanded by Him from whom we learn what to pray for, and through whom we obtain what we pray for. He says: *'In this manner shall you pray: "Our Father Who art in heaven, hallowed be Thy name. Thy kingdom come, Thy will be done on earth, as it is in heaven. Give us this day our daily bread. And forgive us our debts, as we also forgive our debtors. And lead us not into temptation, but deliver us from evil."'* In every kind of petition we ought first to try to gain the good will of the one we are petitioning, and then to state the object of our petition. We usually try to gain the good will by bestowing praise on the one we are petitioning. And the praise is usually placed at the beginning of the prayer, where in this instance Our Lord has bidden us to say nothing else than, *'Our Father Who art in heaven.'* Praise of God has been expressed in many manners of speech. Anyone can see this as he reads those forms of praise scattered widely here and there throughout the sacred Scriptures. But nowhere is there found any instruction for the people of Israel to say, 'Our Father,' or to pray to God as to a Father. To them He has been proposed as a Master, for they were servants; that is, they were as yet living according to the flesh. When I say this, I am referring to them when they received the commandments of the Law which they were ordered to observe, for the Prophets frequently point out that this same Lord of ours would have been their Father as well, if they did not stray from His commandments.

For instance, there are the following expressions: 'I have begotten children, and exalted them; but they have despised me,'[1] and: 'I have said, "You are gods and all of you the sons of the Most High,"'[2] and: 'If I be a Master, where is my fear? And if I be a Father, where is my honor?'[3] Even if we were to disregard those prophetic sayings that refer to the fact that there would be a Christian people who would have God as their Father—in accordance with that saying in the Gospel, 'He gave them the power of becoming children of God'[4]—there are still many other expressions whereby the Jews are reproved for the fact that by committing sins they refused to be children. The Apostle Paul says: 'As long as the heir is a little child, he differs in no way from a slave,'[5] but he reminds us that we have received the spirit of adoption, by virtue of which we cry, 'Abba, Father.'[6]

(16) Because it is not through our own merits—but through the grace of God—that we are called to an everlasting inheritance in order to be joint heirs with Christ and to come into the adoption of sons,[7] we mention that grace at the beginning of the prayer when we say, 'Our Father.' To children, what is more beloved than their father? So, by this appellation love is enkindled. A suppliant disposition is occasioned when men address God as 'Our Father,' and there is engendered a certain confidence of obtaining what we are about to request. For, even before we ask for anything, we have received so great a gift—the gift of being allowed to address Him as 'Our Father.' Indeed, what is it that He

---

1 Isa. 1.2.
2 Ps. 81.6.
3 Mal. 1.6.
4 John 1.12.
5 Gal. 4.1.
6 Rom. 8.15.
7 Rom. 8.15-23.

would not grant to His children who beseech Him, since He has already given them the singular gift of being His children? Furthermore, when a man says 'Our Father,' with what great solicitude is his mind affected, lest he be unworthy of such a Father! If some venerable senator were to permit a plebeian to call him father, the latter would certainly tremble and would scarcely dare to comply, for he would at once be mindful of his own lowliness of birth, his lack of wealth, and the low estate of a plebeian person. How much the more ought a man fear to address God as 'Father,' if there is such defilement and sordidness in his morals that God would repel those vices from relationship with Himself far more justly than that senator would spurn the penury of the beggar? That senator despises in the beggar the very thing to which he himself can be reduced through the instability of human possessions, but God can never fall into sordid morals. All thanks to the mercy of Him who does not exact—as a requisite for His becoming our Father—anything that can be purchased for a material price, but demands only what can be gained by good will. In this there is an admonition for those of wealth or high estate in the world, to the effect that when they become Christians they are not to despise the poor and the lowly. For, in common with those latter, they address God as 'Our Father,' and they cannot do this unless they acknowledge themselves as the brothers of these.

Chapter 5 (Matt. 6.9)

(17) So, let that new people which is called to an everlasting inheritance use the language of the New Testament, and say: *'Our Father Who art in heaven.'* This means that He is in the saints and the just, for God is not confined by local space. Of course, the heavens are the lofty bodies of the universe, but they are bodies nonetheless, and they can-

not be unless they be in a place. And, if God is believed to be in heaven as though He were dwelling in the upper portions of the world, then the birds would be of greater merit than man, for they would be living closer to God. It is not written that the Lord is near to those on high or to those who dwell on mountains; it is written: 'The Lord is nigh unto those of contrite heart.'[1] Although this more properly refers to humility, yet, in contrast with the sinner, the righteous man can be called heaven, just as the sinner was called earth when he was told: 'Earth thou art, and unto earth shalt thou go,'[2] for the righteous are told: 'The temple of God is holy, and this temple you are.'[3] So, if God dwells in His temple and if the saints are His temple, then the clause, *'Who art in heaven,'* is rightly understood as meaning, 'Who art in the saints.' And this is a most apposite comparison, for it shows that, in the spiritual realm, the just differ from sinners to such an extent as the heavens differ from the earth in the material sphere.

(18) For the purpose of signifying this truth, when we stand at prayer[4] we face the East,[5] where the rise of the

---

1 Ps. 33.19.
2 Gen. 3.19.
3 1 Cor. 3.17.
4 With regard to public, or liturgical, prayers, he writes: 'On the days which are celebrated after the Lord's Resurrection . . . we pray standing. This symbolizes the Resurrection. Hence, at the altar the practice is followed on all Sundays . . . I do not know whether *standing* during those days and on all Sundays is observed everywhere' (*Epist.* 55.15.28; id. 17.32). As regards private prayers, he writes: 'Those who pray compose their bodily members in a manner befitting suppliants when they fix their knees, extend their hands, and even prostrate themselves' (*De cura pro mort.* 5.7). Both the standing and the kneeling postures are sanctioned in Scripture. (Cf. Mark 11.25; Luke 22.41).
5 A reference to the orienting of churches. Long before Christianity, pagan temples were so constructed 'that the people would be taught to turn toward the East when they faced the images' (Clement Alex., *Stromata* 7.17.43). From a very early date—probably from the very earliest—Christians made it a practice to place the altar at the

heavens begins. This is not to signify that God is dwelling there, as though He had forsaken the other parts of the world—for God is present everywhere, not in habitations of place but in power of majesty. It is done so that the mind may be admonished to turn toward God while its body is turned toward a heavenly body. For, just as the heavenly body is higher than the earthly one, so God is a higher substance than the human mind. Furthermore, it is in conformity with the degrees of religion, and it is also expedient that an intimation of God be rightly engendered in the sentiments of all, both little and great. Therefore, with regard to those who are still devoted to visible beauties and are as yet unable to conceive of anything as corporeal, if they think God is in the heavens rather than on earth, their opinion can be somewhat tolerated. Even though they have as yet the same conception of God as of a body, they necessarily reckon the heavens superior to the earth. Accordingly, when they have once learned that the dignity of a soul is greater than even a heavenly body, they may seek God in the soul rather than even in a heavenly body. And just as—while they were still wise according to the flesh—they would not dare place Him on the earth, but in the heavens, so afterwards—when they have once learned how great is the difference between the souls of sinners and the souls of the just—by a better faith or understanding they may seek Him in the souls of the just

---

eastern end of the church. This practice either occasioned or strengthened the pagans' accusation that Christians were sun-worshipers. (Cf. Origen, *Contra Celsum* 8.67; Tertullian, *Ad mat.* 1.3; *Apolog.* 16.) Gregory of Nyssa, in the fourth century, explained this 'orienting' as a symbol of the Christians' yearning for happiness through reunion with God, for the Orient contains the paradise of happiness from which man was expelled because of sin (*De orat, domin.* in P. G♦ 44.1183). The orienting of churches (with the exception of the Roman basilicas where the celebrant used to face the congregation) continued down through the Middles Ages, and medieval writers enlarged upon its symbolism. (Cf. Aquinas, *Summa theol.* II-II, qu. lxxiv, a. 3.)

rather than in the souls of sinners. Therefore, the expression, *'Our Father Who art in heaven,'* is rightly understood to mean that He is in the hearts of the just, as though in His holy temple. And it also means that the person engaged in prayer should wish that He whom he is invoking may dwell in him also, and that he should hold fast to righteousness while he is striving for this indwelling. By the performance of this duty, God is invited to dwell in the soul.

(19) Since we have discussed the person and the abode of Him to whom our petitions are addressed, let us now see what petitions we ought to make. The first of all petitions is this: *'Hallowed be Thy name.'* The making of this petition does not imply that the name of God is not holy; it is made so that this name may be held holy by men, that is, so that God may become known to them in such a way that they will deem nothing more holy, nothing which they would be more fearful to offend. Merely, because it has been said that 'In Judea God is known, His name is great in Israel,'[6] we are not to understand it as though He were a greater God in one place than in another. Indeed, His name is great wherever He is named according to the greatness of His majesty; likewise, His name is said to be hallowed wherever He is named with awe and reverence. And this is what is now being done as long as the Gospel—by becoming known throughout the various nations—is making the name of God revered through the ministration of His Son.

Chapter 6 (Matt. 6.10)

(20) The next petition is: *'Thy kingdom come.'* As the Lord Himself teaches in the Gospel, the Day of Judgment will be at hand when the Gospel will have been preached in all

---
6 Ps. 75.2.

the nations.¹ And this pertains to the hallowing of the name of God, for the petition, *'Thy kingdom come,'* is not made here as if God were not reigning now. It may, perchance, be said that the word, *'come,'* is intended to mean *'come upon the earth.'* As if He were not now reigning also on the earth, and had not been reigning there always from the foundation of the world! *'Thy kingdom come,'* therefore, is to be understood as meaning 'May Thy kingdom be made manifest to men.' Just as a light that is present is absent to those who are blind or who shut their eyes, so also the kingdom of God —although it never departs from the earth—is absent to those who know it not. But no one will be allowed to be ignorant of the kingdom of God when—to judge the living and the dead—His Only Begotten Son will have come from heaven, not merely in a manner recognizable by the intellect, but even visibly in the person of the Lord.² After this judgment —that is to say, when the distinction will have been made between the just and the unjust, and their separation accomplished—then God will so dwell in the just that there will then be no need for anyone to be taught by men; for, as is written, 'they all shall be taught of God.'³ Then the blessed life will be totally perfected in the saints for all eternity, just as the heavenly angels are holy and happy in the highest degree, and are wise and happy because God alone is shedding His light upon them. For the Lord has made this promise to those who are His: 'At the resurrection they will be as angels in heaven.'⁴

(21) Therefore, after the petition in which we say *'Thy kingdom come,'* the very next petition is *'Thy will be done*

---

1 Matt. 24.14.
2 Literally, 'in the man of the Lord.' See *Retract.* 1.19.8.
3 John 6.45; Isa. 54.13; Jer. 31.33f.
4 Matt. 22.30.

*on earth, as it is in heaven.'*⁵ The meaning is this: May Thy will be done in Thy saints who are on earth, as it is done in Thy angels who are in heaven. The angels cleave to Thee exclusively and enjoy Thee, because no error beclouds their wisdom and no misery impedes their happiness. But Thy saints have been fashioned from the earth as regards their bodies, and, even though they are to be changed and taken up into a heavenly abode,⁶ it is from the earth that they are to be taken up. There is a longing for this also in the hymn of the angels, 'Glory to God in the highest and peace on earth among men of good will.'⁷ So, when our good will leads us and follow Him who calls, then the will of God is done in us as it is done in the heavenly angels, and no adversity impedes our blessedness. This is peace. But the petition, *'Thy kingdom come,'* can also be rightly understood as meaning: May Thy commandments be obeyed on earth, even as they are obeyed in heaven; that is to say, may they be obeyed by men, even as they are obeyed by angels. Indeed, the Lord Himself says that the will of God is being accomplished when His commandments are being obeyed, for He says: 'My food is to do the will of Him Who sent me';⁸ 'I have come, not to do my own will, but to do the will of Him Who sent me';⁹ and: 'Behold my mother and my brethren; and whoever does the will of God, he is my brother and mother and sister.'¹⁰ Therefore, the will of God is certainly in those who do the will of God. This does not mean that they cause God to will; it

---

5 In expounding this petition, Augustine follows closely—and, at times, verbatim—St. Cyprian *(De oratione dominica* 14). In a much later work, Augustine cites this work of Cyprian, and quotes it extensively (Cf. *De dono persever.* 2.4ff.).
6 1 Cor. 15.52; 1 Thess. 4.16.
7 Luke 2.14.
8 John 4.34.
9 John 6.38.
10 Matt. 12.49-50.

means that they do what God wills, that they act according to God's will.

(22) There is also that other understanding of the petition, *'Thy will be done on earth, as it is in heaven,'* namely, the interpretation that can be expressed by saying: May Thy will be accomplished in sinners also, even as it is accomplished in the saints and the just. And this interpretation can again be taken in two ways. First, we are to pray even for our enemies (for what else are we to consider those who are opposed to the propagation of the Christian and Catholic faith?). According to this understanding of the petition, *'Thy will be done on earth, as it is in heaven,'* it is intended to convey the following meaning: In the manner in which the just do Thy will, in like manner may sinners do it also, so that they may be converted to Thee. Secondly, the interpretation may be taken in the sense that *'Thy will be done on earth, as it is in heaven'* is to be understood as a petition for the rendering of his just due to every man. This will be done at the Last Judgment, when the lambs will have been separated from the goats;[11] the just will then receive a reward, while sinners will receive the penalty of condemnation.

(23) By no means absurd, but—on the contrary—in perfect accord with our faith and hope, is the interpretation by which we understand heaven and earth as spirit and flesh.[12] We see indeed that God's will has been done in the mind, which is the spirit, for the Apostle says: 'With my mind I serve the law of God, but with my flesh the law of sin.'[13] But, when 'death will have been swallowed up in victory, and this mortal body will have put on immortality'[14] (and this

---
11 Matt. 25.32-46.
12 Matt. 26.41.
13 Rom. 7.25.
14 1 Cor. 15.54.

will be done through the resurrection of the flesh and through the change which, according to the preaching of the same Apostle,[15] is promised to the just), then shall the will of God be done on earth even as in heaven. This means that the body will not then be resisting the spirit—that is, the soul—just as the spirit is not now resisting God. For the spirit is following the will of God and trying to do it, but that spirit—or soul—is being harassed by the weakness of the body and inclined toward the way of the flesh. The power not only of willing the good, but also of accomplishing it —that is the perfection of consummate peace in the life eternal. 'For now,' says the Apostle, 'to will is present with me; but to accomplish the good, is not with me.'[16] The will of God has not yet been accomplished on earth in the same way as it is done in heaven; that is to say, it is not yet being done in the flesh in the same way as it is being in the spirit. Of course, it is being accomplished on earth; it is being accomplished even in our misery as long as we are enduring through the flesh the sufferings that are due to the mortality which is justly ours, because our nature has brought it upon itself by committing sin. But we ought to pray that it be done on earth in the way it is done in heaven. This means that we ought to pray for the accomplishment of that bodily change in us,[17] so that through neither earthly delights nor earthly sorrows will any part of our nature be in conflict with that delight which is ours when the mind 'is delighted with the Law according to the inner man.'[18]

(24) Without being necessarily in error, we may also understand the petition, *'Thy will be done on earth, as it is*

---

15 1 Cor. 15.42-55.
16 Rom. 7.18; cf. *Vulg.*
17 1 Cor. 15.52-55.
18 Rom. 7.22.

in heaven,' as the equivalent of asking that God's will be done in the Church in the same way as it is done in Our Lord Jesus Christ. It would be as though we were to pray that the Father's will be accomplished in the woman who is espoused to the Son, just as it is accomplished in the Son who has fulfilled the Father's will[19]—for heaven and earth are aptly taken as husband and wife, since the earth is fruitful because the heavens make it fertile.

Chapter 7 (Matt. 6.11)

(25) The fourth petition is: '*Give us this day our daily bread.*' The expression, '*daily bread,*' may be intended to signify any one of the following three things. First, it may mean everything which supplies the needs of this life. In that interpretation the limitation, '*this day,*' is added, for it is the same bread of which he was speaking when he gave the admonition, 'Take no thought for the morrow.'[1] Next, it may signify either the Body of Christ, which we receive every day,[2] or the spiritual food of which the same Lord says: 'Labor for the food that does not perish,'[3] and: 'I am the bread of life that has come down from heaven.'[4] There may be a question as to which of these three opinions is the most probable. Indeed, someone may be disturbed by the thought that we ought to pray for the necessities of this life, such as food and

---
19 'For Christ is the bridegroom; the Church is the bride' (*Enarr. in ps.* 44.3).

1 Matt. 6.34.
2 In a sermon to a group of newly baptized, Augustine says that the Holy Eucharist is a sacrament which 'you are about to receive, and which you ought to receive every day' (*Sermo* 227). For the Africa of an early day, we have St. Cyprian's observation: '. . . we who are in Christ, and receive the Eucharist every day . . .' (*op. cit.* 18).
3 John 6.27.
4 John 6.41.

clothing, for the Lord Himself says: 'Be not solicitous about what you shall eat or what you shall put on.'[5] Could anyone be unsolicitous about something that he is praying to obtain? On the contrary, prayer is to be directed with a mind so intent that we must apply to it not only everything which has been said with regard to the closing of the door of our sleeping rooms[6] but also what the Lord says later: 'Seek first the kingof God and His righteousness, and all those things will be given you besides.'[7] He does not say: 'Seek first the kingdom of God, and then seek those things.' He says: 'All those things will be given you besides'—that is, they will be given to you, even though you do not seek them. However, I do not see how anyone can find a way of showing that a man can be rightly regarded as not seeking whatever he is earnestly beseeching God to enable him to obtain.

(26) Although this bread is called a daily bread, in the Eastern countries there are very many who do not partake of the Lord's Supper every day; nevertheless, they occasion no scandal by not partaking. They are not condemned as disobedient, for their ecclesiastical superiors do not command them to partake.[8] Therefore, in those regions, the sacramental Bread is not understood as a daily bread; if it were so understood, then those who do not partake of it every day would be charged with the guilt of grave sin. Now, in order that these

---

5 Matt. 6.31; Luke 12.22.
6 Matt. 6.6.
7 Matt. 6.33; Luke 12.31.
8 St. John Chrysostom, who became Bishop of Constantinople a few years later, was at this time delivering his celebrated homilies at Antioch. In those homilies, he deplores the infrequency with which many received the Holy Eucharist, and strongly urges the daily reception of that sacrament. (Cf. *In Epist. ad Eph.* 3.3; *in Epist. ad Tit.* 5.3; *In Epist. ad Heb.* 17.4). St Ambrose, Bishop of Milan, had already given voice to similar complaints and exhortations. (Cf. *In Psalmum* 118.8.26.)

may not raise a dispute with regard to the sacrament of the Lord's Body, and cite the example of their churches in support of their opinion on the question—for that example shows that in their countries the sacramental Bread is not understood as a daily bread—to repeat, in order that we may have no argument on either side, reflection ought to suggest the following thought: We have received a rule of prayer from the Lord. It would be wrong to transgress it either by adding something or by taking anything away. Yet, who would dare to maintain that we ought to say the Lord's Prayer only once; or that, even if we ought to say it two or three times up to the hour when we partake of the Body of the Lord, we certainly ought not to say it throughout the rest of the day? For, from that moment onward, we shall not be able to say, *'Give us this day'* what we have already received. In that case, everyone could compel us to celebrate the Sacrament at the very last hour of the day.

(27) It remains for us, therefore, to understand the *'daily bread'* as a spiritual bread. That is to say, we are to understand it as the divine precepts on which we ought to meditate every day and which we ought to perform daily, for it is of these precepts that the Lord says: 'Labor for the food that is not destroyed.'[9] And as long as this present life continues through days that come and go, this food continues to be called a daily food. And in the same way that bread is a daily necessity, so to speak, for him who at times is nourished by food and later feels the need of it, so also the soul—as long as its affection is alternately turning toward the higher things and the lower, namely, the things of the spirit and the things of the flesh—very truly stands in need of a daily bread by which it may be refreshed when hungry and lifted up when

---

9 John 6.27.

it is again sinking. In this life, therefore (that is, before the glorious change),[10] just as our body is refreshed with food because it suffers exhaustion, so also may the soul be refreshed by the food of the precepts, because—through its affections for temporal things—it suffers, as it were, an exhaustion from its intentness on God. However, the expression, *'Give us this day,'* is used as long as *'this day'* is designated; that is to say, during this temporal life. But, throughout eternity after this life, we shall be so provided with spiritual food that it will not then be called a daily bread; for in that life there will not be that revolving of time which makes days to be successive, and from which the expression, *'today,'* receives its designation. For in this text also the meaning of *'this day'* is the same as in the admonition, 'Today if you shall hear His voice.'[11] And in his Epistle to the Hebrews, the Apostle expounds this as meaning, 'As long as it is being called *Today*.'[12] But, if anyone wishes to understand the expression, *'daily bread,'* either as the necessary nourishment of the body or as the sacrament of the Body of the Lord, then all three interpretations ought to be taken conjointly. And then the meaning would be that at one and the same time we are praying for the needful daily bread for the body, and the consecrated visible Bread, and the invisible bread of the Word of God.

Chapter 8 (Matt. 6.12)

(28) The fifth petition comes now: *'And forgive us our debts, as we also forgive our debtors.'* Sins are called debts. This is made clear by the Lord's saying, 'Thou shalt not come

---

10 1 Cor. 15.53.
11 Ps. 94.8.
12 Heb. 3.13.

out of it until thou hast paid the last farthing,'¹ and by the fact that He named as debtors both the men who were reported as killed in the collapse of the tower and those whose blood Herod had mingled with the sacrifice.² For He said that men were of the opinion these were debtors beyond measure, that is, sinners; and He added: 'Amen I say to you, unless you do penance you shall all likewise perish.'³ Therefore, in this petition, no one is urged to remit the financial claim of his debtors, but everyone is urged to forgive whatsoever sins another has committed against him. Rather, it is through the precept that was previously mentioned that we are ordered to forgive a monetary debt: 'If anyone wishes to take thy tunic from thee, and to go to law with thee, give up to him thy garment also.'⁴ We are thereby required to remit the debt, not to everyone who owes us money, but only to the debtor who is so unwilling to pay that he would prefer to contest the claim. 'For,' as the Apostle says, 'the servant of the Lord is not to quarrel.'⁵ A monetary debt, therefore, is to be remitted to one who is unwilling to pay of his own accord or refuses to pay it on demand, for his refusal may be due to the fact that he has not wherewith to pay, or to the fact that he is avaricious and covetous. Each of these reasons arises from a lack of something: the former, from a lack of means; the latter, from a lack of character. Therefore, whoever remits a debt to such a man remits it to one in need. He performs a Christian act, for he observes the rule that he ought to be willing to lose what is due to him. Indeed, if he modestly and mildly makes every effort to have

---

1 Matt. 5.26.
2 The blood was mingled by Pilate, not by Herod. Cf. Luke 13.1-4.
3 Luke 13.5.
4 Matt. 5.40.
5 2 Tim. 2.24.

repayment made to him—not with an eye toward the monetary advantage, but with a view to the correction of a man for whom it is undoubtedly harmful not to repay when he has the wherewithal—in that case, not only will he not sin in seeking repayment, but he will be most helpful toward preventing the other man from suffering the loss of his faith through an eagerness to profit by money which he owes. And this loss is so much more serious a loss that there is no comparison. Hence it is seen that in the fifth petition—in which we say *'Forgive us our debts'*—the import is not, indeed, with regard to money, but with regard to whatsoever sins anyone is committing against us. But, since it is meant in that way, it is meant also with regard to money. For a man commits a sin against you if, having the wherewithal, he still refuses to pay what he owes you. And if you do not forgive this sin, you cannot say *'Forgive us, as we also forgive.'* But, if you forgive, then you also see that, when a man is ordered to offer such a prayer of supplication, he is admonished to forgive even a monetary debt.

(29) Of course, this petition can be treated in such a way as to make it appear that we are not acting against it unless we are refusing to forgive those who are asking forgiveness. For we wish to be forgiven when we are asking forgiveness from a most benign Father, and our petition is: *'Forgive us our debts, as we also forgive.'* There is also that other precept by which we are commanded to pray for our enemies.[6] We are not commanded to pray for those who are asking forgiveness, for men of that disposition are not enemies, but by no means could anyone truly say that he is praying for a man whom he has not forgiven. We must therefore admit that we have to forgive all sins that are committed against us,

---

6 Matt. 5.44. See above, 1.21.69-1.22.77.

if we wish the Father to forgive us the sins that we commit. With regard to vengeance, I believe that subject already has been sufficiently discussed.[7]

Chapter 9 (Matt. 6.13)

(30) The sixth petition is: *'And bring us not into temptation.'* In place of the word, *'bring,'* many codices have the word, *'lead.'* I regard these words as exactly equivalent; for they are both translated from the same Greek word, which is *eisenégkes*. But in making this application, many persons say: 'Suffer us not to be led into temptation.' And in this way they clearly show the intended meaning of the word, *lead*. God does not of Himself lead a man into temptation, but He suffers a man to be led into temptation when—through one's just deserts and in accordance with a most hidden disposition—He leaves him bereft of divine aid. Often, for reasons that are quite evident, He adjudges a man deserving of being abandoned and led into temptation. But, to be led into temptation is one thing and to be tempted is another. Without temptation no one can be proved. He cannot be proved to himself, as it is written: 'He that has not been tried, what manner of things does he know?';[2] nor can he be proved to another, as the Apostle says: 'And your temptation in my flesh, you did not despise.'[3] For their steadfastness was proved to him by the fact that they were not turned away from charity by reason of the tribulations which had

---
7 See above, 1.19-20.

---
1 'Hence, many persons word the petition in this way, and it reads this way in many codices, and blessed Cyprian [Cf. *De orat. dominica* 25] has written it this way, namely, "Suffer us not to be led into temptation"' (*De dono persever.* 6.12).
2 Eccli. 34.11.
3 Gal. 4.13.

befallen the Apostle according to the flesh. But, even before we are tried by any temptations, we are known to God, for He knows all things before they come to pass.

(31) Therefore, with regard to the text of Scripture which reads: 'The Lord your God tries you, so that He may know whether you love Him,' the clause, 'So that He may know,' is used as the equivalent of an expression which means: 'So that He may make you know.'[4] We ourselves use certain expressions in this way. For instance, we say that a day is joyful because it makes us joyful, and that cold is numb because it makes us numb. Countless expressions of this kind are used in ordinary conversation, in learned discourses, and in the holy Scriptures. But, because the heretics who oppose the Old Testament[5] do not understand this, they think that the brand of ignorance, so to speak, is to be placed on Him of whom it is written: 'The Lord your God tries you.' As though in the Gospel it were not written of the Lord: 'But he said this to try him, for he himself knew what he would do.'[6] But, if He knew the heart of the man He was testing, what did He wish to discover by testing? Why, that was done so that the person under trial would become known to himself,[7] so that, when the crowds had been filled with the Lord's bread, he would disapprove his own diffidence in thinking they had had nothing to eat.

(32) Hence, the import of the petition is not that we be not tried, but that we be not brought into temptation. It is as though a man who has to undergo trial by fire would pray, not that he be not touched by the fire, but that he be not

---

4 Deut. 13.3. An instance of Augustine's anticipating the Vulgate (See above, 2.2.9). The Vulgate reads: 'That it may appear,' instead of 'That He may know.'
5 The Manichaeans. See above, 1.20.65. n. 9.
6 John 6.6.
7 'God is said to learn when He makes us learn' (*Sermo* 2.4.5).

consumed by it, for 'the furnace tries the potter's vessels, and the trial of tribulation just men.'[8] Accordingly, Joseph was tried by the allurement of the adulteress, but he was not brought into temptation;[9] Susanna was tried, but neither was she led into or brought into temptation;[10] and many others of both sexes, particularly Job. When those heretics who impugn the Old Testament wish to deride with sacrilegious lips Job's marvelous trust in the Lord, his God, they especially bandy the taunt that Satan asked to havĕ him in order to submit him to temptation.[11] Since those men are blinded by superstition and wrangling, they cannot discern that God does not occupy a portion of space by bodily mass, and that He is not thus present in one place and absent in another, or at least that He is not partly here and partly elsewhere, but that, being everywhere absolute and not divided into parts, He is everywhere present by His majesty. Having no discernment of all this, they put questions to unskillful men who are entirely unable to understand such things, and ask them how Satan could talk with God. But, if they take a carnal view of the saying, 'Heaven is my throne, and the earth my footstool,'[12] (and the Lord Himself bears witness to this passage, when He says: 'You shall not swear: neither by heaven, for it is the throne of God; nor by the earth, for it is the footstool of His feet'),[13] what wonder that the Devil was set upon the earth and stood before the feet of God and spoke something in His presence? When will they understand that God speaks within the conscience of every man who can reason in any manner, even though he be

---

8 Eccli. 27.6.
9 Gen. 39.17ff.
10 Dan. 13.20ff.
11 Job 1.11.
12 Isa. 66.1; cf. above, 1.17.53.
13 Matt. 5.34.

perverse? For, who but God has written the natural law in the hearts of men? This is the law of which the Apostle says: 'For when the Gentiles who have no law do by nature what the Law prescribes, these having no law are a law unto themselves. They show the work of the Law written in their hearts, their conscience being their witness even when conflicting thoughts accuse and defend them, on the day when the Lord will judge the hidden secrets of men.'[14] Even though some rational souls are blinded by cupidity, every rational soul thinks and reasons. Nevertheless, it is not to the rational soul itself that we ought to attribute whatever is true in its reasoning; we must attribute it to the very light of the truth by which it is enlightened, even though feebly in proportion to its capacity, in order that it may be able to perceive some truth in its reasoning. Therefore, although the soul of the Devil is perverse by depraved desire, what wonder that it is represented as having heard by the voice of God—which is the voice of Truth—whatever was true in his thought with regard to a just man whom he desired to tempt? On the other hand, it is to his own cupidity that we must attribute whatever untruth there was in his thought—the cupidity that has earned for him the name of the Devil.[15] Furthermore, as the Lord and Ruler of all things and as the universal Dispenser of merit, God has spoken to both the good and the bad, even though it was generally done through a bodily and visible creature. In this way, He has spoken through angels who appeared in human form, and He has spoken through the Prophets who used to say: 'Thus speaks the Lord.' And so, what wonder that God is said to have spoken to the Devil, even though He may not have spoken through

---
14 Rom. 2.14.
15 The name is derived from the Greek word, *'diábolos,'* which means *slanderer.*

the mere medium of thought, but through some creature adapted for such an operation?

(33) And let them not think that the fact of God's having talked with the Devil is any reward of the Devil's merit or righteousness of a sort, for God was speaking to an angelic spirit—a fatuous and covetous spirit, to be sure—just as He would speak to a fatuous and covetous human soul. Now, let these same men tell us how God spoke to the rich man whose foolish cupidity He would reprove, saying: 'Thou fool, this night is thy soul demanded of thee: those things thou hast provided, whose will they be?'[16] The Lord Himself says this in the Gospel, to which even the heretics bow their heads whether they like it or not. If they are disturbed by the fact that Satan asked God for a righteous man in order to test his righteousness, I am not explaining why it happened, but I am compelling them to explain why it is that in the Gospel the Lord Himself said to His disciples: 'Behold, Satan has asked to have you, that he may sift you as wheat,'[17] and why He said to Peter: 'But I have prayed that thy faith fail not.'[18] When they have explained this to me, they will have given themselves the explanation they are demanding of me. If they are unable to explain it, then let them not dare brazenly censure in any book the very thing about which they make no objection when they read it in the Gospel.

(34) Temptations, therefore, occur through Satan, but they occur through God's permission and not by virtue of Satan's power. And they occur for the purpose either of punishing men for their sins or of proving and exercising them in accordance with the mercy of the Lord. As to the kind of temptation any man falls into—that is a matter of supreme

---

16 Luke 12.20.
17 Luke 22.31.
18 Luke 22.32.

importance. For Judas, the betrayer of his Master, did not fall into the same kind of temptation as Peter, the terrified denier of the Master. There are also, I believe, temptations that arise from human nature; for, in keeping with human frailty, every well-disposed man falls short of some one or other of the counsels. For instance, through eagerness to correct a brother, he may become slightly more impatient than Christian forbearance allows, and thus become angry with that brother. It is of such temptations that the Apostle speaks when he says: 'May no temptation take hold of you but such as is human.'[19] for the same Apostle says: 'God is faithful, Who will not suffer you to be tempted beyond what you are able to bear, but with the temptation will effect a means of escape, that you may be able to bear it.'[20] In that pronouncement, he clearly shows that we ought not to pray to be free from temptation, but that we ought to pray not to be led into temptation, for we are led into temptation if we encounter such temptations as we are unable to bear. But, even though dangerous temptations—into which it would be dangerous to be brought or led—may arise from either prosperity or adversity in temporal affairs, no one is overcome by the trails of misfortune unless he is dazzled by the delights of prosperity.

(35) The seventh and final petition is: *'But deliver us from evil.'* In the sixth petition we pray that we be not led into the evil of which we are free. But we must also pray to be delivered from the evil into which we have been already led. When that deliverance is accomplished, nothing will remain to be dreaded, and then there will be no need to fear any temptation whatever. There is no ground for hope that

---

[19] 1 Cor. 10.13.
[20] *Ibid.*

this can be brought about in our present life, for it cannot come to pass as long as we are carrying about with us the mortality to which we have been brought by the enticement of the serpent. However, we must hope that it will come to pass sometime; this is the hope that is not seen, the hope of which the Apostle was speaking when he said: 'But the hope that is seen, is not hope.'[21] Yet, the faithful servants of God must not lose hope in the wisdom which is granted even in this life. And that wisdom is this: with the utmost caution and vigilance to shun what the Lord's revelation teaches us that we ought to shun, and with most fervent love to seek what the Lord's revelation teaches us that we ought to seek. For in that way, when the remainder of the burden of this mortality will have been laid aside through death itself, then—in seasonable time—man's blessedness will be rendered perfect in all respects. This blessedness has its very beginning in the present life, and it is only during the course of this present life that we can make any effort to grasp and attain it.

Chapter 10 (Matt. 6.9-13)

(36) We must consider and carefully set forth the respective and distinctive notes of those seven petitions: While our present life is passing away like time, our hope is fixed on the life eternal, and while we cannot reach the eternal without first passing through the present life, eternal things are first in importance. So, also, the fulfillment of the first three petitions has its beginning in the life which begins and ends in this world. For, the hallowing of God's name began with the advent of the Lord's humility, and the coming of His kingdom—the coming in which He will ap-

---

21 Rom. 8.24.

pear in brightness[1]—will be made manifest, not after the end of the world, but at the ending of the world; and the perfect fufilling of God's will on earth as in heaven—whether you take the words, *heaven* and *earth,* to mean the righteous and the sinful, or the spirit and the flesh, or the Lord and the Church, or all of these together—will be fully attained through the full attainment of our blessedness, and therefore at the ending of the world. But, all three of these will continue for all eternity; for the hallowing of God's name will continue forever, and of His kingdom there is no end, and there is the promise of everlasting life for our blessedness. Therefore, these three things will continue, completely fulfilled, in the life that is promised to us.

(37) It seems to me that our remaining four petitions pertain to the needs of this temporal life. The first of them is *'Give us this day our daily bread';* the mere fact that it is called a *'daily'* bread shows that it pertains to the present time, the time which the Lord has called *'today.'* This is equally clear, no matter what significance one may attach to the expression, *daily bread;* that is to say, whether we take it as signifying spiritual bread or the bread that is visible either in the Sacrament or in our earthly food. Of course, this opinion does not imply that spiritual food is not everlasting. What the Scriptures call daily food is offered to the soul in the sound of human speech or in some kind of sign that is confined to time. There will be none of these things when everyone will be 'taught of God,'[2] and will be imbibing the ineffable light of truth through mind alone, but not imparting it through any bodily actions. Perhaps that is the

---

[1] Cf. Phil. 2.8; 2 Thess. 2.8. '. . . Christ, whose first coming at the appointed time was humble, and whose second coming is to be glorious' (*Enarr. in ps.* 98.1).
[2] Isa. 54.13; John 6.45; cf. Jer. 31.34.

very reason why this nourishment is called food rather than drink, for, just as food must be broken up and chewed before it can become nourishment for the body, so also is the soul nourished by the Scriptures when it has uncovered and digested their inner meaning. But, whatever is taken in the form of drink is not changed as it flows into the body. Therefore, truth is called food as long as it is being called a daily bread; when there will be no need of breaking it, so to speak, and chewing it, then it will be in the form of drink. This will be the case when there will be no need of discussing and discoursing, when nothing will be needed but a draught of pure and crystal truth. In this life we are both receiving and granting forgiveness of sins, and this is the second of those four petitions. But in eternity there will be no forgiving of sins, because there will be no sins to be forgiven. Temptations make this life troublesome, but there will be no temptations after the fulfillment of the promise, 'Thou shalt hide them in the secret of Thy countenance.'[3] Of course, the evil from which we wish to be delivered is an evil that is present with us in this life, and it is during this life that we wish to be delivered from it. For through God's justice we have by our own deserts made this life mortal, and through the mercy of God we are being delivered from that mortality.

Chapter 11 (Matt. 6.9-15)

(38) It seems to me, furthermore, that this septenary of petitions corresponds exactly to that septenary from which this entire Sermon has proceeded.[1] For if it is by the fear of God that the poor in spirit are blessed because theirs is the kingdom of heaven, then let us pray that the name of

---
3 Ps. 30.21.

---
1 Matt. 5.3-10. See above, 1.3.10, n. 5; 1.4.12, n. 9.

God be hallowed among men through a fear that is 'holy, enduring for ever and ever.'² If it is through piety that the meek are blessed because they shall inherit the land, then let us pray that His kingdom may come both upon ourselves—so that we may become meek, and not resist Him—and also from heaven to the earth in the brightness of the Lord's coming,³ the coming in which we shall rejoice and be praised by His saying: 'Come, blessed of my Father, receive the kingdom prepared for you from the foundation of the world.'⁴ for the Prophet says: 'In the Lord shall my soul be praised, let the meek hear and rejoice.'⁵ If it is through knowledge that the mourners are blessed because they shall be comforted, then let us pray that God's will be done on earth as it is in heaven. For we shall not mourn when the body and the spirit—earth and heaven, as it were—reach accord in total and consummate peace, because there is no other mourning during this life except the mourning that comes when these two are in mutual conflict and force us to say, 'I see another law in my members, warring against the law of my mind,' while they force us also to proclaim our mourning with the tearful cry, 'Unhappy man that I am! Who will deliver me from the body of this death?'⁶ If it is through fortitude that those who hunger and thirst for justice are blessed because they shall be filled, then let us pray that our daily bread be given us, so that we may be supported and sustained and that we may thus be able to arrive at that most copious abundance. If it is through counsel that the merciful are blessed because they shall ob-

---

2 Ps. 8.10.
3 2 Thess. 2.8.
4 Matt. 25.34.
5 Ps. 33.3.
6 Rom. 7.23f.

tain mercy, then let us forgive our debtors their debts and let us pray that our debts be remitted to us. If the clean of heart are blessed through understanding because they shall see God, then let us pray that we be not led into temptation, lest we have a heart that is divided by simultaneously longing for temporal goods and eternal possessions, instead of fixing its affection solely on the good toward which we are to direct all our actions; for, unless we are weakened by the temptations arising from the allurement of the things which men consider good and enjoyable, we shall not yield to the temptations which arise from the things which they consider grave calamities. If it is through wisdom that the peacemakers are blessed because they shall be called the children of God, then let us pray to be delivered from evil, for that same deliverance will make us children of God; that is to say, it will make us His sons, so that in the spirit of adoption we may cry: 'Abba! Father!'[7]

(39) And, certainly, we should not heedlessly neglect to call attention to the fact that, of all the pronouncements in which the Lord has ordered us to pray, He has deliberately attached a very special commendation to the pronouncement which deals with the forgiving of sins. In this pronouncement He wished us to be merciful because that is the only prescribed means of avoiding miseries. Indeed, in no other petition do we pray in such a manner as to make a kind of covenant with the Lord, for we say: *'Forgive us as we also forgive.'* If we default in this covenant, the whole petition is fruitless, for He says: *'If you forgive men their offenses, your Father Who is in heaven will also forgive you your offenses; but if you do not forgive men, neither will your Father forgive you your sins.'*

---
7 Rom. 8.15; Gal. 4.6.

Chapter 12 (Matt. 6.16-18)

(40) The next is a precept on fasting, but it pertains to the same cleansing of the heart which is now under discussion. For in this work, also, we must guard against the subtle entry of a certain kind of ostentation and a craving for human praise, which would divide the heart and not suffer it to be clean and single for knowing God. *'And when you fast,'* says He, *'do not look gloomy like the hypocrites; for they disfigure the face in order to appear to men as fasting. Amen I say to you, they have had their reward. But when you fast, anoint your heads and wash your faces, so that you may not be seen by men to be fasting, but by your Father Who is in secret; and your Father Who is in secret will reward you.'*[1] It is clear that by these precepts our whole intention is to be directed toward the joys that are within, lest we become conformed to this world[2] by seeking a reward that is without, and lest we thus lose the promised blessedness, which is all the more sound and firm according as it is in the inner man—the blessedness by which God has chosen us to become conformed to the image of His Son.[3]

(41) At this stage of the discourse we must particularly point out that vainglory can find a place, not only in the splendor and pomp of worldly wealth, but even in the sordid garment of sackcloth as well, and that it is then all the more dangerous because it is a deception under the pretense of service to God. When a man dazzles by immoderate adornment of the body and its raiment or by the splendor of whatever else he may possess, by that very fact he is easily shown to be desirous of worldly display; he deceives nobody by a crafty semblance of holiness. But if, through extraordinary

---
1 Matt. 6.16-18.
2 Rom. 12.2.
3 Rom. 8.29.

squalor and shabbiness, a man is attracting men's attention to his manner of professing Christianity, and if he is doing this of his own choice and not merely enduring it through necessity, then one may conjecture by his other works whether he is doing it through an indifference toward needless adornment or through ambition of some kind. Indeed, the Lord has forewarned us to beware of wolves in sheep's clothing: 'By their fruits,' says He, 'you shall know them.'[4] When, through trials of one kind or another, these men begin either to lose the very advantages they have gained under that garb or to be denied what they are seeking to gain by it, then inevitably it becomes clear whether it is a case of a wolf under a sheep's skin or a sheep under its own. But, just as sheep ought not to change their skin even though wolves sometimes hide themselves beneath it, so neither ought a Christian try to delight the eyes of men by needless adornment just because pretenders very often assume that scanty garb which necessity demands, and assume it for the purpose of deceiving the unwary.

(42) Wherefore, it is not unusual to be asked to explain the meaning of that saying of His, *'But when you fast, anoint your heads and wash your faces, so that you may not be seen by men to be fasting.'* Now, although we wash the face in accordance with daily usage, no one would properly prescribe that we ought also to keep our heads anointed while we are fasting. Since it is universally admitted that this would be most unseemly, the precept of anointing the head and washing the face must be understood as referring to the inner man. In that case, the anointing of the head refers to joy, and the washing of the face refers to purity, for we rightly understand the head as that which is pre-eminent in man—that by which his other members are manifestly directed and governed. So,

---

4 Matt. 7.16.

a man is anointing his head if he is seeking his joy from within his mind and reason. And he is seeking it from within when he is not seeking it from without, that is to say, when he is not acting like the carnal man who seeks his joy in the praises of men. Since it behooves the flesh to be in subjection, it is by no means the head of the whole man. It is in this sense that the Apostle speaks when he is giving the precept about loving one's wife: 'For no one ever hated his own flesh.'[5] Indeed, he says elsewhere: 'The head of the woman is the man; and of every man, Christ is the head.'[6] Accordingly, whoever wishes to keep his head anointed in accordance with this precept, let him seek an inner joy in his fasting; let him rejoice in his fasting, precisely because he is thereby so withdrawing himself from worldly pleasures that he is becoming subject to Christ. In this way, he will also wash his face; that is to say, he will cleanse his heart. When he is thus rendered strong and steadfast by being cleansed and single-minded, he will see God through that heart, and not through some veil interposed by reason of infirmity contracted through defilements. 'Wash yourselves,' we are told; 'Be clean; take wickedness away from your minds, and from the sight of my eyes.'[7] Our faces, therefore, must be cleansed of the stain by which the sight of God is offended, for, with faces unveiled, we shall reflect the glory of God as in a mirror and we shall be transformed into His very image.[8]

(43) The mind's occupation with the things that are needful for our present life often mars and sullies our inner eye, and it generally divides the heart. For this reason, then, even our seemingly righteous conduct toward men does not

---
5 Eph. 5.29.
6 1 Cor. 11.3.
7 Isa. 1.16.
8 2 Cor. 3.18.

spring from the kind of heart which the Lord prescribes; that is to say, those righteous actions of ours are performed, not because we love our fellow men, but because we seek thereby to gain some advantage with reference to the needs of this life. But we ought to do good to men for the sake of their salvation, not for the sake of our own temporal gain. Therefore, 'may God incline our heart to His testimonies, and not to emolument';[9] for 'the purpose of the precept is charity, from a pure heart and a good conscience and faith unfeigned.'[10] But, when a man consults the interests of a brother for the sake of his own needs in this life, he is certainly not doing it through charity; for he is consulting his own interests, not those of a man whom he ought to love as he loves himself. Rather, he is not even consulting his own interests, because he is making his own heart double and he is thereby being impeded from seeing God. It is only in seeing God that sure and everlasting blessedness consists.

Chapter 13 (Matt. 6.19-23)

(44) Because the Lord insists that our heart be cleansed, He therefore goes further and gives a command, saying: *'Do not collect treasure on earth, where the moth and corrosion destroy, and where thieves dig up and steal; but lay up for yourselves treasures in heaven, where neither moth nor corrosion destroys, nor thieves dig up and steal. For where thy treasure is, there thy heart also will be.'* Now, if a man does something with the intention of gaining earthly profit, his heart is on the earth. And how can a heart be clean while it is wallowing on the earth? On the other hand, if it be in heaven it will be clean, for whatsoever things are heavenly are clean. A thing becomes defiled if it is mixed with a baser

---
9 Ps. 118.36.
10 1 Tim. 1.5.

substance, even though that other substance be not vile in its own nature; for instance, gold is debased by pure silver if it is mixed with it. So also is our mind defiled by a desire for the things of earth, although the earth itself is pure in its own class and in its own order. Let us not think that in this text the word, '*heaven*,' signifies the universe of heavenly bodies, for the word, '*earth*' includes every kind of body, and a man ought to disregard the whole world when he is laying up treasure for himself in heaven. Therefore, the reference is to that heaven of which it is said: 'The heaven of heaven is the Lord's.'[1] Moreover, since we ought to fix our treasure and our heart on that which will abide forever and not on something which will pass away, the heaven here mentioned means the spiritual firmament, for, 'heaven and earth will pass away.'[2]

(45) The Lord now shows that it is with reference to the cleansing of the heart that He is giving us all these precepts. He shows this when He says: *'The lamp of thy body is thine eye. If therefore thine eye be single, thy whole body will be full of light. But if thine eye be evil, thy whole body will be full of darkness. Therefore if the light that is in thee is darkness, how great is the darkness!'* This passage is to be understood as meaning that we know that all our works are pure and pleasing in the sight of God, if they are performed with a single heart; that is, if they are performed out of charity and with an intention that is fixed on heaven, because 'charity is the fulfillment of the Law.'[3] Therefore, in this passage we ought to understand the eye as the intention with which we perform all our actions. If this intention be pure and upright and directing its gaze where it ought to be directed,

---
1 Ps. 113.16.
2 Matt. 24.35.
3 Rom. 13.10.

then, unfailingly, all our works are good works, because they are performed in accordance with that intention. And by the expression, *'whole body,'* he designated all those works, for the Apostle also designates certain works as our *'members'*— works which he reproves and which he orders us to mortify. 'Therefore,' says he, 'mortify your members, which are on earth: fornication, uncleanness, covetousness,'[4] and all other such things.

(46) In all our actions, therefore, it is the intention, and not the act, that ought to be considered, for the intention is indeed the light within us. Through this light it is made clear to us that, whenever we are doing anything, we are doing it for a good purpose, 'for all that is made manifest is light.'[5] But there is uncertainty with regard to the result of even the deeds which we perform with the intention of benefiting our fellow men; on this account, the Lord calls those deeds darkness. For instance, when I am handing money to a needy beggar, I do not know what he will do with it or what evil he may suffer on account of it. And it is possible that he will do some evil with it or suffer some evil from it— an evil which, when giving him the money, I neither willed nor intended to happen. Now, if I performed that act with a good intention, that intention was known to me at the time; for this reason, it is called light. And my deed also is illumined, no matter what result it may bring; nevertheless, it is called darkness because its result is uncertain and unknown. On the other hand, if I performed that act with a bad intention, then—although even a bad intention is light— my intention is darkness as well. It is called light because a man knows with what intention he is acting, even when acting with a bad intention. However, that same light is darkness

---
4 Col. 3.5.
5 Eph. 5.13.

when the intention is not a single intention directed toward heavenly things, but is deflected toward the things beneath; it is as though it were causing an eclipse when the heart is divided. *'Therefore if the light that is in thee is darkness, how great is the darkness!'* This means that if even the intention of the heart, which is known to you, and through which you are performing your action—if this intention is sullied and darkened by a seeking after the temporal things of earth, how much more darksome is the deed itself of which the result is uncertain! Even though someone may benefit from the deed which you perform with an intention that is neither upright nor clean, yet what is imputed to you is, not how it turned out for him, but how you performed it.

Chapter 14 (Matt. 6.24)

(47) And to this same intention is to be referred what He now sets forth when He says: *'No man can serve two masters.'* Indeed, He explains it forthwith, saying: *'For either he will hate the one and love the other, or else he will bear with the one and disregard the other.'* These words must be carefully considered, although He at once reveals who the two masters are, for He says: *'You cannot serve God and mammon.'* Riches are said to be called *'mammon'* among the Hebrews,[1] and in the Punic the word has a corresponding meaning, for in that language the word *'mammon'* signifies profit. Therefore, whoever serves mammon is the servant of him who—in retribution for his perversity—has been placed over the things of this world, and is therefore designated by the Lord as 'the prince of this world.'[2] Consequently, a man will either hate the one and love the other,

---
1 See Introduction, n. 16.
2 John 12.31; 14.30; 16.11.

who is God, or else he will put up with the one and disregard the other. For, whoever serves mammon puts up with a harsh and harmful master. Entangled in the toils of his own cupidity, he puts himself under the Devil, but he does not love him. (Indeed, who could love the Devil?) Nevertheless, he puts up with him, just as in some large household a man who is intimate with another's maidservant puts up with a harsh servitude because of his own passion, even though he has no love for the man whose maidservant he loves.

(48) But *'he will disregard the other.'* He does not say that he will hate the other, for scarcely anyone's conscience could hate God.[3] But he disregards God; that is to say, he does not fear Him—as though he were presuming on His goodness. From this negligence and baneful confidence, the Holy Spirit recalls us when He says through the Prophet: 'Son, do not add sin to sin; and do not say, "The mercy of God is great"'[4] and when He says: 'Knowest thou not that the patience of God invites thee to repentance?'[5] For, whose mercy can be accounted as great as the mercy of Him who forgives all their sins to those who are converted to Him, and who makes the wild olive a partaker of the fatness of the olive tree; at the same time, whose severity can be accounted as great as the severity of Him who has not spared the natural branches, but has broken them off because of unbelief?[6] Therefore, whoever wishes to love God and to beware of offending Him, let such a one disengage the upright intention of his heart from all duplicity; in this way, he will 'think of the Lord in goodness, and seek Him in simplicity of heart.'[7]

---

3 See *Retract.* 1.19.8.
4 Eccli. 5.6.
5 Rom. 2.4.
6 Rom. 11.17-22.
7 Wisd. 1.1.

Chapter 15 (Matt. 6.25-30)

(49) *'Therefore,'* says He, *'I say to you not to be anxious for your soul as to what you shall eat, nor for your body as to what you shall put on'*—lest perchance the heart become divided on account of those necessities even when nothing superfluous is being sought after, and lest our intention be deflected to seek to gain those needful things for ourselves even while we are acting again as if performing a work of mercy; that is to say, lest our intention become so warped that—while we wish to appear as if consulting the interests of some one else—we would be more intent on our own profit from our actions than on the benefit which someone else would derive from them, and lest we seem to ourselves to be avoiding sin, just because the things we seek are needful things, and not superfluous. Now, the Lord admonishes us to remember that, since God has made us and composed us of soul and body, He has given us what is far more important than food and clothing, and that He does not wish us to have a heart divided through solicitude for those two things, for He says: *'Is not the soul a greater thing than the food?'* He says this so that you may bear in mind that He who gave the soul will much more readily give the food. *'And the body more than the clothing?'*—that is to say: Is it not a greater thing than the clothing? And so, you should likewise understand that He who gave the body will much more readily give the clothing.

(50) But, since this food is bodily nourishment, and since the soul is not a bodily substance, a question is usually asked as to the meaning of this text, namely, whether this food pertains to the soul. Let us bear in mind that the word, *'soul,'* has been used here to signify this present life, of which this corporeal food is the support. It is in accordance with this

meaning of the word that the following pronouncement also has been made, 'He who loves his soul, loses it.'[1] Unless we accept this pronouncement as referring to the present life (the life which it behooves us to lose for the sake of the kingdom of God, and it has been made clear that the martyrs were able to do this), then this precept will be in opposition with the maxim which says: 'For what does it profit a man, if he gain the whole world, but suffer the loss of his own soul?'[2]

(51) He then says: *'Look at the birds of the air: they do not sow, or reap, or gather into barns; yet your heavenly Father feeds them. Are not you of more value than they?'* This means that you are more highly esteemed, for in the order of nature, of course, the rational animal, or man, ranks above the irrational animals, such as birds. *'For which of you,'* says He, *'by being anxious about it can add to his stature a single cubit? And as for clothing, why are you anxious?'* Your body can also be clothed by the providence of Him through whose power and dominion it has come to pass that your body should be brought to its present stature. And from the fact that—even if you are anxious and desirous—you are unable to add a single cubit to this stature, it can be seen that your body has not come to its present stature through any care of yours. Therefore, as to clothing for the body, leave the care of that also to Him through whose care you see it to have come to pass that you have a body of such stature.

(52) But, it was expedient to give an example with reference to the clothing, just as an example has been given with reference to the food. Therefore He continues, and says: *'Consider the lilies of the field: they neither toil nor spin; yet I say to you that not even Solomon in all his glory*

---
[1] John 12.25.
[2] Matt. 16.26.

was arrayed like one of these. But if God so clothes the grass of the field, which today is alive and tomorrow is thrown into the oven, how much more you, O you of little faith!' Now, these examples are not to be analyzed like allegories. We must not inquire about the significance of the birds of the air or the lilies of the field; these examples are proposed so that more important things may be suggested from things of less importance. They are like the example of the judge who feared neither God nor man, and who nevertheless yielded to the widow importuning him to adjudge her case; he yielded, not through piety or kindliness, but through fear of suffering annoyance.³ By no means does that unjust judge furnish an allegorical representation of God. But from the example of an unjust man who, although he yields for the mere sake of avoiding annoyance, nevertheless cannot disregard those who importune him with incessant pleadings —from this example the Lord wishes us to infer how much care God bestows on those who beseech Him, for God is both just and good.

Chapter 16 (Matt. 6.31-33)

(53) He says: *'Therefore do not be anxious, saying, "What shall we eat?" or "What shall we drink?" or "What shall we put on?" (for the Gentiles seek after all these things); for your Father knows that you need all these things. But seek first the kingdom of God and His justice, and all these things shall be given you besides.'* At first, He makes it abundantly clear that these things are not to be sought as if they were for us the kind of blessings for the sake of which we ought to make all our actions good actions, but that they are necessities nevertheless. Then He says: *'Seek first the kingdom of God*

---

3 Luke 18.2-5.

and His justice, and all these things shall be given you besides.' In this sentence, He clearly shows the difference between a good that ought to be sought as an end, and a necessity that ought to be used as a means. Our good is, therefore, the kingdom of God and His justice; we ought to seek this good, and fix our aim upon it. Let us perform all our actions for the sake of it. Yet, since we are waging war in this life in order to be able to reach that kingdom,[1] and since this life cannot be maintained unless those necessities are supplied, He says: *'These things shall be given you besides, but seek you first the kingdom of God and His justice.'* Now, when He said that the one is to be sought first, He clearly intimated that the other is to be sought later—not that it is to be sought at a later time, but that it is to be sought as a thing of secondary importance. He showed that the one is to be sought as our good, that the other is to be sought as something needful for us, but that the needful is to be sought for the sake of the good.

(54) For instance, we ought not to preach the Gospel in order that we may eat, but we ought to eat in order to be able to preach the Gospel. For, if we preach the Gospel in order that we may eat, we esteem the Gospel as of less value than the food; in that case, our good would be in the eating, and our need would be in the preaching of the Gospel. The Apostle also forbids this when he says that he did not use the right to have the necessaries of this life from the Gospel, although he was permitted to do so, because it is granted by the Lord that those who preach the Gospel should have their living from the Gospel.[2] For there were many who were seeking opportunity to receive the Gospel and

---
1 2 Cor. 10.3.
2 1 Cor. 9.14.

to sell it, and, because the Apostle wished to lessen their opportunity, he sustained his life with his own hands.[3] Elsewhere he says of those men: 'That I may cut off the occasion from those who are seeking occasion.'[4] But, even if he—like the other good Apostles, and with the Lord's permission—were making his livelihood from the Gospel, he would not on that account be making that mode of life the fixed purpose of his preaching. On the contrary, he would be making the preaching of the Gospel the fixed purpose of his living in that manner. In other words, he would not be preaching the Gospel for the sake of obtaining food and sundry other necessities, but he would be using those things in order to fulfill the duty of preaching the Gospel. Otherwise he would be preaching the Gospel, not of his own free will, but under the compulsion of necessity; this is the very thing he reproves when he says: 'Do you not know that they who minister in the temple eat what comes from the temple; and that they who serve the altar, have their share with the altar? So also the Lord directed that those who preach the Gospel should have their living from the Gospel. But I have made use of none of these rights.'[5] Hence, he shows that this is a permission, and not a command; if it were a command, he would be understood to have acted against the Lord's precept. Then he goes on to say: 'But I have written this, not so that this provision may be observed with regard to me; for it were better for me to die than that anyone should make my boasting vain.' He said this because he had already resolved—because of certain opportunity-seekers—to gain his livelihood by his own hands. 'For,' says he, 'even if I preach the Gospel, no praise is due to me.' He means that, if he were

---
3 Acts 20.34.
4 2 Cor. 11.12.
5 Cf. 1 Cor. 9.13-17.

to preach the Gospel in order to obtain the necessities of life, he would be making food and drink and clothing the purpose of his preaching the Gospel. Why would he be deserving of no praise? He gives the answer when he says: 'For I am under necessity.' He means that he would be under necessity to preach the Gospel because he would not have wherewith to live; he would be under the necessity of gaining a temporal benefit from the preaching of eternal blessings. In that way, there would be no willingness in his preaching the Gospel; there would be a necessity. 'For woe to me,' he says, 'if I do not preach the Gospel.' In what manner ought he to preach the Gospel? He ought to preach it in such a way that he will reckon his reward in the Gospel itself and in the kingdom of God; in that way he can preach it willingly, and not through constraint. 'For,' says he, 'if I do this willingly, I have a reward; but if I do it unwillingly, a stewardship is entrusted to me.' It is as if he were to say: 'If I preach the Gospel because I am constrained to do so by the lack of those things which are needful for this temporal life, then others—because they will love the Gospel through my preaching—will receive the reward of the Gospel through me. But I shall not receive it, because what I love is, not the Gospel, but the reward of the Gospel insofar as that reward is made up of those temporal things. And it would be wrong to have it come to pass that anyone would minister the Gospel, not as a son, but as a slave to whom the stewardship has been committed. It would be wrong for anyone to minister the Gospel as if he were dispensing from another's goods, and were himself receiving no reward thereby but the eatables that are given, not by reason of his sharing in the kingdom, but as an extrinsic prop to support the misery of his servitude.' In another passage, however, the same Apostle calls himself a steward.⁶ But, even a slave, once he has acquired the status of son by adoption, can properly administer the joint inheritance for those who share it with him. So, when the Apostle now says: 'But if I do it unwillingly, a stewardship is entrusted to me,' he means the kind of steward who administers another's property without receiving any share of it himself.

(55) And so, whenever a benefit is being sought for the sake of something else, it is of course of less esteem than the thing for whose sake it is being sought. Consequently, the primary thing is that for the sake of which you are seeking the benefit; it is not the benefit itself, for you are seeking that for the sake of the other thing. So, if we are seeking the Gospel and the kingdom of God for the sake of food, then we are esteeming food as our primary object, and the kingdom of God as something secondary; our motive is such that if we were not in need of food we would not be seeking the kingdom of God. This would be to seek the food first, and then the kingdom of God, for it would be attaching primary importance to the food, and secondary importance to the kingdom of God. Contrariwise, if we seek food in order that we may have the kingdom of God, then we follow the precept, *'Seek first the kingdom of God and His justice, and all these things shall be given you besides.'*

Chapter 17 (Matt. 6.32-34)

(56) When we are seeking the kingdom of God and His justice—in other words, when we are placing it before all other things so that we are seeking the other things for its sake—we ought to have no lurking anxiety about the necessities of this life; we ought to have no fear that they will

---
6 1 Cor. 4.1.

be lacking to us on account of the kingdom of heaven, for the Lord has said: *'Your Father knows that you need all these things.'* When He had said: *'Seek first the kingdom of God and His justice,'* He did not then say: 'Seek these things afterwards,' although they are necessary. But He did say: *'All these things shall be given you besides.'* This means that these things will follow if you so seek them that they will not become such a hindrance to you that—instead of seeking them for the sake of the kingdom of God—either your intention would be withdrawn from that kingdom or you would pursue two purposes by seeking the kingdom of God for its own sake and also seeking these things as ends in themselves. Sought without becoming such a hindrance, they will not be wanting to you, but you cannot serve two masters. And a man is trying to serve two masters if, while he is indeed seeking the kingdom of God as a great treasure, he is also seeking these temporal things for their own sake. In that case, he cannot keep the eye single, and he cannot serve the Lord God exclusively. He cannot serve God alone unless that is his sole purpose in using whatsoever other things are necessary, that is to say, unless he is using those other things for the sake of the kingdom of God. But, just as all soldiers receive subsistence and pay, so all who preach the Gospel receive food and clothing. And just as there are some soldiers who serve merely for the sake of the pay which they receive and not for the welfare of the state, so also among those enrolled in the service of God there are some who minister, not for the welfare of the Church, but for the sake of the temporalities which they receive by way of subsistence and salary.[1] Perhaps they minister for the one purpose and the other, although it has been said that *'You cannot serve two masters.'* With a single heart,

---

1 Cf. *Epist.* 21.1.

therefore, and exclusively for the sake of the kingdom of heaven, we ought to do good to all men. And in this welldoing we ought not to think about temporal rewards; we ought not to think about them either exclusively or conjointly with the kingdom of God. For it is with reference to all these temporal things that the Lord used the word, *'tomorrow,'* when He said: *'Do not think about tomorrow.'*[2] For that word is not used except in the realm of time, where the future succeeds the past. Therefore, when we perform any good deed, let us think about eternal things and pay no heed to the temporal. Then, our deed will be not only good but also perfect. *'For tomorrow,'* says He, *'will have anxieties of its own.'* By this He means that you are to take food or drink or clothing when it behooves you to do so. When the need for them is pressing, these things will be at hand; our Father knows that we need all these things. *'For sufficient for the day,'* He says, *'is its own evil.'* In other words, when the need is urgent, we have sufficient reason for using these things. I suppose that this necessity is called evil because it partakes of the nature of punishment for us since it is part of the frailty and mortality which we have merited by committing sin.[3] To this penalty of temporal necessity, therefore, do not add something more troublesome; do not bring it about that you not only suffer the lack of these things, but that you would even serve in the army of God for the sake of supplying that want.

(57) On this point, however, when we see some servant of God making provision against the lack of these necessities —either for his own sake or for the sake of those whose care has been committed to him—we must be exceedingly careful not to conclude that he is acting against the precept

---
2 Matt. 6.34.
3 See *Retract.* 1.19.9.

of the Lord and that he is anxious about the morrow. For the Lord Himself—even though angels used to minister to Him[4]—nevertheless condescended to have a purse with money in it, from which the demands of practical necessity could be supplied; of which purse, as it is written, Judas the traitor was at once the keeper and the thief.[5] Of course, the Lord did this for the sake of example, so that afterwards no one would suffer scandal when he noticed some servant of the Lord attending to these necessities. For instance, even the Apostle Paul might seem to have been thinking about the morrow when he said: 'Now concerning the collections for the saints, as I have ordered the churches of Galatia, do you also. On the first day of the week, let each one of you put aside at home and lay up whatever he has a mind to, so that the collections may not have to be made after I have come. But when I am with you, whomsoever you may authorize by credentials, them will I send to carry your gift to Jerusalem. And if it be important enough for me also to go, they shall go with me. But I shall come to you after passing through Macedonia (for I shall pass through Macedonia); but with you I shall perhaps remain, or even spend the winter, so that you may speed me wherever I may be going. For I do not wish to see you just now in passing by; for I hope to stay some time with you, if the Lord permits. But I shall stay on at Ephesus until Pentecost.'[6] Likewise, in the Acts of the Apostles it is written that, on account of an imminent famine, the necessities of life were provided for the future, for we read the following: 'Now in those days some prophets from Jerusalem came down to Antioch, *and there was great rejoicing*. And, when we were

---

4 Matt. 4.11.
5 John 12.6.
6 1 Cor. 16.1-8.

assembled, one of them named Agabus got up and revealed through the Spirit that there would be a great famine all over the world (this famine occurred in the reign of Claudius Caesar). Then the disciples determined—each one according to his means—to send relief to the presbyters for the brethren dwelling in Judea. And they sent it by the hands of Barnabas and Saul.'[7] In view of the fact that needful provisions—which were wont to be offered—were put aboard for the same Apostle when he was sailing, it does not seem that the food thus procured was just enough for one day.[8] Of course, there are those who misunderstand the same Apostle when he writes: 'He who has wont to steal, let him steal no longer; but let him labor, doing good with his hands, that he may have something to give to one who has need.'[9] For, when he is ordering such persons to work so efficiently with their hands that they will have something to bestow on others also, his misinterpreters believe that he is going counter to the instruction which the Lord gives when He says: 'Look at the birds of the air: they do not sow, or reap, or gather into barns . . . Consider the lilies of the field: they neither toil nor spin.'[10] He does not seem to have imitated the birds of the air and lilies of the field. He has repeatedly said of himself that he was working with his own hands so as not to burden anyone,[11] and it is written of him that he joined with Aquila because of the similarity of their handicraft, so that they might work together to maintain a livelihood.[12] From these and other such passages of the Scripture it is clear enough that our Lord does not reprove a man for procuring these things in the usual manner, but that He reproves

---
7 Acts 11.27-30. The italicized words are not found in the Vulgate.
8 *Id.* 28.10.
9 Eph. 4.28.
10 Matt. 6.28.
11 Acts 20.34; 1 Cor. 4.12; 1 Thess. 2.9; 2 Thess. 3.8.
12 Acts 18.3.

a man who would serve in the army of God for the sake of these things, a man who in his works has his eye fixed, not on the kingdom of God, but on the acquisition of these things.

(58) This entire precept is reduced, therefore, to the following rule: namely, that even in the procuring of these things we should keep our mind on the kingdom of God, and that in the service of the kingdom of God we should give no thought to these things. In this way, even if these things be lacking at times (and God permits this usually for the sake of exercising us), not only do they not weaken our resolve, but they even strengthen it for trial and approval. For the Apostle says: 'We exult in tribulations, knowing that tribulation works out endurance, and endurance trial, and trial hope. And hope does not disappoint, because the charity of God is poured forth in our hearts by the Holy Spirit Who has been given to us.'[13] And in the recital of his tribulations and labors, the same Apostle recounts that he has been in distress not only in prisons and in shipwrecks and in many molestations of this kind, but also in hunger and thirst and cold and nakedness.[14] We have been told to seek first the kingdom of God and His justice, and that all these things shall be given us besides. So, even when we read the Apostle's recital of sufferings, let us not think that God has wavered in His promises because that Apostle suffered hunger and thirst and nakedness while seeking the kingdom of God and His justice. The Physician to whom we have unreservedly entrusted ourselves and from whom we have the promise of the present life and of the life to come—that Physician sees these things as helpful remedies.[15] He places them before us or takes them away according as He judges it expedient for us, for He governs us and guides us so that we may be consoled and exercised

---
13 Rom. 5.3-5.
14 2 Cor. 11.23-27.
15 See above, 1.19.57.

in this life, and so that in the life to come we may be established and confirmed in eternal rest. For even a man does not discontinue to care for his beast of burden, although he very frequently removes the fodder from it; rather, he does this in the exercise of care for the beast.

Chapter 18 (Matt. 7.1-2)

(59) But, when a man is either setting these things aside for the future or keeping them for the mere reason that there is no reason for expending them, he may be acting with either a single or a double heart; for his intention is unknown to others. Wherefore, the Lord adds the apposite injunction: *'Do not judge, that you may not be judged; and with what measure you measure, it shall be measurèd to you.'* I believe that in this text nothing else is prescribed for us but to adopt the better interpretation whenever there is doubt as to the intention with which deeds are being performed. For, there is also that other text, 'By their fruits you shall know them.'[1] This has been spoken with reference to manifest actions which cannot be performed with a good intention: for instance, lewdness, blasphemies, thefts, drunkenness, and all other such things. We are allowed to judge of these things, for the Apostle says: 'What have I to do with judging those outside? Is it not those inside whom you judge?'[2] Now, all kinds of human food can be eaten indiscriminately with a good intention and a single heart, and without the vice of concupiscence. With regard to food, therefore, the Apostle forbids abstainers from meat and wine to pass judgment on those who are making use of that kind of nourishment: 'Let not him who eats despise him who does not eat, and let not

1 Matt. 7.16.
2 1 Cor. 5.12.

him who does not eat judge him who eats'; and then he adds: 'Who art thou to judge another's servant? To his own master he stands or falls.'³ Those men were of a mind to pass judgment with regard to things which can indeed be done with a bad intention, but which can also be done with an upright and simple and magnanimous intention. Although they were men, they wished to judge the secrets of the heart—secrets of which God alone is the judge.

(60) And this is also the purport of what he says in another passage, 'Pass no judgment before the time, until the Lord comes, who will both bring to light the hidden things of darkness and make manifest the thoughts of the heart; and then everyone will have his praise from God.'⁴ Therefore, some actions are indifferent, and, since we do not know with what intention they are performed, it would be rash for us to pass judgment on them, and most rash for us to condemn them. The time for judging these actions will come when the Lord 'will bring to light the hidden things of darkness and make manifest the thoughts of the heart.' And in another passage the same Apostle also says: 'Some men's sins are manifest even before the judgment, but some sins afterwards.'⁵ When it is clear with what intention they are committed, he calls them manifest sins, and these sins precede judgment. This means that if judgment follows them at once, it will not be rash judgment. But concealed sins follow judgment, because not even these will remain hidden in their proper time. And this is to be understood about good works as well, for he thus continues: 'In like manner also the good works are manifest, and whatever things are otherwise cannot be hidden.'⁶ On things that are manifest, therefore, let us pass

---
3 Rom. 14.3-4.
4 1 Cor. 4.5.
5 1 Tim. 5.24.
6 *Id.* 5.25.

judgment, but, with regard to hidden things, let us leave the judgment to God. For, whether the works themselves be bad or good, they cannot remain hidden when the time comes for them to be revealed.

(61) There are two cases in which we ought to beware of rash judgment: first, when there is no certainty as to the intention with which an act has been performed; second, when it is uncertain what kind of man he is to become who now seems to be either a good man or a bad man. For instance, if some one complained about his stomach and refused to fast, you would judge rashly if you disbelieved him and attributed his refusal to the vice of gluttony. Even if you knew a case of manifest gluttony or drunkenness, you would nevertheless judge rashly if you reproved the man as though he could never be corrected and changed. Therefore, let us not reprehend actions when we do not know the intention with which they are being performed. As to the things that are manifest, let us not so reprehend them as if we had lost all hope of a cure.[7] In this way, we shall avoid the kind of judgment that is mentioned here, *'Do not judge, that you may not be judged.'*

(62) The following saying of His may occasion anxiety: *'For with what judgment you judge, you shall be judged; and with what measure you measure, it shall be measured to you.'* Does this mean that if we judge by a rash judgment, God will also judge rashly of us? Or does it mean that if we measure by an unjust measure, God also has an unjust measure by which it will be measured to us in turn?

---

7 'The reason why a wicked man lives is either that he may amend or that, through him, a good man may be exercised. . . . In the holy Scriptures, the Devil and his angels are revealed to us as destined for eternal fire. Of them alone is there no hope of correction. Against them we have the hidden wrestling of which the Apostle warns us' (*Enarr. in ps.* 54.4; cf. Matt. 25.41; *Eph.* 6.12).

I think that by the word, *measure,* judgment itself is meant. Of course, God does not judge rashly, nor does He make recompense to anybody by an unjust measure. But this expression has been used because the very rashness by which you punish another will inevitably punish yourself—unless, indeed, we must believe that injustice does harm to the very man against whom it is directed, but no harm whatever to the man from whom it proceeds. On the contrary, it often does no harm to the man who suffers the injustice, but it must of necessity do harm to the man who perpetrates it. Indeed, what harm did the injustice of persecutors do to the martyrs?[8] Nevertheless, it did great harm to the presecutors themselves, for, although some of them made amends, their malice was blinding them while they were inflicting persecution. So, a rash judgment generally does no harm to the man who is rashly judged, but the rashness itself must necessarily do harm to the man who judges rashly. I believe that the following saying is also in accordance with this rule: 'Everyone who strikes with the sword, shall die by the sword.'[9] For, how many men strike with the sword, and yet—like Peter himself—do not die by the sword! But, lest anyone think that the forgiveness of his sins enabled Peter to escape this kind of penalty for striking with the sword, is there anything more absurd than to think the penalty of the sword more severe than the penalty of the cross? Yet Peter escaped the one, and endurend the other.[10] Furthermore, what could

---

8 'Worldly men are sadly successful; martyrs are successfully sad' (*Enarr. in ps.* 127.5). 'By punishing wrongdoers, God avenges those who suffer the wrong' (*Enarr. in ps.* 145.15).
9 Matt. 26.52.
10 Cf. John 21.18f. The historical references to St. Peter's death by crucifixion at Rome date from the second century. Irenaeus tells us that St. Peter lived there (*Contra haer.* 3.3.1). Tertullian writes: 'There [at Rome] Peter was girded by another, for he was bound to the cross'

anyone say with regard to the robbers who were crucified with the Lord?[11] The one who obtained forgiveness obtained it after he had been nailed to the cross; the other did not obtain it at all. Or could it be that those robbers had crucified all whom they had slain, and therefore deserved crucifixion? It would be ridiculous to think so. Then as to the saying, 'Everyone who strikes with the sword, shall perish by the sword' —what else can it mean but that the soul perishes by whatsoever sin it commits?

Chapter 19 (Matt. 7.3-5)

(63) Because the Lord here wishes to admonish us with regard to rash and unjust judgment (for whatever we do, He wants us to do it with a heart that is single and intent on God alone); and because there are many things on which it would be rash to pass judgment (since we do not know with what kind of heart they are done); and because for the most part those who judge and readily condemn things that are indifferent are those who love to find fault and to condemn, rather than to improve and to correct (and this is the vice of pride or envy)—because of all this, He straightway continues, and says: *'But why dost thou see the speck in thy brother's eye, and yet dost not consider the beam in thy own eye?'* So that, for instance, if perchance he has sinned through anger, you would reprove him through hatred. There is, so to speak, as much difference between anger and hatred as there is between a speck and a beam, for hatred is inveterate anger which has acquired, as it were, so much strength through long duration that it may aptly be called a

---

(Scorpiace 15.2-5; cf. *De praescrip.* 36.3). Origen adds that he was crucified head downward. (Cf. Eusebius, *Hist. eccl.* 3.1.)
11 Cf. Luke 23.33-43.

beam. Even though you are angry with a man, you nevertheless wish him to amend, but if you hate a man, you cannot wish him to change for the better.

(64) *'For how canst thou say to thy brother, "Let me cast out the speck from thy eye"; and behold, there is a beam in thy own eye? Thou hypocrite, first cast out the beam from thy own eye, and then thou wilt see clearly to cast out the speck from thy brother's eye.'* In other words, first rid yourself of hatred, and then you will immediately be able to correct the man you love. The word, *'hypocrite,'* is aptly employed here, since the denouncing of evils is a matter for upright men of good will. When evil men engage in it, they impersonate others; like masqueraders, they hide their real selves beneath a mask, while they portray another's character through the mask. You are therefore to understand that the word, hyprocrites, signifies pretenders. Most especially ought we to shun that meddlesome class of pretenders who, under the pretense of seeking advice, undertake the denouncement of all kinds of vices, because they are moved by hatred and malice. Therefore, whenever necessity compels us to reprove or rebuke someone, we ought to proceed with piety and caution. First of all, let us consider whether the man's fault is such as we ourselves have never had, or whether it is one that we have overcome. Then, if we have never had such a fault, let us remember that we are human, and could have had it. But, if we have had it and are rid of it now, let us remember our common frailty, in order that mercy—and not hatred—may lead us to the giving of reproval or rebuke. In this way, whether the rebuke occasions the amendment or the worsening of the man for whose sake we are giving it (for the result cannot be foreseen), we ourselves shall be secure through our singleness of eye. But, if on reflection we

find that we ourselves have the same fault as the man we are about to rebuke, let us neither reprove nor rebuke him; rather, let us bemoan the fault, and induce that man to a like effort, without asking him to submit to our correction.

(65) There are those who—for the sake of supporting their own detestable pretense by the authority of such an example—would have us believe that the Apostle was pretending when he was doing what he mentions in the following: 'To the Jews I became a Jew, that I might gain the Jews; to those who are under the Law, as one under the Law (although I myself was not under the Law), that I might gain those who are under the Law; to those who were without the Law, as one without the Law (although I was not without the Law, but was under the law of Christ), that I might gain those who were without the Law. To the weak I became weak, that I might gain the weak. I became all things to all men, that I might gain them all.'[1] He certainly was not acting through pretense; he was doing it through love, and because of that love he regarded as his own the weakness of everyone whom he wished to help. In fact, he sets this down beforehand by saying: 'For although I was free from all men, yet I have made myself the servant of all, that I might gain more men.'[2] And so that you may understand that this is not done through pretense, but that it is done through that charity by which we share the sufferings of weak men as if we ourselves were weak, he gives the following admonition in another passage, where he says: 'Brethren, you have been called to liberty: only do not use liberty as an occasion for sensuality, but by charity serve one another.'[3] Now, this cannot be done unless each one con-

---
[1] 1 Cor. 9.20-22; cf. *Epist. 40* 4.6; *Epist. 75* 4.12,17.
[2] 1 Cor. 9.19.
[3] Gal. 5.13.

siders as his own the weakness of another for whose welfare he is solicitous, so that he may bear it with equanimity until that other is freed from it.

(66) Rebukes are to be administered but rarely, therefore, and only under great necessity. Even then they are to be so administered that in giving the rebukes we shall insist that submission be made, not to ourselves, but to God, for He is the end for whose sake we ought to do nothing with a double heart.[4] We are not to administer rebukes until we have removed from our eye the beam of envy or malice or pretense, so that we may have clear vision to cast out the speck from a brother's eye. For we shall then see that speck with the eyes of the dove, the kind of eyes that are commended in the Spouse of Christ,[5] the glorious Church which God has chosen for Himself, the Church which has neither spot or wrinkle,[6] that is, the Church which is pure without guile.

Chapter 20 (Matt. 7.6)

(67) Of those who are anxious to obey the commands of God, many may be so deluded by the word, *'simplicity,'* that they would think it just as wrong not to proclaim the truth on every occasion as to utter a falsehood on any occasion. By thus revealing certain facts to persons who are unable to bear such things, they may do more harm than if they always kept such things completely concealed. So, the Lord very fittingly adds: *'Do not give to dogs what is holy; neither cast your pearls before swine, lest they trample them under their feet, and turning upon you, rend you asunder.'* Certainly, the Lord Himself never told a lie; yet, He showed

---

4 *De gratia et lib. arbitr.* 17.34; cf. 1 Cor. 16.14.
5 Cant. 4.1.
6 Eph. 5.27; see *Retract.* 1.19.9.

that He was keeping some truths unrevealed when he said: 'Many things I have yet to say to you, but you cannot bear them now.'[1] And the Apostle Paul says: 'I could not speak to you as to spiritual men but only as carnal, as to little ones in Christ. I fed you with milk, not with solid food; for you were not yet ready for it. Nor are you ready for it now, for you are still carnal.'[2]

(68) Now, in this precept whereby we are forbidden to give a holy thing to dogs or to cast pearls before swine, we must diligently seek to determine the import of the words, *holy, pearls, dogs,* and *swine.* A holy thing is whatever it would be impious to profane and tear apart; even an attempt renders the will guilty of this impiety, although the holy thing may by its very nature remain inviolable and indestructible. Pearls signify all spiritual things whatsoever that are worthy of being highly prized. And because these things lie hidden in secret, it is as though they were being drawn up from the deep; because they are found in the wrappings of allegories, it is as though they were contained within shells that have been opened. It is clear, therefore, that one and the same thing can be called both a holy thing and a pearl. It can be called a holy thing because it ought not to be destroyed: a pearl, because it ought not to be despised. Everyone tries to destroy whatever he does not wish to leave intact, and a man despises whatever he deems worthless, as though he considered it beneath him. Hence, whatever is despised is said to be trampled under foot. Therefore—because dogs rush madly to tear apart whatever they attack, and do not leave intact whatever they tear apart—the Lord says: *Do not give to dogs what is holy.*' For, although the holy thing itself

---
1 John 16.12.
2 1 Cor. 3.1-2.

cannot be rent and destroyed, but remains intact and unharmed, what must be considered is the desire of those who resist the truth with the utmost violence and bitterness and do everything in their power to destroy it, if its destruction were possible. Although swine—unlike dogs—do not attack by biting, they befoul a thing by trampling all over it. Therefore, *'Do not cast your pearls before swine, lest they trample them under their feet, and turn and rend you.'* Hence we, may rightly understand that the words, *dogs* and *swine,* are now used to designate respectively those who assail the truth and those who resist it.

(69) By saying *'Lest they turn and rend you'* He does not say 'Lest they rend the pearls themselves.' For, by trampling on the pearls even when they turn round to hear something further, they lacerate the man who cast the pearls they have already trampled on. Of course, it would not be easy to find anything that would please a man who would trample on pearls, that is to say, anyone who would despise divine truths which have been discovered with great labor. But I do not see how anyone who tries to teach such people will not be rent asunder by indignation and disgust, for both dogs and swine are unclean animals. Therefore, we must be careful not to reveal anything to one who cannot bear it, for it is better that he make a search for what is concealed rather than assail or despise what is revealed.[3] Indeed, it is only through hatred or contempt that men refuse to accept truths of manifest importance. Hence, for one reason some are called dogs, and for the other reason some are called swine. But all this uncleanness is begotten of a love for temporal things, which is a love for this world, although

---

3 See above, 2.2.7, n. 7.

we are ordered to renounce it so that we may be clean. So, the man who seeks to keep his heart clean and single ought not to consider himself at fault if he is concealing something from one who is unable to receive it. But we must not therefore believe that it is lawful to tell a lie, for it does not follow that falsehood is spoken when truth is not revealed. Therefore, an effort must first be made to remove the hindrances through which it comes to pass that a man is not receiving the truth. If it is through defilements that he is not receiving it, then, of course, he is to be cleansed—to the best of our ability—either by word or deed.

(70) Our Lord is found to have spoken many truths which many of his hearers did not receive, for they either resisted those truths or despised them. Nevertheless, we are not to think that He gave a holy thing to dogs or cast pearls before swine, for He did not give those truths to those who were unable to receive them. He delivered those truths to those who were able to receive them, and who, although they were assembled with the others, could not rightly be neglected because of the uncleanness of those others. While tempters were asking Him questions and He was giving the kind of answer that they were unable to gainsay, others, indeed, were profitably hearing many truths through the opportunity thus occasioned by the tempters. For those others were able to receive the truth, while the tempters were wasting away from their own poisons, rather than being filled with the food of the Lord. I have mentioned this so that, when someone finds himself unable to give an answer to a questioner, he may not perchance believe himself excused by this maxim, and therefore say that he does not wish to give a holy thing to dogs or to cast pearls before swine. For he ought to give the answer, if he knows what answer to give; he ought to do this especially for the sake of others,

because their faith becomes weakened if they believe that the question put forward cannot be answered. But this has reference to useful matters that pertain to the instructing unto salvation,[4] for of the inquiries that can be made by the idle, many are useless and empty and generally harmful. Yet, some observation ought to be made on those inquiries, but the thing that ought to be made manifest and plain is this, namely, the reason why such inquiries ought not to be made. Sometimes, therefore, we ought to give an answer to a question that is put to us on matters that are useful, just as the Lord did with reference to the woman who had seven husbands. When the Saducees asked Him whose wife would she be at the Resurrection, He replied that at the Resurrection they will neither marry nor be given in marriage, but will be as the angels in heaven.[4] At times, however, the questioner ought to be asked another question in return. He ought to be asked a question of such a nature that, if he answers it, he himself will be giving the answer to the question he has asked, and if he refuses to answer it the bystanders will not think it unfair if he receives no answer to the question he has asked. Another question was submitted to those who were trying to put Him to a test[6] when they asked Him whether tribute should be rendered. When they had proffered a coin, they were asked whose image it had; when they gave the reply that it had Caesar's image, then to a certain extent they gave themselves the answer to the question they had put to the Lord. And from that reply of theirs He constructed the practical solution: 'Render therefore to Caesar what belongs to Caesar; and to God, what belongs to God.'[7] When the chief priests and

---

4 2 Tim. 3.15.
5 Matt. 22.23-30.
6 Matt. 22.17.
7 Matt. 22.20-21.

the elders of the people had asked Him by what authority He was doing those things, He questioned them about the baptism of John. And because they would not answer that question—for, on the one hand, they would not give the answer which they knew would be against themselves, and, on the other hand, they would not dare to say anything against John, because they were afraid of the bystanders— the Lord said to them: 'Neither shall I tell you by what authority I am doing those things.'[8] And the bystanders considered this a most just refusal, for those others had declared that they did not know something which in fact they did know, but were unwilling to admit. It was certainly fair that those who were desirous of an answer to their own question should first do what they wished to have done for themselves. And if they had done that, they would, of course, have answered their own question, for they had sent messengers to John to ask him who he was.[9] Or, rather, the priests themselves and the Levites had been sent, because they thought that he was the Christ. John told them that he was not the Christ, but he gave testimony regarding the Lord. If they were willing to acknowledge this testimony, they would thus inform themselves by what authority Christ was doing those things. But in the present instance, they had asked the question as if they did not know the answer, and they had asked it in order to find occasion for making false accusations.

Chapter 21 (Matt. 7.7-11)

(71) But when the precept had been announced that a holy thing should not be given to dogs and that pearls should

---
8 Matt. 21.23-27.
9 John 1.19-27.

not be cast before swine, a hearer might propose a question. Mindful of his own ignorance and frailty, and hearing it prescribed that he was not to give away something which he felt he had not yet received, he might therefore ask: 'What holy thing do you forbid me to give to dogs, and what pearls do you forbid me to cast before swine? For I do not see that I have as yet received them.' Most aptly, then, did the Lord go on to say: *'Ask, and it shall be given you; seek, and you shall find; knock, and it shall be opened to you. For everyone who asks, receives; and he who seeks, finds; and to him who knocks, it shall be opened.'* The asking refers to the obtaining of soundness and strength of mind through prayer, in order that we may be able to fulfill the precepts that are being given; the seeking refers to the finding of truth. For the blessed life is made up of doing and knowing:[1] the doing requires a store of strength, while contemplation requires the manifestation of truths. Of these two, we are to ask for the first, and we are to seek for the other, in order that the one may be given, and that the other may be found. In this life, however, knowledge consists in knowing the way toward that blessedness, rather than in possessing it. But, when anyone has found the true way, he will arrive at that possession. And yet, it is to him who knocks that the door is opened.

(72) In order that these three things[2]—the asking, the

---

1 'Two powers of the human soul are made manifest. The one is active; the other, contemplative. Through the former, we advance; through the latter, we arrive. Through the former, we labor to cleanse the heart for seeing God; through the latter, labor ceases and God is seen. The former is exercised in fulfilling the precepts which govern the conduct of this temporal life; the latter, in the doctrine of the life which is eternal. Therefore, the former engages in works, for it is exercised in the cleansing of sinners; the latter rests from labor, for it is exercised in the illumination of the cleansed. (*De consensu evangel.* 1.5.8.)

2 See *Retract.* 1.19.9.

seeking, and the knocking—may be illustrated by an example, let us consider the case of a man who is unable to walk because of weak limbs. Of course, he must first be healed and strengthened for walking. Hence the Lord said: '*Ask.*' But, if that man now goes astray through devious paths, of what benefit to him is the fact that he is able to walk, or even to run? Consequently, the next requirement is that he find the way that leads to his desired destination. But, when he has followed this way, and has reached the abode which he is seeking, what if he finds it closed? Unless that abode be opened to him, then neither the fact that he was able to walk nor the fact that he actually walked will be of any benefit to him. Hence the Lord said, '*Knock.*'

(73) The Lord does not deceive us by His promises; hence He has given—and still gives—great hope by saying: '*Everyone who asks, receives; and he who seeks, finds; and to him who knocks, it shall be opened.*' Perseverance is therefore needed in order that we may receive what we ask and find what we seek, and in order that the door may be opened to our knocking. Just as the Lord had mentioned the birds of the air and the lilies of the field in order that our hope might rise from lesser things to greater, and lest we should begin to fear that food and clothing might be lacking to us, so also in the present instance He says: '*Or what man will there be among you, who, if his son asks him for bread, will hand him a stone; or if he asks for a fish, will hand him a serpent? Therefore, if you—evil as you are—know how to give good gifts to your children, how much more will your Father Who is in heaven give good things to those who ask Him!*' But, how do evil men give good things? Those whom He called evil are sinners and such as are still lovers of this world. And it is in accordance with their notion of good that their gifts are to be called good; that is to say, their

gifts are to be called good, because the givers consider them good. Although those things are good in the order of nature, they are, nevertheless, temporal things pertaining to this feeble life. Moreover, whenever an evil man bestows them, he is not giving of his own, for 'the earth and the fulness thereof is the Lord's, . . . Who made heaven and earth, the sea, and all things that are in them'[3] Now, since we—although we are evil—know how to give what is asked, how much more confidence ought we to have that God will give us good things when we ask Him, and that we cannot be so deceived as to receive one thing instead of another when we ask of Him! For we do not deceive our children, and, whatever good gifts we bestow, we give what is His, and not what is our own.

Chapter 22 (Matt. 7.12)

(74) Steadfastness and a certain vigor of stride along the path of wisdom are based on good morals; good morals, in turn, are reduced to purity and singleness of heart. Discoursing on this at some length, He sums up as follows: *'Therefore all good things whatever you would that men should do to you, even so do you also to them; for this is the whole Law and the Prophets.'* In the Greek codices, the passage reads: 'Therefore all things whatever you would that men should do to you, even so do you also to them.' I think that the word, *'good,'* has been added by the Latins for the sake of clarifying the maxim. For it occurred to them that if someone should wish to have something outrageous done to himself, and were to quote this instruction to justify his doing that same outrageous thing to someone else, it would be ridiculous to think that he was observing this instruction. For

---
[3] Ps. 23.1; 145.6.

instance, if a man should wish to be challenged to drink to excess and to get drunk in carousals, he might first offer the challenge to the man from whom he would wish to receive it. I think that this perturbed the Latins, and that a word was therefore added to clarify the meaning; that is, the word, *'good'* was added to the expression, *'Therefore all things whatever you would that men should do to you.'* And if this word is lacking in the Greek codices, they, too, ought to be emended. But who would dare to do that?[1] So we must understand that the instruction is complete and perfect, even without the addition of that word. But in that case, the expression, *'Whatever you would,'* is not to be accepted in the usual sense. We must make a distinction, and accept the expression in its proper sense. Properly speaking, the will is operating in good deeds only. In evil and shameful deeds the desire is not properly called will—it is called cupidity.[2] This does not imply that the Scriptures always use words in their proper sense. Whenever necessary, they keep to the proper term so absolutely as not to permit any misunderstanding.[3]

(75) Because He says elsewhere that there are two precepts on which the whole Law and the Prophets depend,[4] the present precept seems to concern only the love of neighbor, and not the love of God as well. Of course, if He had said: 'All things whatever you wish to have done to you, do you also those things,' He would then have embraced those two precepts in the one maxim, for it would be readily understood that everyone would wish to be loved by both God and men. So, when a man would be given that one pre-

---
1 See Introduction, note 18.
2 'Cupidity is a depraved will' (*De lib. arbitrio* 3.17.48).
3 Examples of symbolic interpretation of Scripture are numerous in Augustine's writings. See Introduction, note 9.
4 Matt. 22.40.

cept—when he would be ordered to do whatever he would wish to have done to him—then he would of course be given the other precepts as well; that is to say, it would be prescribed that he should love both God and men. But it would seen that the present maxim means nothing more than 'Thou shalt love thy neighbor as thyself,'[5] for it is very expressly restricted to men, since it reads: *'Therefore all things whatever you would that men should do to you, even so do you also to them.'* However, we must pay close attention to His further observation on this point; for He says: *'This is the Law and the Prophets.'* Now, in the case of the above-mentioned two precepts, He did not say merely that 'the Law and the Prophets depend' on them; He said that 'the *whole* Law and the Prophets depend' on them; for that is the sum total of Prophecy. But, by omitting the word, *'whole,'* in the present instance, He reserved a place for the other precept—the precept which pertains to the love of God. At any rate, the present instruction is one that was most apt for the occasion when He was expounding the precepts that pertain to singleness of heart. For there is reason to fear that a man may have a double heart toward men, since the heart is hidden from them, but there is hardly anyone who would wish that others would deal double-heartedly with him. It is impossible for a man to render service single-heartedly to another unless he renders it in such a way that he looks for no temporal advantage from it. And he cannot do this unless he is motivated by the kind of intention that we have sufficiently discussed earlier, when we were speaking about the eye that is single.[6]

(76) When the eye has been rendered clean and single, it will be suitably adapted for beholding and contemplating its

---
5 Matt. 22.39.
6 See above, 2.13.45.

own inner light, because such an eye is an eye of the heart. And a man can have such an eye. For, if he is seeking to perform acts that are truly good, and is therefore not performing them through a desire to please men; and, even if he happens to be pleasing men, if he is directing that human praise toward the salvation of men and the glory of God rather than toward his own vainglory; and if the acquiring of things needful for maintaining this present life is not the purpose of whatever good deeds he performs for the sake of men's salvation; and if he does not condemn any man's intent and purpose whenever it is not evident with what intent and purpose that man's deed has been performed; and if he is not looking for any temporal advantage from whatever benefit he is bestowing on men, but is bestowing it in the way he would wish such benefits to be bestowed on himself—if a man is doing all this, then he has such an eye. Such a man has an eye that is clean and single, and his heart also will be pure and single—a heart in which God is being sought. Therefore: 'Blessed are the pure of heart, for they shall see God.'[7]

Chapter 23 (Matt. 7.13-14)

(77) Because men of this character are very few, He at once begins to speak about the search and possession of wisdom, which is the tree of life.[1] And, of course, it is for the purpose of searching for this wisdom and possessing it by contemplation that such an eye has been led through

---

7 Matt. 5.8.

---

1 Gen. 2.9. Commenting on Gen. 3.24, Augustine writes: 'We may believe that plenitude of knowledge and the flaming sword guard the tree of life, for no one can reach the tree of life except through the suffering of tribulations and through plenitude of knowledge' (*De Gen. contra Manich.* 2.23.35).

all the stages mentioned above, and has reached the point where the close way and the narrow gate can now be seen. So, He goes on to say: *'Enter by the narrow gate. For wide is the gate and broad is the way that leads to destruction, and many there are who enter through it. How narrow the gate and close the way that leads to life! And how few there are who find it!'* He says this, not because the Lord's yoke is rough or His burden heavy, but because there are few who wish their labors to end. They do not put their full trust in the Lord when He cries: 'Come to me, all you who labor, and I will give you rest. Take my yoke upon you, and learn from me, for I am meek and humble of heart. . . For my yoke is smooth, and my burden light.'[2] Hence, the humble and the meek of heart are named at the very beginning of this sermon.[3] But, because there are many who spurn this smooth yoke and this light burden, it comes to pass that the way which leads to life is close and the entry gate is narrow.

Chapter 24 (Matt. 7.15-20)

(78) Most especially, therefore, must we beware of those who promise wisdom and a knowledge of the truth which they do not possess, for instance, the heretics who generally allege their fewness in number as a proof of their possession of wisdom.[1] So, lest they should foist themselves upon us by

---
2 Matt. 11.28-30.
3 The Sermon on the Mount; cf. Matt. 5.3-10.

---
1 'As though wisdom belonged to the few, he commends the fewness of those in his error. . . . All heretics boast of their fewness' (*Contra advers. Legis* 2.12.42). 'This is the boast of all heretics, ancient and modern. It has become smooth and grimy through prolonged use (*Contra Julianum* 5.1.1; cf. *Contra Julianum opus imperf.* 2.3; *Enarr. in ps.* 31.11).

the double claim that they are few in number and that the Lord has said that they are few who find the narrow gate and the close way, He immediately goes on to say: *'Beware of false prophets, who come to you in sheep's clothing, but inwardly they are ravenous wolves.'* Of course, they do not deceive the eye that is single, the eye that knows how to judge a tree from its fruits, for the Lord has also said: *'By their fruits you will know them.'* And now He gives a similitude, saying: *'Do men gather grapes from thorns, or figs from thistles? Even so, every good tree bears good fruit. A good tree cannot bear bad fruit, nor can a bad tree bear good fruit. Every tree that does not bear good fruit will be cut down and cast into the fire. Therefore, by their fruits you will know them.'*

(79) On this point, one must very carefully avoid the error of those who think that they find in these two trees a reason for believing that there are two natures, and that one of them is the nature of God, but that the other neither belongs to God nor depends on Him.[2] This error has been rather fully discussed in other books, and if that is not sufficient it will receive still further treatment later.[3] but we must now show that these two trees furnish no argument in support of it. First of all, in that similitude the Lord is speaking about [two kinds of] men. This is so obvious that if anyone will but read the passages which respectively pre-

---

2 The Manichaeans (See above, 1.11.32, n. 20). Some ten years later, a Manichaean advanced this argument in a public debate with Augustine: 'Manichaeus . . . is now censured because he says there are two natures, a good and a bad. In the Gospel, Christ says there are two trees. . . . Behold! The two natures' (*De actis cum Felice* 2.2).
3 Incidental refutation of Manichaean tenets is found in many of Augustine's earlier works, e. g., *De vera religione*. At this date, he had composed four works expressly against the Manichaeans; later, he composed six others.

ceed and follow it, he will be amazed at the blindness of those misinterpreters. Again, they fix their attention on the saying, '*A good tree cannot bear bad fruit, nor can a bad tree bear good fruit,*' and then they think that an evil soul cannot be changed into a better, nor a good soul into a worse. As though, in truth, the saying were: 'A good tree cannot become a bad tree, nor a bad tree become a good tree'! But, what has been said is that '*a good tree cannot bear bad fruit, and a bad tree cannot bear good fruit.*' Of course, the tree is the soul itself—that is, the man himself—and the fruits are the man's works. So, a bad man cannot perform good works, nor can a good man perform bad works. If a bad man wishes to perform good works, let him first become a good man. The Lord says this very clearly in another passage: 'Either make the tree good, or make the tree bad.'[4] Now, if by these two trees He were representing the two natures supposed by those misinterpreters, He would not have used the word, '*make.*' For, in the whole world, what man is able to make a nature? Furthermore, when He had made mention of these same two trees, He immediately added: 'You hypocrites, how can you speak good things, when you are evil?' Therefore, as long as anyone is evil, he cannot bear good fruit, for, if he bears good fruit, he is no longer evil. The expression, 'Snow cannot be warm,' would likewise be absolutely true, for, as soon as it begins to be warm, we no longer call it snow; we call it water. Of course, it can happen that what used to be snow is no longer snow, but it can never come to pass that snow be warm. And it can likewise happen that a man who used to be evil is no longer evil, but it cannot come to pass that an evil man does good. Even though he is sometimes useful, it is not he that brings this about; it

---

4 Matt. 12.33.

is accomplished in his regard through the guidance of Divine Providence. In this sense, it was said of the Pharisees: 'Do what they say, but not what they do.'[5] Through no merit of theirs were they speaking good things, and through no merit of theirs were their words being listened to and acted upon, for the Lord says: 'They sit on the chair of Moses.' So, they were of no profit to themselves while they were proclaiming the Law of God, but through Divine Providence they could be of profit to their hearers. Of such men it has been said elsewhere through the Prophet: 'You have sown wheat, and you shall reap thorns,'[6] for they were giving good precepts, but performing evil deeds. So, those who were hearing them and fulfilling the commands they were giving—these hearers and doers were not gathering grapes from thorns. Through the thorns, they were gathering grapes from the vine, for if a man were to put his hand through a hedge and pluck a grape from a vine, or even if he were to pluck a grape from a vine entangled in a hedge, the fruit would be from the vine, and not from the thorns.

(80) It is very fitting, therefore, that we should inquire as to the kind of fruit the Lord wishes us to recognize, so that we may be able to distinguish the tree. Many persons reckon as fruits certain things which are indeed the suitable clothing of sheep, for instance, fastings, prayers, and almsgivings. Such people are deceived by wolves, for, if these things could not be done also by hypocrites, the Lord would not have previously said: 'Take heed not to practise your righteousness before men, in order to be seen by them.'[7] And when He had given that instruction, He straightway went on to discourse on those very three things—almsgiving, prayer, and

---
5 Matt. 23.2-3.
6 Jer. 12.13.
7 Matt. 6.1.

fasting. Many persons bestow much upon the poor, not through mercy, but for the sake of display; many persons pray—or, rather, they seem to pray—without directing their attention toward God, but seeking to please men; and many persons fast and display a wonderful degree of self-denial before those who think such things difficult and praiseworthy. But, by these artifices, pretenders deceive their admirers; they use one thing in order to decoy, and another thing to rob or ruin those who cannot recognize them as wolves in sheep's clothing.[8] Therefore, these are not the fruits by which a tree can be recognized in accordance with the Lord's admonition. When these things are truly done with a good intention, they are rightly called the clothing of sheep; when they are deceitfully done through an evil intention, they are only a covering for wolves. However, sheep are not to hate their own clothing just because wolves often hide themselves beneath it.

(81) The Apostle tells us what are the known fruits by which we may recognize a bad tree. He says: 'Now the works of the flesh are manifest: they are immorality, uncleanness, licentiousness, idolatry, witchcraft, enmity, contention, jealousy, animosity, quarrels, heresies, faction, envy, drunkenness, carousings, and such like things. And concerning these I warn you, as I have warned you, that those who do such things will not possess the kingdom of God.'[9] And he goes on to tell us also what are the fruits by which we may recognize a good tree, for he says: 'But the fruit of the spirit is: charity, joy, peace, patience, kindness, goodness, faith, modesty, continency.'[10] With regard to that other instruction

---
8 For specific instances, see *De moribus Manichaeorum* 13, 19, 20 *et passim*.
9 Gal. 5.19-21.
10 Gal. 5.22-23.

'All things whatever you would that men should do to you, even so do you also unto them,' we have already noted that the word, *'will,'* is used in its proper sense, and that evil men are not exercising the faculty which is properly denoted by that term.[11] So, also, in the present instance the word *'joy'* is likewise used in its proper sense, for evil men are not said to rejoice, but to exult. Taken in that sense, rejoicing is not attributed to any but the good. It is in this proper sense that the Prophet also uses the word when he says: 'Rejoicing is not for the wicked, says the Lord.'[12] And the word, *'faith,'* also is used here in its proper sense, for, of course, it does not mean any and every kind of belief: it means the true faith. In wicked and deceitful men there are also certain semblances of the other virtues which are mentioned in that passage. Hence, such men thoroughly deceive anyone who does not keep clear and single the eye through which one is able to recognize those virtues. So, in accordance with the best method of procedure, the cleansing of the eye was discussed first, and then we were told what we are to guard against.

Chapter 25 (Matt. 7.21-29)

(82) No man can look into another's heart. He cannot do that, no matter how thoroughly cleansed his eye may be, that is to say, no matter how sincere and single his heart may be during the course of this life. So, it is through temptations that disclosure is made of whatever cannot be made manifest by words or deeds. And there are two kinds of temptation: one kind of temptation consists in the hope of some temporal gain; the other, in the fear of some temporal loss. While

---

11 See above, 22-24.74, n. 2.
12 Isa. 57.21; cf. Vulgate version.

we are striving after the wisdom which is found only in Christ, 'in whom are hidden all the treasures of wisdom and knowledge,'[1] we must be very cautious lest the mere name of Christ become an occasion of our being deceived by heretics or any kind of misinterpreters, or by the lovers of this world. So, the Lord goes on to give us a warning, when He says: *'Not everyone who says to me, "Lord, Lord," shall enter the kingdom of heaven; but he who does the will of my Father Who is in heaven, he shall enter the kingdom of heaven.'* He thus forewarns us against thinking that the goodness of the fruit consists in anyone's saying 'Lord, Lord,' to our Lord, lest we therefore believe that every such praise-giver is a good tree. Rather, the fruit is this: to do the will of the Father who is in heaven. And our Lord has deigned to show us Himself as the example of the doing of his Father's will.

(83) But one may be truly perturbed by the seeming inconsistency between this pronouncement and the statement which the Apostle makes when he says: 'No one speaking in the Spirit of God says, "Anathema," to Jesus. And no one can say that Jesus is Lord, unless he says it in the Holy Spirit.'[2] We cannot say that anyone who has the Holy Spirit will fail to enter the kingdom of heaven if he perseveres to the end; neither can we say that the Holy Spirit is possessed by those who do not enter the kingdom of heaven, although they say that Jesus is Lord. How is it, then, that no one says that Jesus is Lord, unless he says it in the Holy Spirit? It is because the Apostle uses the word, *'says,'* in the strict sense, for, when the word is used in that sense, it denotes an expression of the speaker's intellect and will. On the other hand, the Lord used that same word in accordance with common

---
1 Col. 2.3.
2 1 Cor. 12.3.

usage when He said: *'Not everyone who says to me, "Lord, Lord," shall enter the kingdom of heaven.'* For a man seems to be saying even that which he neither wills nor understands when he is uttering it. In the strict sense, however, a man says something when he makes vocal sounds to reveal his will and understanding. In the same way—as we noted a short while ago—when *'joy'* was enumerated among the fruits of the Spirit, the word was used in its strict sense. It was not used in the sense in which the Apostle uses it elsewhere, when he says that charity 'does not rejoice over wickedness.'[3] As though anyone could rejoice over wickednss! That kind of elation belongs to the emotion of a man who is wildly exulting. It is not joy, for only the good can rejoice. So, men seem to be saying something whenever they are producing a vocal sound, even though they be merely uttering something which they neither perceive with the intellect nor act upon with the will. Using the word in this sense, the Lord says: *'Not everyone who says to me, "Lord, Lord," shall enter the kingdom of heaven.'* In the strict and proper sense, however, they who say something are those whose vocal sound is in conformity with their mind and will; it is in this sense that the Apostle uses the word when he says: 'No one can say that Jesus is Lord, unless he says it in the Holy Spirit.'

(84) And this is a most timely warning to us when we are striving toward the contemplation of truth, so that we may not be deceived through the name of Christ by those who have the name but not the works, and so that we may not be deceived even by certain feats and prodigies. For, although the Lord Himself performed miracles for the sake

---

3 1 Cor. 13.6.

of unbelievers, He has nevertheless cautioned us against being so deceived by such wonders as to think that the invisible Wisdom is present wherever we see a visible marvel. Therefore, He now subjoins, and says: *'Many will say to me in that day, "Lord, Lord, did we not prophesy in thy name and cast out devils in thy name?" And then I will say to them, "I never knew you. Depart from me, you workers of iniquity!"'* Therefore, He will acknowledge no one but the man who acts righteously. Indeed, He forbade His own disciples to rejoice in such things as these; that is to say, He forbade them to rejoice over the fact that demons were subjected to them. 'But rejoice,' says He, 'because your names are written in heaven.'[4] They are written, I believe, in that city of Jerusalem which is in heaven[5]—the city where none will reign but the just and holy. For the Apostle says: 'Do you not know that the unjust will not possess the kingdom of God?'[6]

(85) But, perhaps someone would say that the unjust cannot perform those visible miracles. He may therefore think that they will be speaking untruly when they say: 'In thy name we have prophesied and cast out demons and worked many miracles.' Let such a man, therefore, read what great wonders the Egyptian magicians wrought when they were resisting Moses, the servant of God.[7] Or, if he refuses to read that account because the magicians did not work those wonders in the name of Christ, then let him read what the Lord Himself says about false prophets. He speaks as follows: 'Then if anyone say to you, "Behold, here is the Christ," or, "There he is," do not believe it. For false christs and false prophets will arise, and will show great signs and

---
4 Luke 10.20.
5 Heb. 12.22.
6 1 Cor. 6.9.
7 Exod. 7.22.

wonders, so as to lead astray [if possible] even the elect. Behold, I have told it to you beforehand.'[8]

(86) Since there are so many deceptions and errors of wicked and perverse men clamoring against wisdom, how great is the need of a clean and single eye in order to find the path to wisdom! To escape all of these is the same as to reach the utmost security of peace and the unchangeable abode of wisdom. The noise of wranglers is of little account unless a man becomes a hindrance even to himself. But this can be seen by only a few, and there is great danger that no one may see it in the midst of contention and strife. This is the purport of the Apostle's saying: 'For the servant of God must not quarrel, but be meek towards all, ready to teach, patient, gently admonishing those who disagree; in case God should give them repentance to know the truth.'[9] Therefore: 'Blessed are the peacemakers, for they shall be called the children of God.'[10]

(87) Above all, we must very carefully note the fear-inspiring conclusion of the whole Sermon, as now presented: *'Therefore, who hears these my words and acts upon them, is like a wise man who built his house on a rock.'* For, unless a man acts upon what he hears or perceives, he does not fix it firmly. So, if Christ is the rock (as many testimonies of the Scriptures proclaim),[11] then a man builds on Christ if he acts upon what he hears from Christ. *'The rain fell, the floods came, the winds blew and beat against that house; but it did not fall, because it was founded on a rock.'* So that man fears neither the fog of superstition (for what else is understood by the word, *'rain,'* when it is used in the sense of some-

---
8 Matt. 24.23-25.
9 2 Tim. 2.24-25.
10 Matt. 5.9.
11 1 Cor. 10.4.

thing bad?), nor the murmurings of men (for I think that these are compared with the winds), nor the flux of this life (which floods the earth, as it were, with carnal lusts). Whoever dwells beneath the pleasing promises of those three things is crushed by their calamities. But, if a man has his house founded on a rock, he fears none of those things. He is the man who not only hears the Lord's precepts, but also acts upon them. If a man hears those precepts, but does not act upon them, he is precariously dependent on all those other things, for he has no solid foundation. By hearing all the precepts and not acting upon them, he is building for a fall. So the Lord goes on to say: '*And everyone who hears these my words and does not act upon them, shall be like a foolish man who built his house on sand. The rain fell, the flood came, the winds blew and beat against that house, and it fell, and was utterly ruined. And it came to pass when Jesus had finished these words, that the crowds were astonished at his teaching; for he was teaching them as one having authority, and not as their Scribes.*' This is what I have already said to have been signified by what the Prophets says in the Psalms: 'I will deal confidently in his regard. The words of the Lord are pure words: as silver tried by the fire, purged from the earth, refined seven times.'[12] It was through this number that I was reminded to compare those precepts with the seven maxims on which the Lord based this entire Sermon when He discoursed on

---

12 Ps. 11.6-7. Elsewhere, Augustine writes: '*"I will deal confidently in his regard"* corresponds with what is said in the Gospel: *"He was teaching them as one having authority, and not as their Scribes."*' (*Enarr. in ps.* 11.6-7). According to the latest authorized Latin translation of the Psalter (See above, 1.12.72, n. 12), the English translation would read: '*I will give salvation to him who desires it.*'

blessedness,¹³ and also with those seven operations of the Holy Spirit which the Prophets Isaias enumerates.¹⁴ But, whether we ought to observe this same order or some other, we must act upon what we have heard from the Lord—if we would build upon rock.

---

13 Matt. 5.3-9.
14 Isa. 11.12. See above, 1.3.10, n. 5; 1.4.11, n. 1; 2.11.38, n. 1.

APPENDIX A

THE RETRACTATIONS
Book I: Chapter 19

URING THE SAME PERIOD of time,[1] I wrote two volumes on *The Lord's Sermon on the Mount, according to Matthew*. Concerning the pronouncement, 'Blessed are the peacemakers, for they shall be called the children of God,' I made the following observation in the first of those two volumes: 'Wisdom corresponds with the peacemakers, for with peacemakers all things are reduced to proper order, and no passion is in rebellion against reason, but everything is obedient to man's spirit because that spirit is itself obedient to God.'[2]

I have good reason to feel dissatisfied with this expression. For, in this life, it cannot happen to anyone that a law warring against the law of the mind be entirely absent from his members,[3] because that law would still be waging war even if man's spirit were offering it such resistance as not to fall into any assent with it. However, since the peacemakers—by subduing the lusts of the flesh—are doing their utmost to reach that full and perfect peace, the statement that no passion is in rebellion against reason can be taken in a correct sense.

(2) And it was with reference to the same Gospel maxim, 'Blessed are the peacemakers, for they shall be called the

---
1 Some period during the years 393-4.
2 See 1.4.11.
3 Rom. 7.23.

children of God,' that I made the following observation, although I made it in another passage, where I said: 'And all these grades of perfection can be reached even in this present life, as we believe them to have been fully attained in the case of the Apostles.'[4]

This statement is to be accepted, not as meaning that we believe that no passion of the flesh was resisting the spirit in the case of the Apostles while they were living in this life, but as meaning that we believe that these things can be as fully accomplished in this life as we believe them to have been accomplished in the case of the Apostles, namely, in as great a degree of human perfection as there can be perfection in this life. For the statement does not read: 'These things can be fully accomplished in this present life, since we believe them to have been fully accomplished in the case of the Apostles.' It says: 'as we believe them to have been fully accomplished in the case of the Apostles'—so that what it means is that these things can be as fully accomplished as they have been accomplished in the case of the Apostles. That is to say, they can be accomplished in that degree of perfection of which this life is capable, but not in the manner in which they are to be accomplished in that full and perfect peace which we hope for when that word will be fulfilled, 'O death, where is thy strife?'[5]

(3) And when I introduced the quotation, 'for not by measure does God give the spirit,'[6] I had not yet discerned that this is more truly understood as proper to Christ. For, unless the spirit were indeed given by measure to other men, then Eliseus would not have asked for a spirit twice as great as was the spirit in Elias.[7]

---
4 1.4.12.
5 1 Cor. 15.55.
6 1.6.17.
7 4 Kings 2.9.

And also, when I was expounding the text, 'Not one iota or one tittle shall pass from the Law till all things have been fulfilled,' I said that this could be understood as nothing else than a vehement expression of perfection.[8] But one may now rightly ask whether this perfection can be understood in such a way that it is nevertheless true to say that in this life no one lives without sin while using free will.[9] Could the Law be fulfilled even to the last tittle, except, indeed, by a man who observes all the divine commandments? As a matter of fact, in those commandments we are bidden to say: 'Forgive us our sins, even as we forgive those who sin against us,'[10] and to the end of the world the whole Church is saying that prayer. Therefore, all the commandments are accounted as fulfilled when forgiveness is granted for whatever is not fulfilled.

(4) In subsequent discourses of mine I have certainly given a better and more apt exposition of the Lord's pronouncement: 'Therefore whoever breaks one of these least commandments, and so teaches,' and so forth, up to the place where He says: 'Unless your justice exceeds that of the Scribes and Pharisees, you shall not enter the kingdom of heaven.'[11] It would be tedious to insert that exposition into this review.[12] But the sense of it is reduced to this, that the justice of those who teach and fulfill is greater than the justice of the Scribes and Pharisees, for, with regard to the

---
8 1.8.20.
9 Cf. 1 John 1.8.
10 Matt. 6.12. For the use of the word, *'sins,'* instead of *'debts,'* see Book 2.8.28.
11 1.9.21.
12 'With regard to the Scribes and Pharisees, Christ says: "You shall not enter the kingdom of heaven unless your justice exceeds theirs," that is, unless you do—rather than undo—what you teach' (*De civ. Dei* 20.9.1; cf. *In Joan. evangl.* tr. 122.9; *Enarr. in ps.* 146.17; *De fide et operibus* 26.48).

Scribes and Pharisees, the Lord Himself says in another passage: 'They say, but do not.'[13]

And afterwards we also had a better understanding of that statement, 'He who is angry with his brother,' for the Greek codices do not have the phrase, *'without cause,'* although the sense is the very same.[14] We said that we must pay close attention to what is meant by being angry with one's brother, because he who is angry with a brother's sin is not angry with a brother. Therefore, a man is angry without cause if he is angry with a brother, and not with a sin.

(5) As to my statement that 'this pronouncement is to be understood with regard to both father and mother and the other ties of kinship, in the sense that in them we should hate what has fallen to the lot of the human race through the facts of birth and death.'[15] This sounds as if there would be no such kinships if—there being no preceding sin of human nature—no one were subject to death. I have already disapproved that interpretation,[16] for there would be blood relationships and affinities even if there were no original sin and the human race were increasing and multiplying without any death. Therefore, another solution must be found for the question as to why God has commanded that enemies be loved, although in another passage He commands that parents and children be held in hatred. The solution is—certainly not the one that we gave in that passage—but the

---
13 Matt. 23.3.
14 1.9.25 Cf. C. a Lapide, *Comment. in S. Script. Matt.* 5.22.
15 1.15.41.
16 'I absolutely disapprove that interpretation. And I have already disapproved it in the first book of the work, *On Genesis, against the Manichaeans* [19.30]. For it would lead to the necessity of our believing that, if those first spouses had not sinned, they would not have begotten posterity... Even if no one had sinned and no one were to be subject to death, there would still be those cognations and affinities' (*Retractations* 1.13.8).

one that we have often given afterwards,[17] namely, that we should love enemies in order to gain them for the kingdom of God, but that in kinsmen we should hate whatever impedes the path to the kingdom of God.

(6) In this book also I have very conscientiously discussed the precept by which it is forbidden that a wife be put away except because of fornication.[18] But we must repeatedly ponder the question as to what kind of fornication the Lord wished to be understood as the fornication on account of which it would be allowable to put away a wife: whether it is the kind of fornication that is condemned in unchastity, or the kind that is meant in the expression, 'Thou hast destroyed everyone who has fornicated from thee.'[19] Of course, the former is included in the latter, for, if a man takes the members of Christ and makes them members of a harlot,[20] he is not guiltless of fornicating from the Lord.

In a question so important and so difficult of precise discernment, I do not wish to have a reader believe that that disquisition of ours is sufficient for him. Rather, let him read other works as well—either those works of ours which were written later,[21] or the works of other men which have been more carefully treated and considered. Or let the reader himself—if he is able—vigilantly and understandingly analyze those points which may cause him just concern in this question. Not that every sin is fornication, for God does not destroy everyone who commits a sin, although He destroys everyone who fornicates from Him. Indeed, every day He graciously hears the prayer of His saints as they say:

---

17 Cf. *Epist.* 243.2-12; *Contra Adimant.* 1.6.
18 1.16.43.
19 Ps. 72.27.
20 1 Cor. 6.15.
21 Cf. *De divers. quaest.* 83, qu. 83; *De bono conjug.* 7.7; *De conjug. adult.* 1.1.1; id. 12.13.

'Forgive us our sins.'²² But to what extent and within what limits is this kind of fornication to be understood, and whether a man is also allowed to put away his wife on account of it—that is a very intricate question. However, there is no doubt that this is allowed because of the fornication that is committed in unchastity.

When I said that this is allowed but not commanded, I did not advert to another text of Scripture which says: 'He that keeps an adulteress, is foolish and wicked.'²³ But I would not say that that famous woman ought to have been considered an adulteress if she obeyed the Lord's injunction after she had heard Him say to her: 'Neither will I condemn thee. Go thy way, and henceforth sin no more.'²⁴

(7) In another passage I defined a brother's sin unto death, the sin of which the Apostle John says: 'I do not mean that anyone should pray as to that.' I defined it by saying: 'I suppose that a brother's sin is a sin unto death, if he assails the brotherhood after he has come to the knowledge of God through the grace of Our Lord Jesus Christ, and is inflamed by the fire of envy against the very grace by which he was reconciled to God.'²⁵ Although I did not positively affirm this, merely saying that I supposed, yet the following qualification ought to have been added, namely, 'if he should end this life in that impious perversity of mind.' For, of course, we ought not to lose hope for even the worst of men as long as he continues in this life, and it is not rash to offer prayers for whomsoever hope is not lost.

(8) And, also, in the second book, I say: 'No one will be allowed to be ignorant of the kingdom of God when—to

---

22 See n. 10.
23 Prov. 18.22.
24 John 8.11.
25 1.22.73.

judge the living and the dead—His Only Begotten Son will have come from heaven, not merely in a manner recognizable by the intellect, but even visibly in the person of the Lord.'[26]

Now, although the man Christ Jesus,[27] who is the Mediator between God and men, is certainly the Lord, I am not sure that He may be rightly called the 'Man of the Lord.' For, what man is there in His holy household who may not be called a man of the Lord? Yet, in the works of a certain Catholic commentators on the divine Scriptures, I certainly read that I could say this.[28] But, no matter why I said it, I wish I had not said it, for afterwards I saw that it ought not to have been said, even though it could be defended by considerable reason.

Furthermore, I do not see that I ought to have made the following statement of mine, namely, 'Scarcely anyone's conscience could hate God,'[29] for there are many of whom it is written: 'The pride of them who hate thee.'[30]

(9) In another passage, I stated that the reason why the Lord said: 'Sufficient for the day is its own evil,' is the fact that necessity itself will force us to take food. I then made the following observation: 'I suppose that this necessity is called evil because it partakes of the nature of punishment for us, since it pertains to that frailty [and mortality] which we have merited through sin.'[31] In making that observation, I did not advert to the fact that even in Paradise bodily nourishment had been given to our first parents before they had merited the punishment of death on account of their sin-

---

26 2.6.20.
27 1 Tim. 2.5.
28 Perhaps in the *Expositio fidei* of Athanasius, and in the *Ancoratus* of Epiphanius.
29 2.14.48.
30 Ps. 73.23.
31 2.17.56.

ning. For, in a body that was sentient but not yet spiritual, they were immortal in such a way that they were nevertheless using bodily nourishment in that kind of mortality.

When I said: 'God has chosen for Himself this glorious Church which has neither spot nor wrinkle,'[32] I did not mean that it is already such a Church in all respects. But, since it has been chosen for this, there can be no doubt that it will be such a Church when Christ, its life, will have appeared; for then it, too, will appear with Him in glory.[33] It is because of this glory to come that it has been called a glorious Church.[34]

Furthermore, because the Lord says: 'Ask, and you shall receive; seek, and you shall find; knock, and it shall be opened to you,' I thought that the respective differences of these three acts ought to be carefully explained.[35] But all three are preferably reduced to a very earnest asking. Indeed, the Lord shows this when He includes them all under one word, saying: 'How much more will your Father, who is in heaven, give good things to those who ask Him!' For He does not say: 'to those who ask, and seek, and knock.'

---

32 2.19.66; cf. Eph. 5.27.
33 Cf. Col. 3.4.
34 'The Church . . . is without spot or wrinkle, not only in the case of those who are taken away from the contagion of this life immediately after the laver of regeneration . . . but also in the case of those to whom the Lord grants the same mercy of departing from this life with washed feet.' [That is, without any stain of sin.] (*In Joan. evang.* 46.5; cf. *id.* 46.4; Tit. 3.5.)
35 2.21.71.

SELECTED SERMONS

SERMON 53[1]

On the Beatitudes

(Matt. 3.5-8)

ON THE OCCASION of the feast of a holy virgin who has given testimony of Christ and who has merited to receive testimony from Christ, a virgin who was put to death in public and received a crown in secret, I am reminded to address you, dearly beloved, on the exhortation which the Lord has just now delivered from the Gospel, wherein He says that there are many causes of that blessed life which no one wishes to be without. Surely, we can find no one who does not wish to be blessed. Would that men were as willing to fulfill the condition as they are eager to obtain the reward! Is there anyone who would not run with alacrity when it is said to him: 'You shall be blessed'? Then, let everyone lend a willing ear when the condition is announced: 'If you do this.' If one loves the reward, let him not decline the labor. Rather, let the thought of the reward enkindle the mind to alacrity in the labor. What we wish for, what we desire, what we are seeking—all that is in the future. What we are bidden to do for the sake of what is in the future—all that is here and now. So, begin to reflect upon the divine sayings—both the precepts and the rewards of the Gospel: *'Blessed are the poor in spirit, for theirs is the kingdom of heaven.'* Be poor in spirit now, and the kingdom of heaven will be yours afterwards. Do you wish the kingdom of heaven to be yours here-

---

1 This sermon is said to have been delivered in a basilica at Carthage. Cf. Florus, *Ad Eph.* 3.

after? See to what kingdom you belong now. But, you may ask me: 'What does it mean to be poor in spirit?' Whoever is puffed up is not poor in spirit. Therefore, the poor in spirit is the humble man. The kingdom of heaven is on high, but 'he that humbles himself shall be exalted.'[2]

(2) Give heed to the following: *'Blessed are the meek,'* says He, *'for by inheritance they shall possess the earth.'* You wish to possess the earth now; then see to it that you are not possessed by the earth. If you are meek, you will possess it; if you are not meek, it will possess you. So, when you hear that possessing the earth is the proffered reward, do not spread the cloak of avarice by wishing to possess it now, to the very exclusion of your neighbor. Let no such notion deceive you, for you will truly possess the earth when you cleave to Him who has made both the heaven and the earth. To be humble means to be so submissive to God that you seek to please Him—and not yourself—in all your good works, and that you are displeased with yourself—and not with Him—in whatever ills you justly suffer. It is no small matter to please God while displeasing yourself, but you will displease Him if you please yourself.

(3) Note the third saying: *'Blessed are they who mourn, for they shall be comforted.'* The labor consists in mourning; consolation is the reward. But, what kind of consolations do they have who mourn according to the flesh? They have troublesome and frightening consolations, for the mourner is consoled by the very thing which he fears may cause him to mourn again. For instance, the death of a son brings grief to the father, and the birth of another son brings him joy; he has borne one son to the grave, and he has received another into the world; he is in sorrow for the one, and in fear for

---

2 Matt. 23.12.

the other. Therefore, he has consolation in neither one nor the other. The true consolation will be that which gives what will never be lost. Consequently, those who mourn their present pilgrimage may rejoice in the fact that they shall have consolation hereafter.

(4) Let us go on to the fourth saying—both the labor and the recompense: *'Blessed are they who hunger and thirst for justice, for they shall be satisfied.'* Do you wish to be fully fed? Wherewith? If the body craves abundance of food, you will suffer hunger again when the abundance of food is digested. The Lord says: 'Who drinks of this water will thirst again.'[3] If a wound is healed by the remedy which is applied to it, there is no more pain. Food is the remedy applied against hunger, but it is applied to give relief only for a little while, for the hunger returns when the fullness is past. The remedy of fullness is applied every day, but the wound of weakness is not healed. Let us hunger and thirst for justice, therefore, so that we may be filled with the justice for which we hunger and thirst; then we shall be filled with that for which we hunger and thirst. Therefore, let our inner man hunger and thirst, for it has its own proper food and drink. The Lord says: 'I am the bread that has come down from heaven.'[4] Behold, the bread of the hungry. Pant after the drink of the thirsty as well, for 'with Thee is the fountain of life.'[5]

(5) Give heed to the next saying: *'Blessed are the merciful, for they shall obtain mercy.'* Do, and it shall be done. Do unto another so that it may be done unto you, for you have an abundance and you suffer a want. You have an abundance of temporal goods, and you are lacking in ever-

---

3 John 4.13.
4 John 6.41.
5 Ps. 35.10.

lasting blessings. You hear the voice of a beggar, but, before God, you are yourself a beggar. Someone is begging from you, and you yourself are begging. As you treat your beggar, so will God treat His. You are empty, although you are filled. Out of your fullness fill an empty man, so that your own emptiness may be filled from the fullness of God.

(6) Give heed to what follows: *'Blessed are the pure of heart'* [that is, those who are clean of heart], *'for they shall see God.'* This is the end of our love. But it is the end by which we are to be perfected, not the end by which we are to cease to exist. Food is finished, and a garment is finished; food is finished when it is consumed in the eating, and a garment is finished when it is completed in the weaving. Both are finished, but the former's finish means destruction; the latter's, perfection. Whatever we do, whatever good deeds we perform, whatever we strive to accomplish, whatever we laudably yearn for, whatever we blamelessly desire, we shall no longer seek any of those things after we have attained to the vision of God. Indeed, what would a man search for when he has God before his eyes, or what would satisfy a man who would not be satisfied with God? Yes, we wish to see God. Who does not have this desire? We strive to see God. We are on fire with the desire of seeing God. But, pay attention to the saying, *'Blessed are the pure of heart, for they shall see God.'* Provide yourself with this means of seeing God; for—to speak in terms of the senses—why desire to see a sunrise while your eyes are bleary? Let the eyes be sound, and that light will be gladsome; if they are not sound, that light will be a torment. Unless your heart is pure, you will not be permitted to see what cannot be seen unless the heart be pure. You will be repelled and removed. You will not be able to see, for, *'Blessed are the pure of heart, for they shall see God.'* How many classes of the blessed has the Lord already enumerated? What reasons for their blessedness—

labors, recompenses, merits, and rewards? Yet, in no instance has it been said that *'they shall see God.'* *'Blessed are the poor in spirit, for theirs is the kingdom of heaven.'* *'Blessed are the meek: by inheritance they shall possess the earth.'* *'Blessed are they who mourn: they shall be comforted.'* *'Blessed are they who hunger and thirst for justice: they shall be satisfied.'* *'Blessed are the merciful: they shall obtain mercy.'* Nowhere has it been said that *'they shall see God.'* But, when we come to the pure of heart, the vision of God is promised to them. The reason for this is the fact that the eyes by which God is seen are within the heart. Speaking of those eyes, the Apostle Paul uses the expression, 'the enlightened eyes of your heart.'[6] At the present time, those eyes are enlightened by faith insofar as their weakness allows, but hereafter they will be enlightened by sight in accordance with their strength. For, 'as long as we are in the body we are exiled from the Lord, for we walk by faith and not by sight.'[7] What is the saying with regard to us as long as we are in this faith? 'We now see through a mirror in an obscure manner, but then face to face.'[8]

(7) Do not imagine a corporeal face in this connection; for if, in your longing to see God, you were to prepare your own corporeal face for the act of seeing, then you would be expecting the face of God to be the same as yours. However, if your concept of God is at least so spiritual that you do not imagine Him to be corporeal (and whether we accomplished anything or not, we treated of this matter at some length yesterday);[9] if in your heart, as in the temple

---

6 Eph. 1.18.
7 2 Cor. 5.6-7.
8 1 Cor. 13.12.
9 This remark is believed to refer to *Sermon 23*. In addition to the fact that the vision of God is treated in that sermon, there is also the fact that according to an annotation in the manuscripts it was delivered in another basilica at Carthage.

of God, I have destroyed the image of human form; if the passage in which the Apostle expresses detestation of those who, 'professing to be wise, have become fools, and have changed the glory of the incorruptible God for an image made like to corruptible man'[10]—if that passage has entered deeply into your minds, and has settled in your inmost hearts; if you detest and resist such impiety; if you are purifying His temple for its Creator; if you wish Him to come to you and to make His abode with you[11]— then, 'Think of the Lord in goodness, and seek Him in simplicity of heart.'[12] And, if you say: 'My heart has said to Thee: I will seek Thy face,'[13] remember to whom you say it, and let your heart also say it. Then add: 'I will seek Thy face, O Lord,' for you are making a good search when you are seeking with your heart. Mention is made of the face of God, the arm of God, the hand of God, the feet of God, the throne of God, and the footstool of God. Do not imagine these as members of a human body. If you would be a temple of the Truth, shatter the idol of falsehood. The hand of God signifies His power; the face of God, a knowledge of Him; the feet of God, His presence. You are the throne of God, if you wish to be. Would you, perchance, dare to deny that Christ is God? 'I would not,' you reply. Do you admit this, also, that 'Christ is the power of God and the wisdom of God'?[14] 'I admit that,' you reply. Then listen. The soul of a just man is the seat of wisdom.[15] And where has God His seat except where He dwells? And where does He dwell except in His temple? 'For the temple of God is holy, and this

---
10 Rom. 1.22-23.
11 John 14.16.
12 Wisd. 1.1.
13 Ps. 26.8.
14 1 Cor. 1.24.
15 Cf. Wisd. 1.

temple you are.'¹⁶ Take heed, therefore, as to how to receive God. 'God is spirit, and one must adore God in spirit and in truth.'¹⁷ Let the ark of the covenant now enter into your heart, and let Dagon fall to pieces.¹⁸ Therefore, take heed now and learn how to long for God. Learn how to make ready the medium through which you will be able to see Him. *'Blessed,'* says He, *'are the pure of heart, for they shall see God.'* Why do you prepare the bodily eyes? If anything can be seen in that way, the thing that can be seen will be in a place. But He who is entire in every place is not contained in any place. Cleanse the medium through which He may be seen.

(8) Listen, and if I am able to explain it with God's aid (and may He aid us toward understanding all these previously mentioned labors and rewards), see how fittingly the corresponding rewards and labors are conjoined. Indeed, where is there a mention of any reward which is not in agreement and harmony with the labor? Because the humble seem as though they were aliens from a kingdom, He says: *'Blessed are the poor in spirit, for theirs is the kingdom of heaven.'* Because those who are meek are easily kept away from their own land, He says: *'Blessed are the meek, for by inheritance they shall possess the earth.'* All the other sayings are plain and clearly understod in themselves; there is no need to discuss them once they are mentioned. *'Blessed are they who mourn.'* What mourner does not desire consolation? *'They,* says He, *'shall be comforted.' 'Blessed are they who hunger and thirst for justice.'* Who is there who does not seek his fill when he is hungry and thirsty? He says: *'They shall be filled.' 'Blessed are the merciful.'* Who is merciful but the

---
16 1 Cor. 3.17.
17 John 4.24
18 1 Kings 5.3.

man who wishes that for his own merciful deed a return be made to him by God, so that it may be done to him as he does unto a poor man? *'Blessed are the merciful,'* He says, *'for God will show mercy unto them.'* How appropriate throughout are the rewards attached to the several labors. In the reward, nothing is added which is not in keeping with the precept. The precept is that you be poor in spirit; the reward, that you shall possess the kingdom of heaven. The precept is that you be meek; the reward, that you shall possess the earth. The precept is that you mourn; the reward, that you shall be comforted. The precept is that you hunger and thirst for justice; the reward, that you shall be filled. The precept is that you be merciful; the reward, that you shall obtain mercy. Thus, the precept is that you cleanse the heart; the reward is that you shall see God.

(9) But, from these precepts and rewards, do not conceive such a notion that, when you hear *'Blessed are the pure of heart, for they shall see God,'* you will think that the poor in spirit will not see Him, or that the meek, the mourners, those that hunger and thirst for justice, the merciful, will not see Him. Do not so think of the pure of heart as if they alone will see God, while all others will be excluded from the sight of Him. For the very same persons constitute all these classes. They shall see. It is not because they are poor in spirit that they shall see, nor is it because they are meek or mourning or hungering and thirsting for justice or merciful—but because they are pure of heart. It is as though bodily operations were severally assigned to the corresponding bodily members, and some one would say, for instance: Blessed are they who have feet, for they shall walk; blessed are they who have hands, for they shall work; blessed are they who have voice, for they shall cry aloud; blessed are they who have lips and tongue, for they shall

speak; blessed are they who have eyes, for they shall see. In like manner, as though disposing spiritual members, the Lord has shown what pertains to each member. Humility is suited for obtaining possession of the kingdom of heaven; meekness, for possessing the earth; mourning, for consolation; hunger and thirst after justice, for fullness; mercy, for obtaining mercy; a pure heart, for seeing God.

(10) So, if we wish to see God, with what shall that eye be cleansed? Who would not be solicitous about the thing by which he may see what he longs for with all his affection? Who would not seek wherewith to cleanse it? Divine testimony has named it: it uses the expression, 'cleansing their hearts by faith.'[19] The faith of God makes the heart pure, and the pure heart sees God. But, sometimes this faith is taken in such a narrow sense by certain self-deceivers that belief alone would seem to suffice. For, there are some believers who lead sinful lives, yet promise themselves both the sight of God and the kingdom of heaven. Incensed against such men, and as though indignant through a love that is spiritual, James the Apostle says in his Epistle: 'Thou believest that there is one God.' You commend yourself for your belief, for you notice that many impious persons think there are many gods, and you rejoice because you believe that God is One. You do well. 'The devils also believe, and tremble'[20]—shall they also see God? They who are pure of heart shall see Him. Who would say that unclean spirits are pure of heart? Nevertheless, they believe and tremble.

(11) Our faith must not be the same as that of devils. Our faith makes the heart pure, while their faith makes them guilty. Their works are evil; therefore, they say to the

---
19 Acts 15.9.
20 James 2.19.

Lord: 'What have we to do with thee?'[21] When you hear the devils say this, do you think they do not acknowledge Him? 'We know who thou art,' they say; 'Thou art the Son of God.'[22] Peter says this, and he is commended; the Devil says it, and he is condemned. What is the reason except that the heart is different, while the voice is the same? Let us, therefore, analyze our faith; let not belief alone suffice. That is not the kind of faith that makes the heart pure. There is the saying, 'Cleansing their hearts by faith.'[23] But, by what faith, by what kind of faith except the kind that the Apostle Paul defines when he says: 'Faith which works by charity'?[24] That faith differs from the faith of devils, and it differs from the shameful and profligate morals of men. 'Faith,' says he. What faith? The faith that works by charity, and hopes for what God promises. There is nothing more exact and perfect than this definition. Therefore, the following are the three essentials. (1) Whoever has the faith that works by charity must necessarily hope for whatever God promises. (2) Therefore, hope is associated with faith, for hope is necessary as long as we do not see what we believe, lest we fail by neither seeing nor hoping. We are saddened because we do not see; but we are consoled because we hope to see. Therefore, hope is present; it is conjoined with faith. (3) And charity, also —charity by which we long for, and strive to reach, our end; by which we are inflamed, and hunger and thirst. So charity also is included, and there are faith, hope and charity. Indeed, how could charity be not there, since charity is nothing else than love, and since this faith is the faith that is described as working through love? Take away faith; whatever you

---

21 Luke 4.34.
22 Matt. 16.16.
23 Acts 15.9.
24 Gal. 5.6.

believe, vanishes. Take away charity; whatever you do, vanishes. For, it is through faith that you believe, and it is through charity that you work. If, indeed, you believe without loving, you do not apply yourself to a good work, or, if you apply yourself, you will do it like a slave and not like a son—through fear of punishment, not through love of justice. Therefore, I say, the faith which works through love makes the heart pure.

(12) But what does that faith do here and now? Through so many testimonies of the Scriptures, through its manifold lesson, through its exhortation so various and plentiful, what does it do but make us 'see now through a mirror in an obscure manner, and afterwards face to face'? But do not again think upon that face of yours. Put your mind on the face of the heart. Force your heart to think on divine things; urge it; compel it. Cast out from your mind any bodily similarity that rushes into it. You are as yet unable to say: 'God is this.' At least, say: 'God is not this.' But when will you be able to say: 'God is this'? Not even when you see Him, for He is ineffable even when you see Him.[25] the Apostle says that he was 'caught up to the third heaven'[26] and heard ineffable words. If the words are ineffable, what is He whose words they are? So, when you had your thought on God, perhaps some wonderful and most extensive greatness in human form occurred to your mind, and perhaps you have placed it before your mental gaze as something great and vastly extended, something grand and massively diffused. But you have set the limits somewhere. If you have set limits, then it is not God. If you have not set limits, then where is the face? You are thinking of a huge body; in order to distinguish

---

25 'There is indeed no small beginning of a knowledge of God if, before we can know what He is, we begin to know what He is not' (*Epist.* 1203.13).
26 2 Cor. 12.2-4.

its parts, you determine its limits. For in no other way could you distinguish its parts but by determining a limit to the extension of the mass. O foolish and carnal cogitation! What are you doing? You have built up a great mass, and you thought that the bigger you made it, the more you were honoring God. Some one else adds a cubit, and he makes it greater.

(13) 'But I have read it,' you say. You who have understood nothing: What have you read? Nevertheless, tell me what you have read. Let us not spurn a child that is happily deluding itself. Tell me what you have read. 'Heaven is my throne, and the earth my footstool.'[27] I say: I have read it, too. Perhaps you think yourself more capable because you have both read it and believed it. I, too, believe what you have said. Let us believe it together. What do I say? Let us examine it together. So, hold on to what you have read and believed: 'Heaven is my throne, and the earth my footstool.' A throne means a seat, for the Greek word, *'thronos,'* corresponds to the Latin word, *'sedes.'* But have you not also read this: 'Who has measured the heaven with the palm of his hand?'[28] I think you have read it, for you recognize it and acknowledge that you believe it. In the same book, we read both of those sayings, and we believe them both. Now, reflect a moment; then become a teacher. I am supposing myself to be a little boy, and I am making you my teacher. Then teach me this, if you please: Who is it that sits on the palm of his own hand?

(14) See what you have done! From a human body you have traced the form and the lineaments of God's members. Perhaps the thought has crept into your mind that with regard to the body we have been made like to the image

---
27 Isa. 66.1.
28 Isa. 40.12.

of God. For the moment, I bring it up for consideration in order to have it analyzed, examined, and rejected through means of discussion. Please listen to me, for I have listened to you in the matter of your opinion. God sits in heaven, and measures the heaven with his palm. Does the same heaven become broad when God sits in it, and narrow when He measures it? Or, when God Himself is seated, is He no wider than the palm of His hand? If this is the case, then God has not made us to His own likeness, for with us the palm of the hand is much narrower than the bodily part on which we sit. So, if God is just as broad in the palm of His hand as He is when seated, He has made our members quite diffearent. Not in this does the likeness consist. For shame! Such an idol in a Christian heart! Therefore, understand the word, *'heaven,'* as signifying all the saints, for the word, *'earth,'* is used to signify all who are on the earth: 'Let all the earth adore Thee.'[29] If, with regard to all those who dwell on earth, we rightly say: 'Let all the earth adore Thee,' then, with regard to those who dwell in heaven, we are equally right in saying: 'Let all the heaven bear Thee.'[30] And heaven also is the hearts' abode of the saints who still dwell on earth and tread it in the flesh. It is not without purpose that they are admonished to have their hearts 'lifted up,' and, when they are thus admonished, they reply that they have them 'lifted up.'[31] And not without purpose is it also said: 'If you have risen with Christ, seek the things that are above, where Christ is seated at the right hand of God. Mind the things that are above, not the things that are on earth.'[32] Therefore, insofar as they have their citizenship there,[33] they

---

29 Ps. 65.4.
30 Cf. 1 Cor. 6.20.
31 From the Preface of the Mass.
32 Col. 3.1-2.
33 Phil. 3.20.

bear God; and they are heaven, for they are the seat of God. And when they announce the words of God, 'the heavens show forth the glory of God.'[34]

(15) Now, return with me to the face of the heart, and prepare that face. Within it is that to which God speaks. The ears and eyes and all the other visible members are either the seat or the organ of something within. It is in the inner man that Christ dwells meanwhile by faith; it is there He will dwell hereafter by the presence of His divinity, when we shall have known 'what is the breadth and length and height and depth, and also Christ's love which surpasses knowledge, in order that we may be filled unto all the fullness of God.'[35] Now, then, if you do not disapprove this interpretation, summon yourself to comprehend breadth and length and height and depth. Do not wander in imagination through the spaces of the world and through the comprehensible extent of a mass so vast as this. Look to yourself for what I am saying. The *breadth* is in good works; the *length* is in longanimity and perseverance in good works; the *height* is in the expectation of the heavenly rewards, and for the sake of this height you are told to have your heart lifted up. For the sake of rewards from God, perform good works and persevere in well-doing. Set no value on earthly things, lest—when you see this earth of ours quaking under some kind of scourge of that wise Being—you may think that you have worshipped God in vain, that you have performed good works in vain, or that you have vainly persevered in good works. For, by doing good works you have had, as it were, the breadth; by persevering in them you have had, as it were, the length; but by seeking earthly things you have not had the height. Pay attention to the depth: it is the grace of God

---
[34] Ps. 18.2.
[35] Eph. 3.17-19.

in the secret of His will. 'For who has known the mind of the Lord, or who has been His counsellor?'[36] and 'Thy judgments are a great deep.'[37]

(16) If you approve this practice of doing good, of persevering in well-doing and of looking for heavenly rewards; if you acknowledge the secret giving of the grace of God, and approve the practice of not complaining because one man receives it in this way while another receives it in that[38]—for there is no injustice with God[39]—if, I say, you approve this practice, if you account it as wisdom and not foolishness, then apply it also to the Cross of your Lord. For, since He had it in His power either to die or not to die, He did not aimlessly choose even such a death as this. Since He had it in His power to die or not to die, how could it be beyond His power to choose this or that manner of death? It is, therefore, not without a purpose that He chose the cross, whereby to crucify you to the world. For, in the cross, the breadth is the transverse beam to which the hands are fastened: it signifies good works. In the cross, the length is that part of the wood which reaches from the transverse beam to the ground —for the body is, as it were, fixed to this part of the cross, and remains standing: this stance signifies perseverance. And in the cross, the height is in that part of the wood which extends from the transverse beam upwards toward the head: the longing for heavenly rewards is thereby signified. But where is the depth? In the cross, it is nowhere else but in the part that is set into the ground. For, grace is secret and out of sight; it is not seen, but it is the well-spring of that which is seen. Then, if you have grasped all this—if you have

---
36 Rom. 11.34.
37 Ps. 37.5.
38 1 Cor. 7.7.
39 Par. 19.7; Rom. 9.14.

grasped it, not merely by understanding it, but also by practicing it, for 'a good understanding to all who practice it'[40] —then reach out, if you can, to grasp a knowledge of Christ's love which surpasses knowledge. When you have reached that point, you will be 'filled unto all the fullness of God,' and the 'face to face'[41] vision will follow. But, your being 'filled unto all the fullness of God' does not mean that God will be filled with you; it means that you will be filled with God. Then search for a bodily face, if you can. Let trifles be cast away from the sight of the mind. Let the little boy throw away his toys, and learn to handle more serious things. In many respects we are children; when we were children in more respects than we are now, we were borne with by our elders. 'Strive for peace with all men, and for that holiness without which no one can see God.'[42] By this, indeed, is the heart made pure, for herein is the faith which works through love. Therefore: *'Blessed are the pure of heart, for they shall see God.'*

---
40 Ps. 110.10.
41 1 Cor. 13.12.
42 Heb. 12.14.

SERMON 54

How to 'let your light shine before men,' and not 'practice your justice before men.'

(Matt. 5.16; 6.1)

(1) In the Sermon related in the Gospel, our Lord Jesus Christ says in one passage: *'Take heed not to practice your justice before men, in order to be seen by them,'* although in an earlier passage He had said: *'Let your light shine before men, in order that they may see your good works and give glory to your Father who is in heaven.'* And this fact, dearly beloved, usually occasions perplexity to many persons, for the mind which does not fully understand those precepts and is anxious to obey both the one and the other is perturbed and perplexed by their difference and opposition. Indeed, it is just as true that no one can obey even one master who gives contradictory orders as it is that no one can serve two masters, and in that same Sermon the Saviour Himself has borne witness to this latter impossibility. What, then, is the wavering mind to do when it thinks itself unable to obey, and dreads the consequences of not obeying? For, if a man places his good works in the light where they will be visible to men, in order that he may obey the precept, *'Let your light so shine before men, in order that they may see your good works and give glory to your Father who is in heaven,'* he will think that he is held accountable for having acted contrary to the precept, *'Take heed not to practice your justice before men, in order*

to be seen by them.' On the other hand, if, in his fear of this transgression and in his precaution against it, he keeps his good works hidden, then he will think that he is not obeying the command of Him who says: *'Let your light shine before men, in order that they may see your good works.'*

(2) But, whoever rightly understands these precepts can fulfill both of them, and will be able to serve the Supreme Master. If that Master were to give commands which could by no means be fulfilled, He would not condemn the slothful servant. Hearken, then, to 'Paul, the servant of Jesus Christ, called to be an Apostle, set apart for the gospel of God,'[1] while he both observes and teaches the one precept and the other. See how his light shines before men, so that they may see his good works. 'We commend ourselves,' says he, 'to every man's conscience in the sight of God.'[2] And again: 'For we take forethought for what is honorable, not only before God, but also in the sight of men.'[3] And yet again: 'Be pleasing to all men in all things, as I myself in all things try to please all men.'[4] On the other hand, see how he takes heed *'not to practice his justice before men, in order to be seen by them.'* For he says: 'But let everyone test his own work, and so he will have glory in himself, and not in comparison with another.'[5] And again: 'For our boast is this, the testimony of our conscience.'[6] And nothing is plainer than this other saying, namely, 'If I were still trying to please men, I should not be the servant of Christ.'[7] Let none of

---
1 Rom. 1.1.
2 2 Cor. 4.2.
3 2 Cor. 8.21.
4 1 Cor. 10.33.
5 Gal. 6.4.
6 2 Cor. 1.12.
7 Gal. 1.10.

those who are disconcerted by the apparently contradictory commands of the Lord Himself become all the more perplexed regarding the Apostle's meaning. Let them not ask *him* how he can say to us: 'Be pleasing to all men in all things, as I myself in all things try to please all men,' while he also says to us: 'If I were still trying to please men, I should not be the servant of Christ.' Rather, may we receive the aid of the Lord Himself, who has spoken through the person of His servant and apostle. May the Lord Himself reveal His will to us, and may He enable us to fulfill it.

(3) Of course, the very words of the Gospel are self-explanatory, but, while they feed the hearts of those who knock, they do not preclude the clamor of those who hunger. One must look into the human heart, to see in what direction it is turned and on what point its gaze is fixed. If a man wishes his good work to be seen by men, and if he then reckons his glory and profit according to the estimation of men and seeks it in the sight of men, he fulfills neither the one nor the other of the commands which the Lord has given in this matter. For, he has sought to practice his justice before men, in order to be seen by them; and his light thus has not shone before men for the purpose of having them see his good works in order that they may give glory to the Father who is in heaven. That man did not wish to have glory rendered to God; he wished to have glory for himself. He did not love the will of God; he sought advantage for himself. Of such men the Apostle says: 'For they all seek their own interests, not those of Jesus Christ.'[8] So, the saying was not completed by the words, *'Let your light so shine before men that they may see your good works,'* for He immediately adds the reason why this should be done; He says: *'that they*

---
8 Phil. 2.21.

may give glory to your Father who is in heaven.' This means that, even though a man is seen by men when he is performing good works, in his conscience he ought to have the intention of a good work, but it is only for the sake of God's glory that he ought to aim toward having it become known. And this aim ought to be directed toward the good of those to whom it becomes known. For it is to their advantage to be well disposed toward God because He bestows this power on a man, in order that they may not lose hope in the possibility of its being given also to themselves if they desire it. Accordingly, the clause, *'in order to be seen by them,'* is the only ending that He gave to this other saying, *'Take heed not to practice your justice before men.'* He did not subjoin the clause, *'that they may glorify your Father who is in heaven.'* Rather, He went on to say: *'Otherwise, you shall have no reward with your Father who is in heaven.'* With regard to those who are not the kind of men He wishes His faithful followers to be, He thereby shows that they seek their reward in the very fact of being seen by men, that they reckon this as their good, that they delight the vanity of their hearts in it, and that they are being emptied and puffed up and swelling and wasting away in it. Why is it not sufficient to say: *'Take heed not to practice your justice before men'?* Why did He add the words, *'In order to be seen by them'?* Only because there are some who practice their justice before men, not in order to be seen by them, but in order that the works themselves may be seen and that glory may be given to the Father who is in heaven and has vouchsafed to grant those works to men who have turned from impiety to justice.

(4) Such men do not account even their justice as their own; they account it as the justice of Him by whose faith they live. Hence, the Apostle says: 'That I may gain Christ and be found in him, not having a justice of my own, which is

from the Law, but that which is from faith in Christ, the justice from God based upon faith.'⁹ And elsewhere he says: 'So that in him may be the justice of God.'¹⁰ Hence, he also reprehends the Jews in this manner: 'Ignorant of the justice of God and seeking to establish their own, they have not submitted to the justice of God.'¹¹ Therefore, if any man wishes his works to be seen by men, in order that glory may be given to the divine Giver of the things that are seen in him, and in order that those who see them may be prompted by the piety of faith to imitate the work—that man's light truly shines before men. The smoke of pride does not belch forth from that man; the light of charity beams forth from him. He takes heed not to practice his justice before men in order to be seen by them, because he neither accounts that justice as his own nor practices it in order to be seen. He practices justice in order that He who is praised in them that are justified may become known, and may endue the praiser with the justice that is praised in another, that is, in order that God may make the praiser praiseworthy. And observe that the Apostle did not stop—as if he had fixed the aim of his intention in the mere pleasing of men—when he had said: 'Be pleasing to all men, as I myself in all things try to please all men.' If he had stopped at that point, he would have spoken a falsehood when he said: 'If I were still trying to please men, I should not be the servant of Christ.' But he at once added the reason why he was trying to please men; he said: 'Not seeking what is profitable to myself but to the many.'¹² So, he was not trying to please men for the sake of any profit to himself, lest he might not be the servant of

---
9 Phil. 3.8-9.
10 2 Cor. 5.21.
11 Rom. 10.3.
12 1 Cor. 10.33.

Christ; at the same time he was trying to please men for the sake of their salvation, so that he might be a fit dispenser of Christ. A 'good conscience in the sight of God' was enough for him; in the sight of men, there shone forth from him the kind of example that they ought to imitate.

SERMON 55

On Taming the Tongue

(Matt. 5.23; 1 James 3.8)

(1) If we have faith, we have been greatly alarmed by the section of the holy Gospel to which we have just now listened while it was being read. But it occasioned no fear in those who have no faith. Because it arouses no fear in them, they are willing to enjoy a false security, for they know not how to discern and distinguish the respective times for fear and assurance. Because man is now leading a life that will come to an end, let him have fear now so that in the next life he may have security without end. Therefore, we were filled with fear. For, who would not fear the Speaker of truth when He says: *'Whoever shall say to his brother, "Thou fool!" shall be liable to the Gehenna of fire'?*[1] Yet, 'the tongue no man can tame.'[2] Although man tames the wild beast, yet he tames not his own tongue; he tames the lion, yet he restrains not his own speech; he himself tames, yet he tames not himself; he tames what he used to fear, yet what he ought to have feared in order to tame himself—that, he does not fear. What happens? A truth is announced, and it has come forth from the oracle of truth: 'But the tongue no man can tame.'

(2) My brethren, what, therefore, shall we do? I know

---
1 For the rendering, *'Gehenna of fire,'* rather than, *'fire of Gehenna,'* see above, Commentary 1.9.22.
2 James 3.8.

233

that I am speaking to a multitude, but let us take counsel as in secret, for we are all one in Christ. No outsider is hearing us; we are one, because we are united. What shall we do? *'Whoever shall say to his brother, "Thou fool!" shall be liable to the Gehenna of fire.'* And 'no man can tame the tongue.' Shall all men, therefore, go to Gehenna? God forbid! 'Lord, Thou hast been our refuge from generation to generation.'³ Thy wrath is just. Thou sendest no one to Gehenna unjustly. 'Whither shall I go from Thy spirit? And whither shall I flee from Thee, except to Thee?'⁴ Therefore, most dearly beloved, let us understand that if no *man* can tame the tongue, we must have recourse to *God,* in order that He may tame our tongue. Even if you should wish to tame it, you are unable, because you are a *man*. 'The tongue no *man* can tame.' Note the similitude taken from the beasts which we are able to tame.⁵ The horse does not tame itself; the camel does not tame itself; the elephant does not tame itself; the adder does not tame itself; the lion does not tame itself. Neither does a man tame himself. A man is needed for the taming of the horse, the ox, the camel, the elephant, the lion, and the adder. For the taming of a man, therefore, let God be sought.

(3) 'Lord, thou hast been our refuge.' Therefore, we have recourse to Thee. Our healing shall be from Thee, for our evil is from ourselves. Because we have abandoned Thee, Thou hast abandoned us to ourselves. May we therefore be found in Thee, for in ourselves we had been lost. 'Lord, thou hast been our refuge.' Why, my brethren, should we doubt that the Lord will make us gentle if we submit ourselves to be tamed by Him? You have tamed the lion, which you

---
3 Ps. 89.1.
4 Ps. 138.7.
5 James 3.3.

did not create. Will your Creator be unable to tame you? What is the source of your power to tame such savage beasts? Are you their equal in bodily strength? By what power, then, have you been able to tame such huge beasts? The so-called beasts of burden are wild by nature; for, if untamed, they could not be endured. But, because you are not accustomed to see them except when handled by men, and under the curb and control of men, you might think that they were born tame. At any rate, consider the savage beasts. The lion roars; who does not fear?[6] And yet, whence your knowledge of the fact that you are more powerful? Not in bodily strength, but in the inner reason of the mind. You are more powerful than a lion, because you have been made to the image of God. The image of God tames a wild beast. Is God unable to tame His own image?

(4) In Him is our hope. Let us be submissive to Him, and beseech His mercy. Let us place our hope in Him. As long as we are being subdued and thoroughly tamed—which means, as long as we are being led to perfection—let us submit ourselves to our Tamer, for, as a rule, our Tamer makes use of the scourge. If you apply the rod and the whip in order to tame your beasts of burden, shall God not exhibit His scourges for taming his beasts of burden! We are God's beasts of burden, but He will make us to be His sons. You tame your horse. But what do you intend to give that horse when it becomes gentle enough to carry you, to submit to your training, to obey your commands—in a word, to be your beast of burden, that is, a support for the burden of your weakness? What do you give that horse? Why, after it dies, you do not even bury its carcass; you throw it where it will be torn to pieces by birds of prey. But God reserves

---

6 Amos 3.8.

an inheritance for you when you are tamed. That inheritance is God Himself. Some time after your death, God will resurrect your body; He will restore it to you, even to the last hair. And He will set you with the angels forever, where you will not need to be tamed, for you will need only to be possessed by His exceeding love. God will then be 'all in all,'[7] and there will be no unhappiness to exercise us, but only happiness to nourish us. Our God Himself will be our sustainer. Our God Himself will be our drink. Our God Himself will be our glory. Our God Himself will be our wealth. Whatsoever things you seek in this present life, God alone will be all those things to you.

(5) In view of this hope, man is being tamed. Shall his Tamer be deemed unbearable? In view of this hope, man is being tamed. If, perchance, his beneficent Tamer exhibit the scourge, should we murmur against Him? You have heard the exhortation of the Apostle, 'If you withdraw from discipline . . . you are illegitimate children and not sons.' (Illegitimates are adulterous.) 'For what son is there whom his father does not correct?' The Apostle continues: 'Furthermore, we had fathers of our flesh to correct us, and we reverenced them. Shall we not much more obey the Father of spirits, and live?'[8] Now, what advantage could your father bestow on you by correcting you, by scolding you, by taking out the scourge and striking you? Could he make you live forever? How could he give you what he could not give to himself? For the sake of a paltry sum of money which he had gained by toil and usury, he disciplined you with scourgings, so that when the fruit of his labor had been left to you it would not be squandered by your loose mode of life. Fearing that the fruit of his labor would perish, he struck

---
7 1 Cor. 15.28.
8 Heb. 12.7-9.

his son—because he was leaving to that son what he himself could neither hold on to in this life nor take with him to the next. For he did not leave you anything in this life which could continue as his own. He withdrew, so that you might take possession. But your God, your Redeemer, your Tamer, your Chastiser, your Father, instructs you. For what purpose? In order that you may receive an inheritance where you will not have to bear your father to the grave, but where you shall have your Father Himself for your inheritance. In view of this hope, you are being instructed. Do you therefore murmur? And if something unpleasant should chance to befall you, would you blaspheme? Whither shall you go from His spirit? Suppose He does not scourge you, but sends you away! Suppose He abandons you when you indulge in blashemy! Shall you, then, escape Him when He sits in judgment? Would it not be better to be scourged while He receives you than to be abandoned while He spares you?

(6) Let us therefore say to the Lord our God: 'Lord, Thou hast been our refuge from generation to generation.' In the first generation and in the second generation, Thou hast been our refuge. When we were not, Thou wast our refuge so that we might be born. When we were evil, Thou wast our refuge so that we might be born anew. Thou art a refuge for the sustaining of those who have forsaken Thee. Thou art a refuge for raising up and directing Thy children. 'Thou hast been our refuge.' We will not withdraw from Thee, for Thou hast delivered us from all those evils of ours, and hast filled us with Thy good gifts. Thou art still giving good gifts. For Thou art dealing gently with us, lest we faint by the way, and Thou art giving reproofs and stripes and lashes and correction,[9] lest we wander from the

---
9 Ps. 88.31-3.

way. Therefore, whether Thou dealest gently with us, lest we faint by the way, or whether Thou dost inflict chastisements, lest we wander from the way, 'Lord, Thou hast been our refuge.'

SERMON 56[1]

On the Lord's Prayer

(Matt. 5.9-13)

(1) When the holy Apostle wished to show that the Prophets had foretold the coming of those times when it should come to pass that all nations would believe in God, he cited the testimony which reads: 'And it shall come to pass that everyone that shall call upon the name of the Lord shall be saved.'[2] For the name of God who has made heaven and earth used to be invoked among the Israelites only. The rest of the nations used to call upon deaf and dumb idols, and were not heard by them; or they invoked demons, and were heard to their own harm. 'But when the fullness of time had come,'[3] then was fulfilled what had been foretold. 'And it shall come to pass that everyone that shall call upon the name of the Lord shall be saved.' Hence, the Jews—even those of them who believed in Christ —begrudged the Gospel to the Gentiles, and maintained that the Gospel of Christ ought not to be preached to the uncircumcised. Against those, the Apostle Paul cited this testimony, 'And it shall come to pass that everyone that shall

---
1 This sermon was delivered to a class of *'competents,'* that is, to a group of catechumens about to be admitted to the reception of the sacrament of baptism. It is on this account that Augustine uses such reserve (particularly in sects. 10-11) when speaking of Holy Eucharist, thus indicating the high esteem of the early Church for this sacrament. See above, *Commentary* 2.2.7, n. 7.
2 Joel 2.33.
3 Gal. 4.3.

239

call upon the name of the Lord shall be saved.'⁴ And because he cited it in order to refute those who opposed the evangelization of the Gentiles, he immediately went on to say: 'But how are they to call upon him in whom they have not believed? And how are they to believe him of whom they have not heard? And how are they to hear if no one preaches? And how are men to preach unless they be sent?'⁵ Because he said: 'How are they to call upon him in whom they have not believed?' you have not first been taught the Lord's Prayer, and then the Creed. You have been taught the Creed first, so that you may know what to believe, and afterwards the Prayer, so that you may know upon whom to call. The Creed contains what you are to believe; the Prayer, what you are to ask for. It is the believer's prayer that is heard.

(2) Many do not know what is expedient for them; hence, they ask what they ought not to ask for. A man must guard against two things when he is praying: he must take heed not to ask what he ought not to ask for, and not to ask from whom he ought not to ask. He ought not to ask anything from the Devil, from idols, or from demons. Whatever we are to ask, we must ask it from 'God . . . Christ Jesus our Lord,'⁶ from God, the Father of the Prophets, Apostles, and Martyrs, from God 'the Father of our Lord Jesus Christ,'⁷ from God 'who made heaven and earth, the sea, and all things that are in them.'⁸ But we must take heed not to ask even God for anything we ought not to ask for. Even though we ought to ask for the necessities of life, what would it profit you to ask this from deaf and dumb idols? Likewise,

---
4 Rom. 10.13.
5 Rom. 14.15.
6 Rom. 6.23.
7 Eph. 3.14.
8 Ps. 145.6.

if you were to wish the death of your enemies, what would it profit you to ask this from God the Father who is in heaven? Have you not heard or read that, in the Psalm in which the reprehensible traitor Judas is forespoken, the prophecy has said of him: 'May his prayer be turned into sin'?⁹ So, if you come forward and pray for evil on your enemies, your prayer will be turned into sin.

(3) In the holy Psalms, you have read that the speaker in the Psalms speaks as if he were hurling many imprecations against his enemies. Now someone objects: 'Most certainly, he who is speaking in the Psalms is just, yet why does he wish so many evils on his enemies?' He does not wish them; he foresees them. The prophecy is a herald's proclamation, not the wish of an imprecator. In spirit, the Prophets knew to whom evil was to come, and for whom good was in store; they pronounced the prophecy as if they wished what they foresaw. And how do you know that the man on whom you beseech evil today will not become a better man than you? You say that you know he is a wicked man. But you also know that you are wicked. Although you may dare to judge another's heart, you do not know it. But you do know that you yourself are wicked. Do you not hear the Apostle saying: 'For I formerly was a blasphemer, a persecutor and a bitter adversary; but I obtained mercy because I acted ignorantly.'¹⁰ Now, brethren, do you think that the Church was praying *against* the Apostle Paul or *for* him when he was persecuting the Christians, binding them wherever he found them, and dragging them to the high priests for questioning and punishment? Of course the Church of God —since she had her instructions from her Lord, who said while He was hanging on the cross: 'Father, forgive them,

---
9 Ps. 108.7.
10 1 Tim. 1.13.

for they do not know what they are doing'[11]—that Church was making like supplication on behalf of Paul (or, rather, on behalf of him who as yet was Saul), so that there might be wrought in him the very change that came about. Indeed, why does he say: 'And I was unknown by sight to the churches of Judea which were in Christ. But they had heard only that he who formerly persecuted us, now preaches the faith which once he ravaged. And they glorified God in me.'[12] How did they glorify God, except by beseeching this of Him before it came to pass?

(4) First of all, then, our Lord excluded loquaciousness, so that you might not address a great many words to God—as though you would teach God by a great many words. Piety, not wordiness, is what you need when you pray, 'for your Father knows your need before you ask Him.'[13] Therefore, do not speak much, for He knows what you need. It might happen that someone would now say: 'If He knows what we need, why should we use even a few words, or why should we pray at all? He knows. Then let Him give us what He knows we need.' Yes, but He wishes you to pray, so that you may be desirous of His gift, lest His gift be lightly esteemed. He Himself has implanted this desire. So, the words which our Lord Jesus Christ has taught in his Prayer are the expression of what our desires ought to be. You are not allowed to ask for anything except what is written in that Prayer.

(5) He says: 'Say you therefore, *"Our Father who art in heaven."*' You see, you have begun to have God for your Father, and you will have Him when you are born anew. But even now, before you are born, you have been conceived

---
11 Luke 23.34.
12 Gal. 1.22ff.
13 Matt. 6.8.

of His seed, for you are about to be born of the font, which is, as it were, the womb of the Church. *'Our Father who art in heaven.'* Remember that of your father Adam you have been born unto death, but of God the Father you will be reborn unto life. What you say, say it in your hearts. Let there be affection in him who prays, and there will be effect from Him who hears it. *'Hallowed be thy name.'* Why should you ask that the name of God be hallowed? It *is* holy. Why, then, do you ask for the hallowing of what is already holy? Moreover, when you ask that His name be hallowed, is it not as though you were asking Him on His own behalf, not on yours? Understand it rightly; then, you are praying on your own behalf. For this is what you are asking, namely, that what is always holy in itself may be hallowed in you. But what is meant by saying: *'Hallowed be thy name'?* It means: May it be accounted holy, may it be not despised. So, you see, when you wish for that, you wish a blessing for yourself. For, if you despise the name of God, it will be an evil thing for you, but not for God.

(6) *'Thy kingdom come.'* To whom do we address this petition? And will the kingdom of God not come unless we ask for it? It is said of that kingdom that it will exist after the end of the world.[14] God has a kingdom forever. He is never without a kingdom, for all creation is subject to Him. Then, what kingdom do we wish for? The kingdom of which it is written in the Gospel: 'Come, blessed of my Father, take possesion of the kingdom prepared for you from the foundation of the world.'[15] Behold, that is the kingdom of which we speak when we say: *'Thy kingdom come.'* May that kingdom come within us and may we be found within that kingdom—that is our petition. Of course it will come,

---
14 Luke 1.33.
15 Matt. 25.34.

but what will that profit you if it finds you at the left hand? So, in this petition also, it is on yourself that you wish a blessing; it is on your own behalf that you pray. For in this petition, this is what you desire and long for, namely, that you may so live as to have a share in the kingdom which shall be given to all the saints. So, when you say: *'Thy kingdom come,'* it is for yourself you pray, for you pray that you may lead a good life. May we partake of Thy kingdom. The kingdom that is to come to Thy saints and Thy just ones—may that same kingdom come also to us.

(7) *'Thy will be done.'* Shall God not accomplish His will unless you make that petition? Remember what you have recited in the Creed: 'I believe in God the Father Almighty.' If He is almighty, why do you pray that His will be done? What is the meaning of this petition, *'Thy will be done'?* It means this: May it be so done in me that I shall not resist Thy will. So, in this petition also, you pray for yourself, not for God. The will of God shall be done in you, even though it be not done by you. As to those to whom He will say: 'Come, blessed of my Father, take possession of the kingdom prepared for you from the foundation of the world'—the will of God shall be so done in them that, being holy and just, they shall receive the kingdom. But, as to those to whom He will say: 'Begone! go to the everlasting fire which was prepared for the devil and his angels'[16]—the will of God shall be so done in them that, being wicked, they shall be condemned to everlasting fire. That the will of God be done in you is one thing; that it be done by you is another thing. For no other reason, therefore, but that it may be well for you, do you pray that God's will be done in you, for, whether it be well or ill with you, it shall be done in you. But may it be done also by you! Why do I say: 'Thy will be done in

---

16 Matt. 25.41.

heaven and on earth,' rather than: 'Thy will be done by heaven and earth'? I say it because it is God that does in you whatever is done by you. Never is anything done by you except what He does in you. Sometimes, indeed, He does in you what is not done by you. But never is anything done by you, unless He does it in you.

(8) Now, what is the meaning of the expression, 'in heaven and on earth,' or, 'on earth as it is in heaven'?[17] This is what it means: The angels do Thy will; may we also do it. *Thy will be done on earth, as it is in heaven.* The mind is heaven; the flesh is earth. The Apostle says: 'With my mind I serve the law of God, but with my flesh the law of sin.'[18] As long as you are saying that—if, indeed, you are still saying it—the will of God is being done in heaven, but as yet it is not being done on earth. However, when the flesh is in such harmony with the mind, and death is so swallowed up in victory, that no carnal desires remain with which the mind may be in conflict; when strife on earth will have passed away, and the war of the heart will be no more; when it will be no longer true to say: 'For the flesh lusts against the spirit, and the spirit against the flesh; for these are opposed to each other, so that you do not do what you would'[19]—when, I say, this war will have passed, and all lust will have been changed into charity; when nothing will remain in the body to resist the spirit, nothing to be tamed, nothing to be bridled, nothing to be trampled on; when the whole man [the spirit and the flesh] will be harmoniously advancing toward justice—then it will have come to pass that the will of God is being done in heaven and on earth.

---

17 Evidently the two forms were in current use. The form 'on earth, as in heaven,' is closer to the Greek, '*hōs en ouranō kai epi gēs.*'
18 Rom. 7.25.
19 Gal. 5.17.

We pray for perfection whether we say: *'Thy will be done in heaven and on earth,'* or: *'Thy will be done on earth, as it is in heaven.'* For, in the Church, the spiritual are heaven, and the carnal are earth. Therefore, *'May Thy will be done on earth, as it is in heaven,'* so that the carnal may be reformed, and serve Thee in like manner with the spiritual. *'Thy will be done on earth, as it is in heaven.'* There is also another very spiritual interpretation of this petition, since we are admonished to pray for our enemies. According to this interpretation, the Church is heaven, and her enemies are the earth. Then, what is the meaning of *'Thy will be done on earth, as it is in heaven'?* It means this: May our enemies believe in Thee, just as we believe. May they become friends, and cease their enmity. They are earth and are therefore against us; may they become heaven, then they will be with us.

(9) *'Give us this day our daily bread.'* It is very plain that in this petition we pray for ourselves. When you say: *'Hallowed be thy name,'* it must be explained to you that you are praying for yourself, not for God. When you say: *'Thy will be done,'* this petition also must be explained to you, lest you think that, instead of praying on your own behalf, you are praying on God's behalf in wishing that His will be done. When you say: *'Thy kingdom come,'* an explanation must likewise be given, lest you think that it is on God's behalf you are wishing that He may reign. But, from this point onwards to the end of the Prayer, it is plain that we are beseeching God on our own behalf. When you say: *'Give us this day our daily bread,'* you confess that you are a beggar in relation to God. But, do not be ashamed of that. No matter how rich a man may be in worldly wealth, he still is a beggar in relation to God. A beggar stands before the rich man's door; the rich man himself stands before the door of Him who is

rich and mighty. Someone is begging from the rich man, and the rich man himself is begging. If he were not in need, he would not make his petition vibrate in the ears of God. And what is he in need of? The rich man, I venture to say, is in need of daily bread. How is it that he has an abundance of all things? Only because God has bestowed it on him. What would he have if God withdrew His hand? Have not many men retired to sleep in wealth, and risen from that same sleep in poverty? If a man is not in want, that is due to the mercy of God—not to man's own ability.

(10) But, dearly beloved, you see that God gives this bread—that is, the bread by which the belly is filled and the body is nourished anew every day—you see that God gives this bread, not only to those who praise Him, but also to those who blaspheme Him. For He 'makes his sun to rise on the good and the evil, and he sends rain on the just and the unjust.'[20] You praise Him; He feeds you. You blaspheme Him; He feeds you. He awaits your repentance; unless you are converted, He condemns you. Now, since the good and the evil receive this bread from God, is there not, think you, some kind of bread which the children seek—the bread of which the Lord has said in the Gospel, 'It is not fair to take the children's bread and to cast it to the dogs'?[21] Plainly, there is. But, what is the first-mentioned bread? And why is it called a daily bread? That bread also is necessary, for we could not live without it; we could not live without bread. While it would be shameless for you to ask God for riches, it is not shameless to ask Him for daily bread. It is one thing to ask for what might make you proud; it is another to ask for what enables you to live. Nevertheless, since that visible and tangible bread is given to the good

---
20 Matt. 5.45.
21 Matt. 15.16.

and to the evil, there is a daily bread which the children seek. And this bread is the Word of God,[22] which is dispensed to us every day. It is our daily bread, the nourishment of our minds—not the nourishment of our bodies. It is necessary for us even now, while we are laborers in the vineyard. It is our food, not our hire. The laborer is entitled to two things from him who hires him for the vineyard: he is entitled to food, lest he lose his strength; to a reward, that he may rejoice in it. Our daily food on this earth is the Word of God, which is always being dispensed in the churches; our reward when the labor is done—that is called life everlasting. So, if in the expression, *'daily bread,'* you see a signification of that which the faithful receive and which you will receive after you are baptized, then we do well when we ask for it, and say: *'Give us this day our daily bread,'* that we may so live as not to be excluded from its altar.

(11) *'And forgive us our debts, as we also forgive our debtors.'* This petition needs no expounding in order to show that it is for ourselves that we make it, for by it we beg that our debts be forgiven us. And we are debtors, not in money, but in sins. Perhaps you now say to me: 'Even you?' We answer, Yes, even we. 'What! Even you holy bishops are debtors?' Yes, even we are debtors. 'Even you! Far be it from you, my Lord; do not so unjustly accuse yourself.' I do not unjustly accuse myself; I am speaking the truth, for we are debtors. 'If we say that we have no sin, we deceive ourselves, and the truth is not in us.'[23] Though we have been baptized, yet we are debtors. Not that anything remained which was not remitted to us in baptism, but because in our life we are contracting something which needs daily

---

22 Cf. above, Commentary 2.7.25, n. 2.
23 1 John 1.8.

remission. As to those who are baptized and then depart from this life—they come forth from the font without any debt and they go forth from this life without any debt. But, as to those who are baptized and then continue to live—these contract some imperfection through the frailty of mortals. Even though the ship is not lost through these imperfections, the pumps must be used, for if the pumps are not used, there is a gradual leakage that may sink the whole ship. By making this petition, we make use of the pumps. Further, we ought not only to pray, but to give alms as well. For, when we are using the pumps to prevent the ship from sinking, we are using both our voice and our hands. We use our voice when we say: *'Forgive us our debts, as we also forgive our debtors'*; we use our hands when we fulfill this command: 'Deal thy bread to the hungry, and bring the homeless needy into thy house,'[24] and 'Shut up alms in the heart of the poor, and it shall intercede for thee before the Lord.'[25]

(12) Even though all sins are forgiven through 'the bath of regeneration,'[26] we should nevertheless be driven into great straits if the daily cleansing of holy prayer were not afforded us. Almsgiving and prayer wash sins away, provided that no such sins be committed as would necessitate our being excluded from the daily Bread. Even though you avoided those debts to which a determined and severe penalty is attached, do not call yourselves righteous, as if you had no reason to say: *'Forgive us our debts, as we also forgive our debtors.'* For, even though you abstain from

---
24 Isa. 58.7.
25 Eccli. 29.15.
26 Tit. 3.5.

idolatry, from the constellations of astrologers,[27] and the spells of enchanters; even though you avoid the deceptions of heretics and the divisions of schismatics; even though you refrain from murder, adultery, fornication, thefts, robbery, false testimony, and whatsoever other such sins—I am not mentioning those sins which have such a deadly effect as to necessitate one's exclusion from the altar, and such a binding on earth as to bring on a very dangerous and deadly binding in heaven unless that which may be loosed in heaven be loosed also on earth—even when all these sins are excepted, there still remain sins which a man may commit. A man sins by willingly seeing what he ought not to see. And who could check the quickness of the eye, since in fact the eye is said to have received its name because of its quickness? Who could restrain the ear or the eye? The eyes can be closed whenever you wish, and they can be closed quickly. It is with an effort that you close the ears, for you must raise the hand to reach them, and, if someone should restrain your hand, you would not be able to close the ears against abusive, impure, cajoling, or deceptive words. When you listen to something you ought not to listen to, do you not sin with the ear, even if you do not act in accordance with what you have heard? For you have willingly heard something evil. How many kinds of sin does a deadly tongue commit? At times, it commits the kind of sin that excludes one from the altar. The sphere of blasphemies belongs to the tongue, and many irrelevant idle words are spoken. But,

---

27 In Augustine's works, the term, *'mathematicus,'* means *astrologer*. He deals with astrology in many works; for instance, in *De doctrina Christiana* (2.21.32-33), he writes: 'From this kind of superstition, we cannot exclude those who are called *'genethliaci'* because of their attention to birthdays, but who are now commonly called *mathematici*. . . . The so-called constellations are a notation of the position of the stars at the time of the person's birth . . .

even if the hand do no evil, if the foot advance toward no evil, if the eye be directed toward nothing lascivious, if the ear be willingly open to no scurrility, if the tongue be exercised on no indecent speech—even then, tell me, who could restrain his thoughts? My brethren, our thoughts are often elsewhere while we pray, as though we forget before whom we stand or lie prostrate. If all these things be reckoned against us, will they fail to overwhelm us because they are small? What does it matter whether it be lead or sand that presses you down? The lead is one compact mass; the sand is composed of many grains, but it crushes you by their multitude. Your sins are small; yet, do you not see that from tiny drops rivers are filled and lands are lessened? Our sins are small, but they are many.

(13) Every day, therefore, let us say: *'Forgive us our debts, as we also forgive our debtors.'* Let us say it with sincerity of heart, and let us fulfill our promise, for we make a promise, a covenant and pleasing agreement with God. What the Lord your God says to you is this: Forgive, and I will forgive. If you have not forgiven, then you yourself—not I —are retaining your sins against yourself. Now, my most dearly beloved, give me your attention. I know what is especially applicable to you in the Lord's Prayer, and, above all, in this sentence of it, *'Forgive us our debts, as we also forgive our debtors.'* You are about to be baptized; forgive everything. Whatever anyone of you has in his heart against anyone let him dismiss it from his heart. Come to the font with this disposition, then rest assured that you are forgiven all the sins which you have contracted—both the sin that is yours by reason of your birth from parents with original sin according to Adam (for it is because of this sin that you join with babes in hastening to the grace of the Saviour), and also whatever sins you may have committed during your lives,

by word, or thought, or deed. All sins are forgiven you, and you shall come forth from the font, as from the presence of your Lord, with the assurance that all your debts are forgiven.

(14) And now, what are you to *do* with regard to those sins of which I have spoken? For, it is on account of those sins that—as though by a kind of daily cleansing—you have to say: *'Forgive us our debts, as we also forgive our debtors.'* Well, you have enemies. Indeed, who could live on this earth without having them? See to it that you love them. In no way can a raging enemy injure you as much as you injure yourself unless you love your enemy. He can damage your farm or your flock; he can injure your household—your man-servant or maid-servant, your son or your wife, or, at most, he can injure your body if he has been given the power. But—unlike you—can he injure the soul? Dearly beloved, strive toward this perfection, I exhort you. Is it I that gave you this? It has been given to you by Him to whom you say: *'Thy will be done on earth, as it is in heaven.'* And do not think it impossible, for I know that there are Christians who love their enemies. I know this, for I have discovered it and proved it. You will not even try to love your enemy if you think it impossible for you to love him. Therefore, begin by believing it possible, and then pray that the will of God be done in you. If your enemy had no wickedness, he would not be an enemy. But, how profitable his wickedness can be for you! Wish him well; let him put an end to his evils, and he will no longer be your enemy. It is not the man's nature that is your enemy; it is his vice. Can it be that he is your enemy because he has a soul and body? In this, he is the same as you. You have a soul, so has he; you have a body, so has he. He is of the same substance as you, from kindred earth you both were made, and from the Lord you have both received the

soul. He is the same as you. Look upon him as your brother. The first two human beings, Adam and Eve, were our parents. He is our father, she is our mother; therefore, we are brothers. Not to mention our first origin, God is our Father, the Church is our Mother; therefore, we are brothers. But, my enemy is a heathen! my enemy is a Jew! my enemy is a heretic! Yes, and therefore I have already said: *'Thy will be done on earth, as it is in heaven.'* O Church, thy enemy is the heathen, the Jew, the heretic; he is the *earth.* If thou art *heaven,* call upon thy Father who is in heaven, and pray for thy enemies. So Saul was an enemy of the Church, but, when prayer was offered for him as an enemy, he became a friend. He not only ceased to be a persecutor, but he labored to become a helper. If you seek the truth of the matter, prayer was offered against him, but it was offered against his malice, not against his nature. So, also, let your prayer be against the malice of your enemy; may his malice die, but may he live. For, if your enemy should die, it would be as though you had one enemy less; but you would not have gained a friend. However, if his malice should die, then you would have lost an enemy and gained a friend.

(15) You are still saying: 'Who can do it, and who has ever done it?' May God do it in your hearts. Very few do it, I know. Those who do it are noble and spiritual. Is it true that all the faithful in the Church, all who approach the altar and receive the Body and Blood of Christ—is it true that all these are such as forgive their enemies? Yet, they all say: *'Forgive us our debts, as we also forgive our debtors.'* Suppose God were to say to them: 'Why do you ask Me to do what I have promised, when you are not doing what I have commanded? What have I promised? I have promised to forgive your debts. What have I commanded? I have commanded you to forgive your debtors. How can you do that, unless

you love your enemies?' Brethren, what, therefore, must we do? Is the flock of Christ reduced to such fewness? If those only who love their enemies ought to say: *'Forgive us our debts, as we also forgive our debtors,'* then I know not what to say, or what to do. Must I tell you that unless you love your enemies, you are not to pray? I would not dare do that. Rather, pray that you may love them. But must I say to you: Unless you love your enemies, then in the Lord's Prayer do not say: *'Forgive us our debts, as we also forgive our debtors'*? Suppose I tell you not to say it? Unless you say it, your debts are not forgiven; if you say it without doing it, your debts are not forgiven. Therefore, in order that our debts be forgiven, we must both *say* and *do*.

(16) I have in mind something with which to console, not merely a select few, but also the multitude of Christians. I know that you are eager to hear it. Christ has said: 'Forgive, that you may be forgiven.'[28] And what do you say in the Prayer in which occurs the petition we are now discussing, *'Forgive us our debts, as we also forgive our debtors'?* You say: 'Forgive, O Lord, just as we forgive.' For you say: 'Thou, Father who art in heaven, *forgive us our debts, as we also forgive our debtors.'* That is what you say. What you must *do* is this: When an enemy asks forgiveness, forgive him at once; unless you do this, you shall perish. Is this too much for you? Even were it too much for you to love him as an enemy raging against you, is it too much for you to love him as a man humbly beseeching you? What do you say? He was raging against you, and you hated him. Would that you had not hated him even then! Would that, even when he was raging against you, you had recalled the saying of the Lord your God, 'Father, forgive them, for they know not what they are doing.'[29] Oh that, even then,

---
28 Luke 6.37.
29 Luke 23.34.

when your enemy was raging against you, you had recalled the Lord your God speaking those words! Perhaps you will say: 'He did it, but He did it as the Lord; He did it because He was Christ, the Son of God, the Only-Begotten, the Word made flesh. But what can I do, since I am a weak and sinful man?' If the example of the Lord your God is too much for you, then let your thought dwell on your fellow servant. St. Stephen was being stoned, and on bended knees he prayed for his enemies while they were stoning him. He said: 'Lord, do not lay this sin against them.'[30] They were casting stones, not asking pardon, but he was praying for them. That is the kind of man I wish that you were. Strive to be such. Why are you always dragging your heart on the earth? Listen, lift up your hearts. Strive upward. Love your enemies. If you cannot love a man while he is raging against you, love him at least when he is asking your pardon. Love the man who says to you: 'Brother, I have sinned; forgive me.' If you do not forgive that man, then I do not tell you to blot out the Prayer from your heart; I tell you that your name will be blotted from God's book.[31]

(17) But, if then at least you forgive him, by all means cast out hatred from your heart. I tell you to cast out hatred, not correction. What if the man who asks forgiveness from you ought yet to be punished by me? Do what you will, for I suppose you love your child even when you chastise him. You pay no heed to his tears while he is being chastised, since you are saving an inheritance for him. So, I tell you to cast out hatred from your heart when an enemy asks you for forgiveness. Perhaps you will say that his words are false and deceptive. So, you are a judge of another's heart! Then, tell me your father's thoughts, or your own thoughts yesterday.

---
30 Acts 7.60.
31 Apoc. 3.5.

That man implores you, and asks for pardon. Then forgive him; forgive him at once. If you refuse to forgive him, the refusal will injure you; it will not injure him, for he knows what to do. If you, a servant, refuse to forgive a fellow sersant, he will go to your Lord and say to Him: 'Lord, I asked my fellow servant to forgive me, and he refused; do Thou forgive me.' Is it wrong for the Lord to loose His servant's debts? When that servant has obtained forgiveness from the Lord, he comes back free; you remain bound. Bound in what way? The time for the Prayer will come, the time for you to say: *'Forgive us our debts, as we also forgive our debtors.'* The Lord will answer you thus: 'Wicked servant, although thou didst owe me such a great debt, thou didst ask me to forgive thee, and I forgave. "Shouldst not thou also have pity on thy fellow-servant, even as I had pity on thee?" '[32] These words are from the Gospel, not from my emotion. On the other hand, if, when you are asked to forgive, you grant forgiveness to him who asks it, then you can say that Prayer. So, even if you are as yet unable to love a raging enemy, you can nevertheless say that Prayer: *'Forgive us our debts, as we also forgive our debtors.'* Let us pass on to the rest of the Prayer.

(18) *'And lead us not into temptation.'* Because of our past sins, we say: *'Forgive us our debts, as we also forgive our debtors,'* for we cannot bring it to pass that those sins have not been committed. You may indeed see to it that you will not do what you have done. But, how could you bring it to pass that what you have done has not been done? With regard to sins that have been committed, your remedy lies in this petition of the Lord's Prayer, *'Forgive us our debts, as we also forgive our debtors.'* But, what shall you do with regard to the sins into which you may fall? *'Lead us not into temp-*

---
32 Matt. 18.33.

tation, but deliver us from evil. Lead us not into temptation, but deliver us from evil'— that is to say, from temptation itself.

(19) Three of those petitions—'*Hallowed be thy name,*' '*Thy kingdom come,*' '*Thy will be done on earth, as it is in heaven*'— these three will not cease, but the other petitions are made for the sake of man's life [on earth]. For, God's name ought to be hallowed in us forever; we ought to be in His kingdom forever; and we ought to be doing His will forever. This will continue for all eternity, but the daily bread is a necessity of this present life. So, from that point onward, the rest of the Prayer pertains to the needs of this present life. The daily bread is a necessity during this present life. It is necessary that our debts be forgiven during this present life, for we shall have finished with debts when we have reached the next life; there is temptation during our life on earth, for our ship is sailing through danger. During our life on earth, there is a certain leakage through the chinks of our frailties, and it has to be pumped out. But, when we shall have become 'as the angels'[33] of God, think not that we shall then ask or implore God to forgive us our debts; there shall be no debts. In this life, therefore, is the daily bread, and it is in this life that debts may be forgiven. It is in this life that we pray to be led not into temptation, for no temptation finds entry in the next life. It is in this life that we pray to be delivered from evil, for in the next life there is no evil. In that life, the eternal good abides.

---
33 Mark 12.25.

SERMON 60

On Almsgiving

(1) Every man who is unequal to the task of extricating himself from a distressful situation in which he finds himself tries to find some prudent person to consult, in order that he may thus learn what he ought to do. Let us suppose, therefore, that the whole world is, as it were, a man who is trying to escape evil and is disinclined to do good. Since it is unequal to the task of extricating itself from the tribulations which are thereby increasing, what counsellor can it find more prudent than Christ? Yes, let it find a better counsellor if it can! Let it follow such a counsellor's advice! But, if it cannot find a better counsellor anywhere, let it come to that Counsellor whom it may find everywhere. Let it consult Him and accept His advice; let it observe the good commandment and escape the great evil. Men shrink from present temporal evils. They murmur exceedingly under those evils, and by their murmuring they so offend their Corrector that they do not find their Saviour in Him. But, assuredly, those present evils are passing evils. Either they pass through us or we pass through them; either they pass away while we live or they are dismissed when we die. Whatever is of short duration is not a great tribulation. When you are thinking of tomorrow, you are not recalling yesterday. On the arrival of the day after tomorrow, tomorrow will then be a yesterday. Now, if men are so convulsed with anxiety to escape temporal tribulations which are passing through them—or,

rather soaring over them—how much thought ought a man to take so that he may escape those tribulations which will continue forever?

(2) Mortal life is a harsh condition. What else is its birth but an entry into a life of toil? Even the infant's cry bears witness to the toil that awaits it. From his burdensome banquet no one is excused. We must drink of the chalice which Adam has filled for us. We have been fashioned by the hands of Truth; yet, on account of sin, we were cast out in the day of vanity. We have been fashioned to the image of God,[1] but we have marred that image by sinful transgression. Thus the Psalm reminds us how we have been made and to what state we have fallen. It says: 'Although man walks in the image of God, yet shall he be disquieted in vain.'[2] He walks in the image of God! Behold what he was made. But to what condition has he fallen? Hear what follows: 'Yet shall he be disquieted in vain.' He walks in the image of truth, and he shall be disquieted in the counsel of vanity. Then see his perturbation. See it, and—as though in a mirror—see yourself, and be not complacent. But why, pray, shall man be disquieted in vain? As though we were asking that question, the Psalm gives the answer: 'He is storing up treasures, and he knows not for whom he is gathering them.'[3] Do you recognize that man? He is, as it were, the whole human race, represented as a man whose resources have failed, who has lost foresight, and whose mind has strayed from the ways of sanity. He is storing up treasures and he does not know for whom he is gathering them. What could be more foolish or fruitless? But, at least, is he not doing it for himself? No, he is not. Why not? Because

---
1 Gen. 1.27.
2 Ps. 38.7.
3 *Ibid.*

he will die. Man's life is short. A treasure endures, but he who stores it passes quickly away. Therefore—with pity for him who is walking in the image of God and confessing truth while he pursues vanity—the Psalm says: 'He shall be disquieted in vain.' I am perplexed: man is storing up treasures and he knows not for whom he is gathering them. Is he gathering them for himself? No, because the man dies, but the treasure endures. Then, for whom is he gathering them? You are taking counsel. Impart it to me, also. You have no counsel to give me! Therefore, if both of us lack counsel, let both of us seek it, receive it, and discuss the matter. The man is disquieted; he is storing up treasures; he is planning and toiling; he is sleepless with anxiety. Throughout the day you are harassed with toil; throughout the night you are troubled with fears. Your mind is feverish with anxiety that your purse may be filled with money.

(3) I am aware of that, and I am saddened by it. You are disquieted, and—as He who is infallible tells us—you are disquieted in vain. Yes, you are storing up treasures. Even though we grant that you are successful in every transaction, even though we say nothing about your losses, even though we make no mention of the great risks and the deaths that accompany every profitable transaction (I do not mean corporeal deaths; I mean the deaths that are occasioned by evil designs—for veracity dies so that profits may increase), yet, you are being inwardly despoiled so that you may be outwardly adorned. Yes, suppose that we ignore those facts, and make no reference to certain other facts; suppose that we disregard your reverses, and consider only your successes. In that case, you are storing up treasures, profits are pouring in from all sides, money is flowing into your coffers as if from a fountain, and whenever a need arises it is engulfed by abundance. Nevertheless, have you not heard: 'If riches

abound, set not your heart upon them.'[4] Yes, you are growing rich; so you are not disquieted unprofitably. Nevertheless, you are disquieted in vain. But you ask me: 'Why am I disquieted in vain? See, I am filling my coffers, and my storehouses can hardly contain the treasures I am acquiring. How, then, am I disquieted in vain?' Because you are storing up treasures, and you know not for whom you are gathering them. Or, if you know it, I beseech you to tell me. I would hear you tell me that. So, if you are not disquieted in vain, tell me for whom you are gathering treasures. 'For myself,' you reply. Do you dare to say that, although you must die? 'For my children,' you reply. Do you dare to say that, since they, too, must die? 'It is a pious duty for a father to store up treasures for his children!' Rather, since a man must die, it is a great vanity for him to store up treasures for those who must die. If it is for yourself, why are you gathering treasures which you must leave behind when you die? This is also the case with regard to your children; they are to succeed you, but they are not to abide forever. I refrain from asking: 'For what kind of children?' Perhaps debauchery may squander what avarice has amassed. By loose living, some one else squanders what you have amassed by your labors. But I leave this out of account. Perhaps your children will be upright, not dissolute. Perhaps they will preserve what you will have left and increase what you have saved, not dissipate what you have gathered. If your children do this, if in this regard they imitate you, their father, then they are just as vain as you are. What I was saying to you, I say to them. To your son, I put this question: 'For whom are you gathering?' To him also I say: 'You are storing up treasures, and you know not for whom you are gathering

---

4 Ps. 61.11.

them.' For, just as you do not know, so neither does he. Even if vanity has remained in him, has truth therefore lost its force for him?

(4) I refrain from saying that you may be gathering treasures for a thief who will take them even while you are alive. During the course of one night he comes and finds ready what has been amassed during the course of so many days and nights. Perhaps you are storing them up for a robber, a plunderer. I say no more on this, lest I remind someone of the wound of past sufferings and rub that wound anew. The treasures which empty vanity has gathered—how many of them does hostile cruelty find ready! I do not mean that I wish for this, but it behooves all of us to fear. it. May God protect us from it. May His own scourges suffice for us. Let us all implore God to protect us from it, and may He spare us who beseech Him. But, if He should ask us for whom we are gathering treasures, what answer could we make? Therefore, O man, whosoever you are that are storing up treasures in vain, what answer do you give me while I am discussing this matter with you, and seeking counsel with you in our common cause? You have spoken and have given these replies: 'I am gathering them for myself, for my children, for my descendants.' I have told you how many things are to be feared even with regard to your children. I do not go so far as to say that they will live to suffer the penalty of spoliation, as your enemy would wish. May your children's lives fulfill their father's hopes. But I have mentioned those misfortunes, and I have reminded you how many have fallen into them. You were horrified, but you were not corrected. What answer can you give except to say that *perhaps* this will not happen to them. But that is how I have spoken, for I said that *perhaps* you were gathering treasures for a thief, a robber, or a plunderer. I

did not say that you were *certainly* doing this; I said that *perhaps* you were doing it. The probability of its not happening implies the probability of its happening. So, you do not know what will happen, and you are disquieted in vain. You see how truly Truth has spoken, and how vainly vanity is disquieted. You have listened, and at length you have understood. Since you say that *perhaps* it is for your children, but do not dare to say that you are certain it is for your children, you do not know for whom you are gathering treasure. Therefore, as I see and as I have already said, you have failed in your purpose. You cannot answer my question; neither can I find the answer for you.

(5) Therefore, let both of us seek the answer; let both of us seek counsel. We have access, not merely to a wise man, but to Wisdom itself. Let both of us listen to Christ. 'To the Jews indeed a stumbling-block and to the Gentiles foolishness; but to those who are called, both Jews and Greeks, Christ is the power of God and the wisdom of God.'[5] Why are you preparing safeguards for your riches? Consider the power of God; there is nothing more powerful. Why are you framing arguments in defense of your riches? Hearken to the wisdom of God; there is nothing more prudent. If, perchance, you should be scandalized when I say this, you would be a Jew; for to the Jews Christ is a scandal. If, perchance, you should deem it foolish, you would be a Gentile; for to the Gentiles Christ is foolishness. But you are a Christian; you have been called. And, 'to those who are called, both Jews and Greeks, Christ is the power of God and the wisdom of God.' When I mention the wisdom of God, do not be sad, do not be scandalized, do not mock it wryly as though it were my foolishness. Let us bear this in mind,

---

5 1 Cor. 1.23.

namely, that Christ has said what I am going to say. Then why should I say it? While you despise the herald, at least fear the judge. Why should I say it? By reading the Gospel to you just now, the lector has relieved me of that task.⁶ I shall not read it. I shall merely call your attention to what has been read. You were seeking counsel, because your own resources were insufficient. Then hearken to the words of the source of right counsel, the fountain from which you fear no poison, no matter how copiously you drink.

(6) 'Do not lay up for yourselves treasures on earth, where moth and rust consume, and where thieves dig down and steal; but lay up for yourselves treasures in heaven, where no thief approaches and where no moth consumes. For where thy treasure is, there thy heart also will be.'⁷ What more do you expect? The matter is plain. The advice is clear, but avarice lies concealed. Rather, it is not concealed, but —what is worse—it, too, is plain to be seen. For robbers have not ceased to plunder, the covetous have not ceased to defraud, and the deceitful have not ceased to swear falsely. For what purpose is all this done? So that treasures may be stored up. Stored up where? On earth. Truly, stored by earth unto the earth. For, when man had sinned—that man by whom, as I have said, a life of toil was pledged for us— it was said to him: 'Earth thou art, and unto earth thou shalt return.'⁸ Accordingly, the treasure is on earth, because the heart is there. How is it, then, that 'we have it lifted up to God'?⁹ You have understood me, repent; if you repent,

---
6 It was customary for the *lector* to read the Scriptural text, and for the bishop to expound it. References to this custom are found in several of Augustine's works. Cf. *Enarr. in ps.* 138.1; *Sermones* 17.1-2; 18.5; 32.23; 67.1; 235.1.
7 Matt. 6.19-21.
8 Gen. 3.19.
9 Cf. Preface of the Mass.

amend your lives. How long will you continue to praise, and not act? This saying is true; there is nothing more true. Therefore, let that which is true be done. We praise the One God, yet we remain unchanged. In this matter, also, may we not be disquieted in vain.

(7) Therefore, whether you have learned by experience, that what is buried in the earth perishes, or whether you fear to experience it, although as yet you have had no such experience, 'Do not lay up for yourselves treasure on earth.' Let experience correct the man whom words do not correct. There will be no arousing or advance unless we all cry out with one voice: 'Woe to us! The world is falling.' If it is falling, why do you not forsake it? If an architect were to tell you that your house was about to crumble, would you not quit it before you began to complain? But the Builder of the world tells you that the world will crumble. Do you not believe Him? Hear His forewarning voice; heed His words of admonition. His forewarning voice is this: 'Heaven and earth will pass away.'[10] These are His words of admonition: 'Do not lay up for yourselves treasure on earth.' Therefore, if you believe His forewarning, and do not disregard His admonition, let that be done which He advises, for He who gives this advice does not deceive you. You will not lose what you have given away, but you will follow what you have sent ahead. Then I give this advice: 'Give to the poor, and thou shalt have treasure in heaven.'[11] You will not remain without treasure, but what you possess on earth with anxiety you shall have with security in heaven. Therefore, transport your possessions. My advice is for preservation, not for loss. 'You shall have,' says He, 'treasure in heaven; and come, follow me.' 'Follow me,' so that I may lead you to your

---
10 Matt. 24.35.
11 Matt. 19.21.

treasure. This is not a loss, but a profit. Why do men remain silent? Let them hear what they ought to fear, or, having experienced it, let them so act as to have no reason to fear. Let them transfer their treasure to heaven. You are sowing grain in the field. Then comes your friend who knows the nature of the grain and of the soil, and he shows you how unskilled you are. He says to you: 'What have you done? You have sown the grain in low ground. The soil is moist. What you have sown will rot, and you will lose your labor.' You ask him: 'What, therefore, should I do?' 'Change to higher ground,' he replies. Do you, therefore, give heed to the advice of a friend with regard to your grain, yet give no heed to God when He advises you with regard to your heart? Are you afraid to sow your grain in the earth, but ready to lose your heart in the earth? Behold, when the Lord your God gives you counsel with regard to your heart, He says: 'For where your treasure is, there your heart also will be.' He bids you lift up your heart to heaven, lest it rot in the earth. This is the counsel of salvation, not of destruction.

(8) If this is true, then how regretful are those who have not acted accordingly! How are they reproaching themselves now? They are saying to themselves: 'We could have stored in heaven what we have lost on earth.' An enemy has broken into the house. Could he have broken into heaven? He has killed the servant who was guarding the treasure. Could he have killed the Lord who would have been preserving it 'where a thief does not approach, and the moth does not consume'? How many are now saying: 'We could have saved our treasure; we could have stored it up where we ourselves would shortly arrive without fear of losing it. Why did we not listen to our Lord? Why did we disregard our Father's admonition? Now we have experienced the enemy's incursion.' So, if this is the advice, let us not be slow to follow such

excellent counsel. If our possessions are to be carried away, let us transfer them to a place where we shall not lose them. The poor to whom we give alms! With regard to us, what else are they but porters through whom we transfer our goods from earth to heaven? Give away your treasure. Give it to a porter. He will bear to heaven what you give him on earth. But you will say to me: 'How does he bear it to heaven, for I see that he consumes it by eating?' Certainly, he eats it. It is by eating it, and not by keeping it, that he bears it to heaven. Have you forgotten the words, 'Come, blessed of my Father, take possession of the kingdom . . . For I was hungry and you gave me to eat . . . When you did it for one of these, the least of my brethren, you did it for me'?[12] If you have not despised a man who was begging of you, remember to whom your alms has come, for Christ says: 'When you did it for one of these, the least of my brethren, you did it for me.' Christ has received what you have given; He who has given you wherewith to give has received what you have given; He who will at length give you Himself has received what you have given.

(9) Indeed, my dear brethren, I have repeatedly called your attention to this text in the Divine Scripture, for, I confess, it impresses me very much, and I am obliged to remind you of it very often. I beseech you to reflect on what our Lord Jesus Christ Himself says, namely that, when He will have come to the judgment at the end of the world, He will assemble all the peoples in His presence. He will then divide all men into two classes, and He will place some at his right hand and others at his left, and He will say to those at the right hand: 'Come, blessed of my Father, take possession of the kingdom which has been prepared for you

---

12 Matt. 25.34-40.

from the foundation of the world,' but to those at the left hand: 'Depart unto the everlasting fire which was prepared for the devil and his angels.' Seek out the reasons for such a reward or for such a punishment, namely, 'Take possession of the kingdom,' and 'Depart unto everlasting fire.' Why are the former to take possession of the kingdom? Because 'I was hungry and you gave me to eat.' And why must the latter depart unto everlasting fire? Because 'I was hungry and you did not give me to eat.' What, I ask you, does this imply? I understand its import with regard to those who are to take possession of the kingdom. They are to possess the kingdom because, like good and faithful Christians, they did not disregard the Lord's words, but gave alms, and did so with the confident hope of receiving the promised rewards. For, even if they had not done this, their moral life could still not rightly be called entirely barren. Indeed, they may have been chaste, they may not have been drunkards or defrauders, they may have kept themselves free from evil deeds, but, if they had not added almsgiving, their lives would have remained fruitless. In that case, they would indeed have observed the command, 'Turn away from evil,' but they would not have observed its complement, 'And do good.'[13] Yet, not even to such as those does He say: 'Come, take possession of the kingdom; for you have lived chastely, you have defrauded no man, you have not oppressed any poor man, you have not plundered any man's property, you have deceived no one by an oath.' That is not what He said. Here are His words: 'Take possession of the kingdom, for I was hungry and you gave me eat.' Since the Lord made no mention of the other commandments, but named only this one, how much greater than all the others must this one be! And now, with regard to those to whom it is said: 'Depart

---
13 Ps. 33.15.

unto the everlasting fire which was prepared for the devil and his angels.' Of how many sins could he accuse the ungodly, if they were to ask Him: 'Why are we departing into everlasting fire?' He could have retorted: 'Adulterers, murderers, defrauders, impious, blasphemers, unbelievers, why do you ask the reason?' But He said none of those things; He said merely: 'Because I was hungry, and you did not give me to eat.'

(10) I see that you are astonished, as I, also, am astonished. The matter is certainly astonishing. To the best of my ability, I am deducing the reason for this astonishing matter. And I shall not keep it hidden from you. It is written: 'As water quenches fire, so does almsgiving quench sin.'[14] It is also written: 'Shut up alms in the heart of a poor man, and it shall supplicate the Lord for thee.'[15] Likewise it is written: 'O king, hear my counsel, and redeem thy sins with alms.'[16] In the Divine Scripture, there are many other passages by which we could show that almsgiving is of much avail for the quenching and erasing of sins. To those, then, whom He is about to condemn—or, rather, to those whom He is about to reward with a crown—He ascribes only almsgiving. It is as though He were to say: 'If I were to examine you closely, and weigh your deeds and scrutinize them diligently, I could hardly fail to find reason to condemn you. Nevertheless, enter into the kingdom, "for I was hungry and you gave me to eat."' Therefore, brethren, you will enter the kingdom of heaven, not because you have not sinned, but because you have redeemed your sins by almsgiving. Then to the others, He said: 'Depart unto the everlasting fire which was prepared for the devil and his angels.'

---
14 Eccli. 3.33.
15 Eccli. 29.15.
16 Dan. 4.24.

And these—since they are evil-doers, sinners since long ago, but only recently filled with fear, and now adverting to their sins—how could they dare to say that they are being undeservedly condemned, that this sentence is being unjustly pronounced against them by so just a Judge? Examining their conscience and gazing at all the wounds of their souls, how could they dare to say: 'We are unjustly condemned?' Of them it has been said in the Book of Wisdom: 'Their iniquities shall stand against them to convict them.'[17] Of course, they will see that they are being justly condemned for their sins and transgressions, but it will be as though He were saying to them: 'No, the reason is not what you think it to be. The reason is this: "Because I was hungry and you did not give me to eat." If you had turned away from all those evil deeds of yours and had turned to Me and had redeemed all those sins and transgressions by giving alms, your almsgiving would now deliver you and free you from the punishment due to such great crimes. For, "Blessed are the merciful, for they shall obtain mercy."[18] But now, "Depart unto the everlasting fire," for "Judgment without mercy to him who has not shown mercy." '[19]

(11) My brethren, this is what I would recommend to you: Give earthly bread, and knock at the door for the Bread of Heaven, which is the Lord, for He says: 'I am the bread of life.'[20] But, how will He give it to you unless you give to one who is in need? Someone needs aid from you; you need aid from another. Since you need another's aid, the man who needs your aid needs the aid of one who is himself in need of aid. But, He whose aid you need is Himself

---
17 Wisd. 4.20.
18 Matt. 5.7.
19 James 2.13.
20 John 6.35.

in need of aid from no one. Do what may be done for you. Here there is no room for those partial reproaches with which friends usually remind one another of favors bestowed. 'I did you a favor,' says one. 'And I did *you* a favor,' the other replies. A man wants us to do him a favor because he has already done some favor for us. God needs nothing from any man, and He is therefore the true Lord. 'I have said to the Lord: thou art my God, for thou hast no need of my goods.'[21] Although He is Lord, and the true Lord, and has no need of our goods, He nevertheless has deigned to be hungry in the persons of the poor, in order that we may be able to do something for Him. He says: 'I was hungry and you gave me to eat . . . Lord, when did we see thee hungry? . . . When you did it for one of these, the least of my brethren, you did it for me.'[22] Briefly, then: Let men hear and rightly consider how meritorious it is to have fed Christ when He was hungry, and how sinful it is to have despised Christ when he was hungry.

(12) Repentance for sins certainly changes men for the better. But, even that repentance seems to be of no avail if it is barren of works of mercy. The Truth gives testimony of this through the voice of John, who said to those who were coming to him: 'Brood of vipers! who has shown you how to flee from the wrath to come? Bring forth therefore fruits befitting repentance, and do not say, "We have Abraham for our father." For I say to you that God is able out of these stones to raise up children to Abraham. For even now the axe is laid at the root of the trees; every tree, therefore, that is not bringing forth good fruit, shall be cut down and thrown into the fire.' Of course this is the fruit of which he speaks above, where he says: 'Bring forth fruits befitting

---
21 Ps. 15.2.
22 Matt. 25.35-40.

repentance.' Therefore, whoever does not bring forth this fruit has no reason for believing that he is gaining forgiveness of his sins through barren repentance. Indeed, John straightway points out what these fruits are, for, after those words of his, the multitudes asked him, saying: 'What then are we to do?' In other words, they asked him: What are those fruits for which you frighten us, and exhort us to bring forth? And in answer, he said to them: 'Let him who has two tunics share with him who has none; and let him who has food do likewise.' My brethren, what could be plainer, more certain or definite than this? What, then, is the import of what he says above: 'Every tree that is not bringing forth good fruit, shall be cut down and thrown into the fire'? What meaning can it have but the same as that which those at the left hand will hear, namely: 'Depart into the everlasting fire . . . for I was hungry, and you did not give me to eat.' So, a withdrawal from sins is not enough if you neglect to heal past offenses, as it is written: 'Son, hast thou sinned? Do so no more.'[23] And, lest he should think himself secure by this only, it says also: 'And for thy former sins also pray that they may be forgiven thee.' But, what will prayer avail you, if you render yourself unworthy of being heard, by not bringing forth fruits befitting repentance, so that you will be cut down and thrown into the fire? If, therefore, you wish to be heard when you pray for forgiveness for your sins, 'forgive, and you shall be forgiven; give, and it shall be given to you.'[24]

23 Eccli. 21.1.
24 Luke 6.37-8.

SERMON 61

On Almsgiving

(1) In the pasage of the Holy Gospel which has been read to us,¹ the Lord exhorts us to pray. He says: 'Ask, and you shall receive; seek, and you shall find; knock, and it shall be opened to you. For everyone who asks, receives; and he who seeks, finds; and to him who knocks, it shall be opened. Or what man is there among you, who, if his son asks him for bread, will hand him a stone; or if he asks for a fish, will hand him a serpent; or when he asks for an egg, will hand him a scorpion? Therefore, if you, although you are evil, know how to give good gifts to your children, how much more will your Father who is in heaven give good things to those who ask Him.'² An astonishing thing, brethren. We are evil, yet we have a good Father. What could be plainer? We have heard our description, for the Lord says: 'Although you are evil, you know how to give good gifts to your children.' Yet, see what kind of Father He shows to those whom He has called evil: 'How much more will your Father who is in heaven?' Father of whom? The Father of those who are evil. And what kind of Father? 'No one is good, but God only.'³

(2) Therefore, brethren, although we are evil, we have a good Father, in order that we may not remain evil forever.

---
1 See Sermon 60, n. 6.
2 Matt. 7.7-11; Luke 11.12.
3 Luke 18.19.

No evil man does good. And, if no evil man does good, how could an evil man make himself good? He who is eternally good can make an evil man good. 'Heal me, O Lord, and I shall be healed: save me, and I shall be saved.'[4] Why do the vain give me this vain counsel, namely: You can save yourself if you wish to do so?[5] Rather: 'Heal me, O Lord, and I shall be healed.' We have been created good by One who is good, for 'God made man right.'[6] Through our own free will we have become evil. It was in our power to change ourselves from good to evil, and we shall be able to be changed from evil to good. But He who is eternally good— He it is that makes an evil man good. Of himself, man is unable to heal himself by his own will. You do not seek a physician for injuring yourself, but, when you have wounded yourself, you seek a healer. But even though we are evil, we know how to give our children the goods that are seasonable for them, goods that are temporal, corporal, carnal. Even those things are good. Who doubts it? A fish, an egg, bread, grain, light itself, and the very air we breathe are good. Even riches, through which men become haughty, and loath to recognize other men as their equals—yes, I say, through which men become haughty, and enamored of distinctive raiment rather than mindful of the skin that is common to all men—even riches are good. And all those goods

---

4 Jer. 17.14.
5 A reference to the Pelagians, who 'say that when a man has learned God's precepts in this life, then, merely through the free choice of his will, and without the aid of the Saviour's grace, he is able to attain such perfect righteousness that he has no further need of saying: *"Forgive us our debts,"* and that the next petition, *"Lead us not into temptation,"* is not to be understood as meaning that we ought to beseech divine aid lest we fall into sin when we are tempted, but that the mere will of man suffices for this, as though the Apostle had erred in saying: *"Not of him who wills nor of him who runs, but of God showing mercy"*' (*Epist.* 176.2; cf. Rom. 9.16).
6 Eccle. 7.30.

which I have mentioned can be possessed alike by good or evil men. But, although they are good, they cannot make men good.

(3) There is, therefore, a good which can make you good, and there is a good through which you can do good. The good which can make a man good is God, for it is only He who is eternally good who can make a man good. Therefore, in order to be good, call upon God. Yet, there is another kind of good. It is the good through which you may do good; it is whatever you possess. Gold and silver are good, but they are not the kind of good that can make you good. They are the kind of good through which you can do good. You have gold, you have silver, yet you are craving for gold and silver. You have them, and you are craving for them. You are full, yet you crave for more. That is not wealth; it is a disease. Men suffer from a disease in which they are full of fluid, and yet are thirsty. How can you be happy with riches when you have this dropsical craving? Yes, you have gold, and it is good. But then you have, not the kind of good by which you become good, but the kind of good through which you may do good. But, you will ask, what good can I do with gold? Have you not heard the Psalm: 'He has distributed, he has given to the poor: his justice remains for ever and ever.'[7] This is good; this is the kind of good by which you are good through righteousness. If you possess the good by which you become good, do good with the good through which you are not become good. You have money? Give it away. By giving it away, you increase your justice, for 'He has distributed, he has given to the poor: his justice remains for ever and ever.' See what is lessened, and what is increased. Money is lessened; justice is increased. There is a lessening of that which you would

---
7 Ps. 111.9.

have to give up, a lessening of that which you would have to leave behind; there is an increase of that which you will possess for ever and ever.

(4) I am telling you how to make profits. Learn how to trade. Do you praise the merchant who sells lead and acquires gold? Then why not praise the trader who gives away money and acquires righteousness? But, you will say: 'Since I do not have righteousness, I do not give away my money. Let the man who has righteousness give his money away. But I do not have righteousness; let me at least keep my money.' Is it precisely because you do not have righteousness that you refuse to give away your money? Rather, give it away so that you may have righteousness. From whom, indeed, will you receive righteousness except from God, the source of righteousness? Therefore, if you would have righteousness, be a beggar in the sight of God, for, in the Gospel just read to us, He admonished you to ask, to seek, and to knock. He knew you were a beggar dependent on Him. And behold! like a householder and a rich magnate—rich in spiritual and everlasting goods—He exhorts you and tells you to ask, to seek, and to knock. 'He who asks, receives; he who seeks, finds; and to him who knocks, it shall be opened.' He exhorts you to ask. Will He refuse your petition?

(5) Consider a similitude that exhorts us to pray. For instance, the comparison with a contrary case, such as that of the unjust rich man of whom the Lord says: 'In a town there was a certain judge who neither feared God nor respected man.'[8] Every day a certain widow used to importune him, and say: 'Render me a just decision.' For a while he refused, but she did not desist. And, what he would not do as a favor, he did because of the annoyance.

---
8 Cf. Luke 18.2.

From a contrary case, therefore, the Lord thus admonishes us to ask.

(6) He goes on to illustrate. A man to whom a guest had come went to the home of his friend, and began to knock, and to say: 'A guest has arrived at my house. Lend me three loaves.'[9] The friend answered: 'I am already in bed, and my servants also are in bed. The man does not desist. He remains, he persists, he knocks, he begs as one friend from another. And what does the Lord say of this? He says: 'I say to you that he rises, and—not through friendship, but on account of the importunity—gives him as many as he wants.' Not through friendship—although he is a friend— but on account of the importunity. What is the force of the expression, 'on account of the importunity'? It means: Because he did not cease to knock, because he did not turn away even after his request was refused. He who was unwilling to give granted the request because the other did not weaken in his petition. How much more will God give, who is good, who exhorts us to ask, who is displeased if we ask not? And when, sometimes, He delays the giving for a little while, He is not denying His gifts; He is making them more desirable. There is an added pleasure in obtaining gifts that have been long desired; what is quickly obtained is less appreciated. Ask, seek, persevere. By asking and seeking, you increase your receptive capacity. What God does not will to give you at once He is preserving for you, so that you may learn to yearn greatly for things that are great. Therefore, 'we ought always to pray, and not to faint.'[10]

(7) Therefore, my brethren, if God has made us His beggars by admonishing and exhorting and commanding

---
9 Cf. Luke 15.11.
10 Cf. Luke 18.1.

us to ask, to seek, and to knock, let us, in turn, consider those who ask from us. We make petitions. From whom do we ask? What are we who ask? What do we ask for? From whom? What are we? What do we ask? We ask of the good God. We are evil, but we ask for justice, whereby to become good. Yes, we ask for that which we may possess forever, that through which we shall never again be in want, once we have been filled with it. Let us hunger and thirst, so that we may be filled with that for which we are asking. By hungering and thristing, let us ask, seek, and knock, for, 'Blessed are they who hunger and thirst, for justice.'[11] Whereby are they blessed? Are they blessed because they are hungry and thirsty? Is want ever a blessing? They are blessed, not because they are hungry and thirsty, but because they shall be filled. But let hunger precede the fullness, lest loathing keep us away from the bread.

(8) Now, we have told you from whom it is that we ask, who we are that ask, and what it is that we ask for. But something is asked from us also. Truly, we are God's beggars. And, in order that He may receive His beggars, let us also take notice of ours. And in this case—when some one is asking from us—let us consider who the askers are, from whom they are asking, and what they are asking for. Who are the askers? They are men. From whom do they ask? From men. Who are the askers? Mortals. From whom do they ask? Mortals. Who are the askers? Frail beings. From whom do they ask? From frail beings. Who are the askers? Wretched beings. From whom do they ask? From wretched beings. Except with regard to worldly wealth, the askers are in the same condition as those from whom they ask. How impudent of you to ask from your Lord while

---

11 Matt. 5.6.

you ignore your own equals! I, says the proud man, am a different kind of man; far be it from me to be on the same level as that man. Clad in silken robes, the haughty man thus speaks of that other man who is clad in rags. Now, I prescind from your clothing. I am not asking what appearance you make when clothed. I am asking about the condition in which you were born. Both of you were naked; both of you were feeble; both of you were beginning a life of misery; hence, both of you were mewling.

(9) You, O rich man, reflect upon your life's beginning. Consider whether you brought any possession with you. You came, and you found a great deal here. But, I pray you, tell us what you brought with you. Or, if you are ashamed to tell us that, then listen to the Apostle: 'We brought nothing into this world.'[12] He says: 'We brought nothing into this world.' Perhaps you will take something away with you, for, although you brought nothing in with you, you have found many things here? Perhaps, because of your love of riches, you are anxious to avow this? Then listen. Let the Apostle—who does not flatter you—tell you this: 'We brought nothing into this world' (he means, when we were born); 'Neither can we take anything out of it' (that is, when we depart from this world). You brought nothing into this world, and you shall take nothing out from it. Then, why are you haughty toward a poor man? When children are born, let the parents, the servants, the dependents, and the obsequious crowd be withdrawn; then try to distinguish the rich from the poor among the mewling infants. Let a rich woman and a poor woman give birth to children at the same time. Let them take no notice of those children. Let them go away from those children for a while.

---

12 1 Tim. 6.7.

Then let them return and distinguish one child from the other. At any rate, O rich man, you brought nothing into this world. Neither can you take anything out of it. What I have said about infants, I say also about the dead. For instance, when by any chance old sepulchres are broken open, try to recognize the bones of the rich. Therefore, O rich man, listen to the Apostle: 'We brought nothing into this world.' Acknowledge that. It is true. 'And neither can we take anything out of it.' Acknowledge that. That also is true.

(10) What does he say next? 'Having food and clothing, let us be content therewith; for those who desire to become rich fall into temptation and into many harmful desires, which plunge a man into destruction and damnation. Indeed covetousness is the root of all evils; and some, pursuing it, have strayed from the faith.'[13] Note what they have cast away. You are sorry because they have cast it away. But, note also in what they have involved themselves. Give heed. 'They have strayed from the faith; and they have involved themselves in many troubles.' Who have done this? Those who desire to become rich. To be rich is one thing; to desire to become rich is something else. A man born of rich parents is rich. However, he is rich, not because he desired it, but because many others have made him their heir. I can see his wealth; I do not question his desires. It is covetousness that is here condemned—not gold or silver or riches, but covetousness. As to those who do not desire to become rich, or who make no effort to become rich, or who are not incited by covetous desires or inflamed with fires of avarice, but who are nevertheless rich—let these also listen to the Apostle. This has been read today: 'Charge the

---

13 Cf. 1 Tim. 6.8-10.

rich of this world.'[14] Charge them what? Charge them most especially not to be proud. Riches beget nothing else so much as pride. Every kind of fruit, every kind of seed, every kind of grain, every kind of tree has its own worm. Of one kind is the worm of the apple; of another, the worm of the pear; of another, the worm of the bean; of another, the worm of the wheat. The worm of riches is pride.

(11) Therefore: 'Charge the rich of this world not to be proud.' He has banned the vice of riches; now let him point out their proper use. 'Not to be proud.' How are they to avoid it? By the advice which immediately follows: 'And not to trust in the uncertainty of riches.' They who do not trust in the uncertainty of riches are not proud. If they are not high-minded, let them fear.[15] If they fear, they are not high-minded. How many were rich yesterday, and are poor today! How many go to bed rich, and—because robbers have come and have taken all their goods—awaken poor! Therefore: 'Charge them not to trust in the uncertainty of riches, but in the living God, who provides all things in abundance for our enjoyment.'

He provides both temporal things and eternal—but, the eternal things for enjoyment, and the temporal things for our use; the temporal things as to travelers, the eternal things as to inhabitants; the temporal things whereby we may do good, and the eternal things whereby we may become good. Let the rich, therefore, do this: Let them not become proud, nor trust in the uncertainty of riches, but let them trust in the living God, who provides all things in abundance for our enjoyment. Let them do this. What should they do with what they have? Hear what they should do: 'Let them be rich in good works; let them give readily.' They have the means.

---
14 1 Tim. 6.17.
15 Cf. Rom. 11.20.

Then, why do they not do it? Poverty is an affliction. Let the rich give readily, for they have the means. Let them 'share with others.' In other words, let them recognize their fellow mortals as their equals. Let them 'share with others, and provide for themselves a good foundation against the time to come.' It is not that I wish to despoil them or to deprive them of clothing or to leave them empty when I tell you that the Apostle says: 'Let them give readily; let them share with others.' I am showing them how to trade with profit when I show them this: 'Let them provide for themselves.' I do not wish them to remain poor. I am not asking them to destroy their riches. I am showing them whither to transfer them. Let them 'provide for themselves a good foundation against the time to come, in order that they may lay hold on the true life.' Therefore, the present life is a false life. Let them lay hold on the true life. For, 'Vanity of vanities, and all is vanity. What abundance has man in all his labor in which he labors under the sun?'[16] The true life, therefore, must be laid hold on; our riches must be transferred to the region of the true life, in order that we may there find what we have here given away. He exchanges them who changes us.

(12) Therefore, my brethren, give to the poor. 'Having food and clothing, with these let us be content.' The rich man gets nothing from his riches except what the poor man is asking him for, namely, food and clothing. What more do you get from all that you possess? You have obtained the necessary food and clothing. I mean what is necssary, not what is useless or superfluous. What more do you get from your riches? Tell me that. At any rate, the time will come when all your possessions will be superfluous for you. Suppose that all your superfluities are necessities for the poor. You say

---
16 Eccle. 1.2.

that your meals are expensive, for you feed on costly fare. And what does the poor man eat? Cheap food. The poor man eats cheap food. But, says the rich man, I feed on costly viands. When both of you have eaten to the full, then I ask you this question: The costly food that enters into you, what does it become after it has entered? Is it not true that if we had windows to the belly we should blush for all the costly food with which you have been sated? The poor man is hungry, and so is the rich man; the poor man seeks to satisfy his hunger, and so does the rich man. But the poor man is satisfied with cheap food, the rich man is filled with costly victuals. Both of them are equally satisfied; both of them attain the goal they are seeking to reach. But the former reaches it by a short cut; the latter, in a roundabout way. But, you will say: 'I relish the costly viands better.' Since you are fastidious, you are not easily satisfied, for you know not the savor which hunger seasons. In saying this, I do not mean to compel the rich to eat the same kind of food as the poor, or to have the same kind of meals as the poor. Let the rich follow the custom induced through their debility, but let them regret that they are unable to do otherwise. They would be healthier if they could do otherwise. If the poor man is not proud of his beggary, why should you be proud of your debility? Yes, use foods that are choice and costly, for you have become accustomed to them; you are unable to do otherwise and you would become sick if you were to change your custom. You are allowed to do this. But, use also what is superfluous for you; give it to the poor who need it. Use the costly foods; give the cheap food to the poor. The poor man is hopefully depending on you; you are hopefully depending on God. The poor man is depending on a hand which—like his own—was made; you are depending on the hand that made you. And it made not only you, but the beggar as well. It has set one path for both of you, namely, this present life. You have met as companions; you are treading the same path. He is carrying nothing; you are overburdened. He is carrying nothing with him; you are carrying more than you need. You are laden; give him some of what you have. Thus, you feed him and you lighten your own burden.

(13) Therefore, give to the poor. I beg you, I admonish you, I charge you, I command you to give. Whatever you wish to give away, give it to the poor. I shall not conceal from you, brethren, the reason why I deemed it necessary to deliver this discourse to you. As long as we have been here, the poor have been beseeching us on our way to the church and on our return, and have been asking us to speak to you so that they may receive something from you. They have urged us to speak to you. When they see that they are receiving nothing from you, they think that we are laboring in vain among you. They expect to receive something even from us. We give as much as we have; we give in so far as we are able.[17] But, are we capable of supplying their needs? Because we are not able to supply their needs, we are, as it were, their ambassadors to you. You have listened; you have applauded. Thanks be to God. You have received the seed. You have responded. That praise of yours increases our obligation, and sends us into danger. We bear it, and tremble beneath it. Yet, my dear brethren, that praise of yours is but as the leaves of the trees. The fruit is being sought for.

---

17 Augustine 'was ever mindful of his fellow poor and for them he spent from the same funds from which he spent for himself and all who lived with him, that is, either from the revenues from the possessions of the church or from the offerings of the faithful. . . . He made no will, because as a poor man of God he had nothing from which to make it' (Possidius, *S. Augustini vita.* 23, 31, translated by Weiskotten, 1919).

SERMON 72

On Almsgiving

(1) The Lord Jesus Christ has admonished us to be good trees, and to be able to bear good fruit, for He says: 'Either make the tree good and its fruit good, or make the tree bad and its fruit bad; for by its fruit the tree is known.'[1] When He says: 'Make the tree good and its fruit good,' this is not a mere admonition; it is a salutary precept which must be obeyed. But, as to His saying: 'Make the tree bad and its fruit bad,' this is not a precept commanding you to do so; it is a caution against your doing so. For He made this pronouncement against those who thought that, although they were evil, they could say good things and do good works. The Lord Jesus Christ says that this is impossible, for, in order that a man's works may be changed, the man himself must first be changed. If a man remains evil, he cannot do good works; if he remains good, he cannot have bad works.

(2) But, inasmuch as 'Christ has died for the wicked,'[2] what man has been found good by the Lord? He therefore found all trees bad, but, to those who believe in His name, 'he gave the power of becoming children of God.'[3] Hence, whoever is now a good man (that is to say, a good tree) was found bad and has been made good. If the Lord had

---

1 Matt. 12.33.
2 Rom. 5.6.
3 John 1.12.

willed to root up the bad trees when He came, what tree would have been left which would not deserve to be rooted up? But He came to dispense mercy beforehand, so that he might afterwards dispense justice, for He is the Lord to whom the Psalmist says: 'Mercy and judgment 1 will sing to thee, O Lord.'[4] He therefore gave remission of sins to those who believe. Of them, He would not even demand an accounting of previous decrees.[5] He gave remission of sins; He made the trees good. He delayed the axe; He removed the threat.

(3) This is the axe of which John speaks when He says: 'Even now the axe is laid at the root of the trees. Every tree that is not bringing forth good fruit shall be cut down and thrown into the fire.'[6] This is the axe of which the householder in the Gospel gives a threat when he says: 'Behold, for three years now I have been coming to this tree, and I find no fruit on it. Now I must clear the place. Let it therefore be cut down.' And the husbandman intercedes, saying: 'Sir, let it alone this year too. I shall dig around it and manure it. If it bear fruit, all is well; but if it does not, then you will come and cut it down.'[7] As though for three years—that is, in three different eras—the Lord has visited the human race. The first era was before the Law; the second, under the Law; the third is now, which is the time of grace.[8] If He did not visit the human race before the Law, whence Abel and Enoch and Noe? whence Abraham and Isaac and Jacob, whose Lord He was pleased to call himself? For, as though He were the God of three men, He to whom all the nations belonged says: 'I am the God of Abraham and Isaac and Jacob.'[9] If He

---

4 Ps. 100.1.
5 Col. 2.14.
6 Matt. 3.10.
7 Luke 13.7-9.
8 See above, *Commentary* 1.16.49, n. 16.
9 Exod. 3.15.

did not visit under the Law, He would not have even given the Law. After the Law, the Householder himself came. He suffered, He died, He rose again. He gave the Holy Spirit, and He caused the Gospel to be preached throughout the whole world. Yet, a certain tree remained barren, for there is still a certain portion of the human race that refuses to amend its ways. The husbandman is interceding; the Apostle is praying for the people. He says: 'I bend my knees to the Father for you . . . so that, being rooted and grounded in love, you may be able to comprehend with all the saints what is the breadth and length and height and depth, and to know Christ's love which surpasses knowledge, in order that you may be filled unto all the fullness of God.'[10] By bending the knee, he is making intercession for us with the Householder, lest we be rooted up. Wherefore, since of necessity He will come, let us so live that He will find us bearing fruit. The digging around the tree signifies the humility of the penitent, for every ditch is low. The manure signifies the filthy robe of repentance. Indeed, what is more filthy than manure? And yet, if you use it rightly, what is more fertilizing?

(4) Let each man, therefore, be a good tree. Let him not think that he is bearing good fruit, if he continues to be a bad tree. No fruit is good except the fruit of a good tree. Change the heart, and the work will be changed. Root out covetousness, and plant charity. For, just as covetousness is the root of all evils,[11] so is charity the root of all good. Why, then, do men indulge in murmurings and contentions, asking: 'What is good?' Oh, that you knew what the good is! What you wish to have is not very good. What you do not wish to be, that is the good. You wish to have bodily health, and bodily health is good. However, do not regard as a great good that

---
10 Eph. 3.14-19.
11 1 Tim. 6.10.

which an evil man possesses. You long to have gold and silver. These also, I admit, are good, provided that you make good use of them. But, if you are an evil man, you are not making good use of them. Accordingly, gold and silver are bad for the bad and good for the good—not that gold or silver makes men good, but because it finds them good and is put to good use. You wish to have honor, and that also is good—if you make good use of it. In how many cases has honor been the occasion of destruction! And in how many cases has it been the ministry of a good work!

(5) Therefore, let us distinguish and compare those goods, if we can, for we are speaking about the good trees. And first of all, in this regard there is nothing which anyone ought to consider more important than to fix his attention on himself, to learn his own case, to examine himself, to scrutinize himself, to search into himself, to discover himself, and then to kill what seems bad, and select and plant what seems good. For, when a man finds himself empty of the better things, how could he be greedy for external goods? And what is the advantage of a locker stocked with goods, if one's conscience is empty? Do you wish to have goods, and yet do not wish to be good? Do you not see that you ought to blush for the goods which you have, if your house is full of goods but has an evil owner in you? Indeed, what is it that you would wish to have evil? Tell me that. Absolutely nothing—neither wife nor son nor daughter, neither man-servant nor maid-servant, neither villa nor tunic, nor even a shoe. Yet, you are willing to have your soul evil. I beg you, place more value on your soul than on your shoe. Everything elegant and beautiful that lies within your sight is prized by you; yet, do you regard yourself as vile and filthy? If the goods with which your house is filled—the goods which you longed to possess and which you have feared to lose—

if those goods could give you their answer, would they not cry out to you, saying: 'Just as you wish to have us good, so do we wish to have our owner good?' Without the sound of voice, they are importuning your Lord against you, saying: 'Behold, you have given so many good things to this man; and he himself is bad. What good is his wealth doing him, as long as he has not Him who has given all things?'

(6) Admonished by—and perhaps smarting under—those words of mine, some one asks what a good is, what is its nature, and whence its goodness. It is well that you have understood that you ought to ask that question. In reply to the questioner, I shall say: What you cannot lose unless you are willing to lose it—that is a good. Even when you are unwilling, you can lose gold, you can lose a house, you can lose honor, you can lose even bodily health. But the good wherewith you are truly good, this you can neither receive nor lose unless you are willing to do so. I therefore ask what kind of good is this. One of the Psalms teaches us an important truth, and perhaps it is the answer to our question. It says: 'O you children of men, how long will you be dull of heart?'[12] How long did that tree continue—that tree of the three years' barrenness? 'O you children of men, how long will you be dull of heart?' What does this dullness of heart mean? 'Why do you love vanity, and seek after lying?' In response to these queries, it tells us what must be sought: 'Know that the Lord has magnified his Holy One.' Christ has now come; He has been magnified; He has risen and has ascended into heaven; His name is now being preached throughout the world. How long will you be dull of heart? Let these past happenings be sufficient. Now that the Holy One has been magnified, how long will you be dull of heart? After three years, what is left but the axe? 'How long will

---

12 Ps. 4.3-4.

you be dull of heart? Why do you love vanity, and seek after lying?' Even after Christ has been magnified, are the vain things, the useless things, the pompous and the fleeting things still being sought after? Truth is now crying aloud; is vanity still being sought after? 'How long will you be dull of heart?'

(7) Deservedly is this world being sorely scourged, for now the world knows its Master's words. He says: 'And the servant who did not know his master's will, but did things deserving of stripes, will be beaten with few stripes.[13] Why? In order that he may seek to know his master's will. The servant who did not know his master's will (that is, the world before God had magnified His Holy One, for it was then a servant not knowing its Master's will), was, accordingly, beaten with few stripes. But the servant who already knows his master's will (that is, the world today, and since the day God magnified His Holy One), and is not doing that Master's will—that servant will be beaten with many stripes. What wonder that the world is being beaten with many stripes? It is a servant who knows his master's will, yet is doing things deserving of stripes. Let it not refuse, therefore, to be beaten with many stripes, for, if it unjustly refuses to heed its Teacher, it will justly suffer punishment from its Chastiser. Therefore, since it knows that it is deserving of stripes, let it not murmur against its Chastiser, so that it may gain mercy through Christ our Lord, who lives and reigns with God the Father and the Holy Spirit for ever and ever. Amen.

---

13 Luke 12.47-48.

SERMON 94

The Slothful Servant
(Matt. 25.14-30)

Their Lordships, my brethren and fellow bishops, have deigned to visit us and to gladden us by their presence, but I know not why they are unwilling to aid me, although I am fatigued. Dearly beloved, I tell you this while they are listening, so that your hearing it may somehow so intercede with them on my behalf that they also will deliver a discourse when I ask them. May they give out what they have received; may they graciously consent to put it to use, rather than to make excuses. Meanwhile, be willing to listen to a few words from me, although I am fatigued and scarcely able to speak. Besides, we have a written list of favors received from God through the holy martyr. Let us willingly listen to the reading of that also.[1] What is it, then? What shall I say to you? In the Gospel, you have heard both the reward of the good servants and the punishment of the bad.[2] The fault of that servant who was reproved and severely punished

---

1 A written account of divine favors which had been received through the intercession of the martyr. In another sermon, Saint Augustine explicitly states that it was the custom to read such a list to the assembled congregation: 'We are accustomed to hear written accounts of the miracles of God which have been wrought through the prayers of the most blessed martyr, Stephen. Today, this account is the very presence of this man [who had been healed]. Instead of a written account, we have the news itself; instead of a paper, the man's face is shown. You know what it used to grieve you to see in this man. Rejoice now to read what you see in him here present' (*Sermo* 320). For further references, see *Sermones* 79, 321, 322, 323.
2 Matt. 25.14-30; Luke 19.12-27.

293

was this and this only, namely, that he would not put to use what he had received. He preserved it intact, but his master was looking for a profit from it. God is avaricious of our salvation. If such condemnation befalls the servant who did not use what he had received, what are they to expect who lose it? Therefore, we are dispensers. We expend; you receive. We expect a profit; on your part, live good lives, for that is the profit from our dispensing. Do not think that you are free from the obligation of dispensing. Of course, you cannot dispense your gifts as from this higher station of ours; but you can dispense them in whatever station you happen to be. When Christ is attacked, defend Him; give an answer to those who murmur; rebuke blasphemers, but keep yourselves far from any fellowship with them. If in this way you gain anybody, you are putting your gifts to use. In your own homes, take our place, for the title, *bishop*, signifies one who superintends, one who takes care of others by watching over them. In every home, therefore, a bishopric necessarily pertains to him who is the head of the household. It is a superintendence of the faith of the members of his household, lest any of them fall into heresy. It extends to the wife, to a son or a daughter; it extends also to a slave, for he also has been redeemed at so great a price. The apostolic teaching places the master above the slave, and the slave beneath the master,[3] but Christ has given the same price for each of them. Do not neglect even the lowliest among your household. With all vigilance, attend to the salvation of those who are yours. If you do this, you dispense your gifts. Then you will not be slothful servants; you will not fear that horrible condemnation.

---

3 Eph. 6.5; Tit. 2.9.

SERMON 109

The Adversary

(Matt. 5.25)

(1) We have heard the Gospel,[1] and therein we have heard the Lord rebuking those who 'know how to judge the face of the sky,'[2] but know not how to discover the time of the promise of the kingdom of heaven which is approaching. Of course, it was to the Jews that He gave this rebuke. But His utterance concerns us, also, for it is thus that our Lord Jesus Christ Himself began to preach His gospel: 'Repent, for the kingdom of heaven is at hand.'[3] In like manner, His precursor, John the Baptist, began to preach: 'Repent, for the kingdom of heaven is at hand.'[4] And the Lord now rebukes those who will not repent while the kingdom of heaven is approaching. As He Himself tells us: 'The kingdom of heaven will come unawares.'[5] And, again, He says: 'The kingdom of heaven is within you.'[6] Let all men, therefore, wisely heed His admonitions as a Teacher, lest they miss the time of His mercy as a Savior, for His mercy is now being dispensed as long as the human race is being spared. Man is being spared now, in order that he be converted and not be the kind of man that will be condemned. Only God knows when the end of the world

---
1 See *Sermon* 60, n. 6.
2 Luke 12.56.
3 Matt. 4.17.
4 Matt. 3.2.
5 Luke 17.20.
6 Luke 17.21.

will come. Now is the season of faith. I know not whether the end of the world will find any of us here. Perhaps it will not find us here. But the time is close at hand for every one of us, for we are mortal. We walk in the midst of mishaps; if we were made of glass, we should have less reason to fear mishaps. What is more fragile than a vessel of glass? Yet, it is preserved and lasts for ages. Although there is reason to fear a fall with regard to a vessel of glass, there is no reason to fear old age or fever with regard to it. Therefore, we are weaker and more frail than glass; for, from day to day, our frailty makes us fear all the mishaps that incessantly occur in human affairs. Even if those mishaps do not occur, time advances. A man can escape a blow; can he escape the stroke of death? He can escape what arises from without. But what originates within him—can that be driven away? Again, the entrails may engender worms, or some disease may suddenly seize him. Finally, when old age at length arrives, there is no way of putting it off.

(2) Let us, therefore, give heed to the Lord; let us do for ourselves what He has laid down for us. Let us see who is that adversary of whom He put us in fear, saying: 'If thou art going with thy adversary to the ruler, take pains to be quit of him on the way, lest perchance he deliver thee to the ruler, and the ruler deliver thee to the officer, and thou be cast into prison, whence thou shalt not come out until thou hast paid the last farthing.'[7] Who is this adversary? If he is the Devil, we have already been delivered from him. What a price has been given for us to be delivered from him! Speaking of this redemption of ours, the Apostle says on this point: 'He has rescued us from the power of darkness and transferred us into the kingdom of his beloved

---
7 Cf. Matt. 5.25; Luke 12.58.

Son.[8] We have been redeemed; we have renounced the Devil. How shall we take pains to be delivered from him, lest he make us captive sinners again? But he is not the adversary against whom He cautions us. In another passage, another Evangelist has worded the saying in such a way that we shall quickly see who this adversary is, if we combine both accounts and compare the words of one Evangelist with those of the other. Note what the Evangelist says in this passage: 'When thou are going with thy adversary to the ruler, take pains to be quit of him on the way.'[9] But the other Evangelist expresses the same saying in these words: 'Be in agreement with thy adversary quickly while thou art with him on the way.'[10] In both of the Evangelists, the rest of the discourse is alike: 'Lest thy adversary deliver thee to the judge, and the judge deliver thee to the officer, and the officer cast thee into prison.' Both Evangelists have given the same reason, but one of them has said: 'Take pains to be quit of him on the way,' and other has said: 'Be in agreement with him.' So, you cannot quit him unless you are in agreement with him. Do you wish to be quit of him? Then, be in agreement with him. Now, could the Devil be the adversary with whom a Christian ought to be in agreement?

(3) Let us try to find out, therefore, who is this opponent with whom we ought to be in agreement, lest he deliver us to the judge and the judge deliver us to the officer. Let us try to find him and be in agreement with him. If you are committing a sin, your adversary is the word of God. For instance, perhaps you may like to get drunk; it says to you: 'Don't do that.' You may like to frequent the circus

---
8 Col. 1.13.
9 Luke 12.58.
10 Matt. 5.25.
11 Exod. 20.13-16.

and indulge in frivolities; it says to you: 'Don't do that.' You may like to commit adultery; the word of God says to you: 'Don't do it.' In whatsoever sins you wish to follow your own will, it says to you: 'Don't do that.' It is the adversary of your will until it becomes the assurance of your salvation. Oh, what an honest and helpful adversary! It does not seek what we wish; it seeks what is good for us. It is our adversary so long as we are opposed to ourselves. So long as you are your own enemy, you have also the word of God as your enemy. Be a friend to yourself, and you are in agreement with it. 'Thou shalt not commit murder.' Heed that injunction, and you are in agreement with this adversary. 'Thou shalt not steal.' Heed that, and you are in agreement with him. 'Thou shalt not commit adultery.' Heed that, and you are in agreement with him. 'Thou shalt not bear false witness.' Heed that, and you are in agreement with him. 'Thou shalt not covet thy neighbor's wife.' Heed that, and you are in agreement with him. 'Thou shalt not covet thy neighbor's goods.' Heed that, and you are in agreement with him. In all these cases, you are in agreement with that adversary of yours. And what have you lost for yourself? Not only have you lost nothing, but you have even found yourself, for you had been lost. 'The way' is this present life. If we are in agreement with that adversary, if we consent with him, then, when 'the way' is ended, we shall not fear the judge, the officer, or the prison.

(4) When is 'the way' ended? Its ending is not at the same hour for all men. Every man has an hour when he must end his journey. This life has been called a journey. When you reach the end of this life, you have finished the journey. We have been traveling, for even to live is to go forward. Or perhaps you think that time moves onward and that we stand still? That cannot be so, for, just as time

moves onward, we also advance. The years do not come to us; rather, they glide away from us. Men are greatly mistaken when they say: 'This boy has little wisdom yet, but years are coming to him, and he will become wise.' Note what you say. You have said: 'Years are coming to him.' I can show that they are going away from him. See how easily I can prove it. Let us suppose that we know his allotted years from birth. To wish him well, let us suppose, for instance, that he is to live eighty years and is to reach old age. Then, write down: 'Eighty years.' Now, suppose he has lived one year. How many years have you in the total? Rather, how many did you have? Eighty. Subtract one. Suppose he has lived ten years. There are seventy left. Suppose he has lived twenty years. There are sixty left. The years have come to him, but what does that mean? They have come so that our years might go away. I say, the years come, so that they may go away; they do not come in order to remain with us. When they pass through us, they wear us down, and make us weaker and weaker. Such is 'the way' on which we are traveling. What are we to do about that adversary—which is the word of God! Be in harmony with that adversary, for you know not when your journey will end. And, when the journey is ended, there still remain the judge, the officer, and the prison. But, if you remain on good terms with your adversary and be of one mind with him, then—instead of a judge—you will find a father; instead of a cruel officer, you will find an angel who will bear you to the bosom of Abraham; instead of a prison, you will find paradise. How quickly you have changed everything while you were on 'the way,' because you have been in agreement with your adversary!

SERMON 346

On Life's Pilgrimage
(2 Cor. 5.6)

(1) Beloved brethren, let us join in recalling that the Apostle has said: 'As long as we are in the body we are exiles from the Lord, for we walk by faith and not by sight.'[1] For, the Lord Jesus Christ has said: 'I am the way, and the truth, and the life';[2] He has, therefore, willed that we walk through Him and to Him. Where, indeed, can we walk except on a way? And what is our destination except truth and life? But that life is the eternal life, for it alone deserves the name of life. In comparison with that life, the mortal life in which we now live is convincingly shown to be death; it is exceedingly variable and inconstant, weak and unstable, and it ends after a very brief course. Consequently, when that rich man had asked: 'Good Master, what good work should I do to attain eternal life?' the Lord replied: 'If thou wilt enter into life, keep the commandments.'[3] Of course, that man was already in some kind of life, for the Lord was not addressing a corpse or a man who was not alive. Yet, although He had made inquiry about attaining eternal life, the Lord did not say: 'If thou wilt enter into *eternal* life, keep the commandments.' Rather, He said: 'If thou wilt enter into life, keep the commandments.' He thus

---
1 2 Cor. 5.6.
2 John 14.6.
3 Matt. 19.16.

intended to signify that the life which is not eternal does not deserve even the name of life, because only the eternal life is a true life. Hence it is that, when the Apostle was advising that almsgiving be counseled to the rich, he said: 'Let them be rich in good works, let them give readily, let them share with others, let them provide for themselves a good foundation against the time to come, in order that they may lay hold on the true life.'⁴ What life did he call a true life, except the eternal life—the life which alone deserves to be called life, since it is the only happy life? The rich certainly possessed the present life in the abundance of its riches; yet, the Apostle said that they were to be counseled to 'lay hold on the true life.' Now, if he considered this present life a true life, he certainly would not have said: 'Let them provide for themselves a good foundation against the time to come, in order that they may lay hold on the true life.' For, in saying this, he gives no other caution but that the life of the rich is not a true life, although fools consider it not only a true life but also a happy one. But, if a life is not true, how can it be happy? A life is not a happy one unless it is true, and it is not true unless it is eternal. We can clearly see that the rich do not yet possess this eternal life through any delights whatever; hence they are counseled to lay hold on it through almsgiving, in order that they may at length hear: 'Come, blessed of my Father, take possession of the kingdom which has been prepared for you from the beginning of the world; for I was hungry and you gave me to eat.'⁵ Almost at once, the Lord Himself inferentially shows that this very kingdom is eternal life, for He says: 'These will go into everlasting fire, but the just will enter into everlasting life.'⁶

4 1 Tim. 6.18-19.
5 Matt. 25.34-35.
6 Matt. 25.46.

(2) Until we lay hold on that eternal life, 'we are exiles from the Lord, for we walk by faith and not by sight,' and the Lord says: 'I am the way, and the truth, and the life.' Our way is in faith, but the truth and the life are in sight. 'We now see through a mirror in an obscure manner, but then face to face.'[7] There is faith *now;* there will be sight *then.* The same Apostle says: 'Unto the progress of the inner man, to have Christ dwelling by faith in your hearts.'[8] This is 'the way'; by following it, 'we know in part.'[9] And he goes on to say: 'To know also Christ's love which surpasses all knowledge, in order that you may be filled unto all the fullness of God.'[10] That will be sight, for in that fullness, 'when that which is perfect has come, that which is imperfect will be done away with.'[11] Furthermore, he says: 'For you have died, and your life is hidden with Christ in God.'[12] That is faith. Then he adds this: 'When Christ, your life, shall appear, then you too will appear with him in glory.' That will be sight. And John also says: 'Beloved, now we are the children of God, and it has not appeared what we shall be.'[13] Then he continues: 'We know that, when he appears, we shall be like to him, for we shall see him just as he is.' The Lord Himself was speaking to the Jews when He said: 'I am the way, and the truth, and the life,' and among them were some who already believed in Him. So, He directed His words to those believers, and said: 'If you abide in my word, you shall be my disciples indeed, and you shall know the truth, and the truth shall make you free.'[14] They already

---

7 1 Cor. 13.12.
8 Eph. 3.16-17.
9 1 Cor. 13.9-10.
10 Eph. 3.19.
11 1 Cor. 13.10.
12 Col. 3.3.
13 1 John, 3.2.
14 John 8.31-32.

believed in Him, for the Evangelist thus relates it: 'Jesus therefore said to the Jews who believed in him, "If you abide in my word, you shall be my disciples indeed, and you shall know the truth, and the truth shall make you free."' They had already become His believers and had already begun, as it were, to walk in 'the way'—that is, they had already begun to walk in Christ. He is, therefore, exhorting them to reach a certain goal by continuing in that way. And what other goal does He mean but the one He mentions when He says: 'The truth shall make you free'? And what is this 'freeing' but the delivery from all vain fickleness and from all corruption of morals? The true life, therefore, is the eternal life. It is the life which we do not lay hold on as long as we are exiles from the Lord, but which we shall lay hold on if we most constantly abide in His word, for we are then walking in the Lord Himself through faith. With regard to his saying, 'I am the way,' this corresponds to His saying, 'If you abide in my word, you shall be my disciples indeed.' And with regard to His saying, 'I am the truth and the life,' this corresponds to His saying, 'You shall know the truth and the truth shall make you free.' My brethren, what then do I exhort you to do during your pilgrimage in this present life—that is, during the time of faith? I exhort you in no other words than in those of the Apostle when he says: 'Having therefore these promises, beloved, let us cleanse ourselves from all defilement of the flesh and of the spirit, perfecting holiness in the fear of God.'[15] Those who desire to have the light of the most pure and unchangeable truth supplied to them before they believe are like blind men who wish to see the corporeal light of the sun in order to be healed of their blindness. Just as the latter cannot see the light

---

15 2 Cor. 7.1.

of the sun until they are healed, so neither can men see the light of incommutable truth except through faith and with a heart that is cleansed. 'Blessed are the pure of heart, for they shall see God.'[16]

---

[16] Matt. 5.8.

SERMON 4 (Den)[1]

Christ: Lamb and Lion
(Isa. 53.7; Apoc. 5.6)

(1) In fulfillment of Holy Writ, the Truth has resounded through the voice of the Apostles, for the Psalmist has sung: 'Their voice has gone forth unto all the earth, and their words unto the ends of the world.'[2] So, also: 'Christ our passover is sacrificed,'[3] for of Him the Prophet had foretold: 'He was led as a sheep to the slaughter, and he was mute as a lamb before its shearer, and he opened not his mouth.'[4] Who is this man? He is the man of whom the Prophet at once goes on to say: 'In humility his judgment was taken away: who shall declare his generation?'[5] I recognize the realization of so much humility in a king of so much power, for He who is as a lamb that opens not its mouth before its shearer is also 'the lion of the tribe of Juda.'[6] Who is

---

1 This and the following six sermons are not to be confused with the sermons listed under the same numbers in any edition of the complete works of St. Augustine. Six of them are from the collection of twenty-five sermons which were first published by Michael Denis at Vienna in 1792. The seventh is one of seventeen sermons which were first published by Dom Germain Morin in *Revue Bénédictine*, intermittently from 1890 to 1929. This sermon was first published in 1922. The present translation is based on the Latin text in the *Miscellanea Agostiniana* 1.21-38; 1.55-64; 1.627-635. (See Introduction, p. 140).
2 Ps. 18.5; Rom. 10.18.
3 1 Cor. 5.7.
4 Isa. 53.7.
5 Isa. 53.8.
6 Apoc. 5.5.

this lamb and lion? He suffered death like a lamb, and He has devoured like a lion.[7] Who is this lamb and lion? Meek, yet courageous; lovable, yet fearsome; innocent, yet powerful; silent under judgment, yet roaring to pronounce judgment. Who is this lamb and lion—suffering like a lamb; rising up like a lion? Rather, is He not at the same time a lamb and lion in both His suffering and His resurrection? Let us discern the lamb in the suffering. 'He was,' as we have just reminded you, 'mute as a lamb before its shearer, and he opened not his mouth.' Let us discern the lion in the suffering. Jacob has said: 'Thou hast risen: resting thou hast slept as a lion.'[8] Let us discern the lamb in the resurrection. When the Apocalypse is speaking of the everlasting glory of virgins, it says: 'They follow the lamb whithersoever he goes.'[9] Let us discern the lion in the resurrection. The Apocalypse also says: 'The lion of the tribe of Juda has overcome to open the scroll.'[10] Why is He a lamb in His suffering? Because, although He was innocent, He suffered death.[11] Why is He a lion in His suffering? Because He slew death when He himself was slain.[12] Why is He a lamb in His resurrection? Because his innocence is everlasting.[13] Why is He a lion in His resurrection? Because His power is everlasting.[14]

(2) Who is this lamb and lion? In what sense do you intend that question? If you wish to know what He was previously, then He 'in the beginning was the Word.' If you wish to know where He was, then 'the Word was with God.'

---
7 Osee 13.8.
8 Gen. 49.9.
9 Apoc. 14.4.
10 Apoc. 5.5.
11 James 5.6.
12 2 Tim. 1.10.
13 Heb. 7.26.
14 Heb. 1.20; Apoc. 5.13.

If you wish to know what kind of Word He was, then 'and the Word was God.' If you wish to know how powerful He was, then 'All things were made through him.' If you wish to know what he became, then 'And the Word was made flesh.'[15] But, if you ask how He was begotten of the Father without a mother, or born of a mother without a Father, then, 'Who shall declare his generation?' Begotten from all eternity, co-eternal with his begetter;[16] becoming flesh, and not ceasing to be the Word;[17] the creator of all times, created at a fitting time;[18] the prey of death, and the despoiler of death;[19] without beauty in the sight of the children of men, and beautiful of form in the sight of the children of men;[20] acquainted with bearing infirmities and with bearing them away;[21] exalted, yet performing works of lowliness; lowly, yet accomplishing the sublime;[22] the God-man and the God of man;[23] the First-begotten, and the Creator of those who are the first-begotten;[24] the Only-begotten, and the brother of many;[25] born of the substance of the Father, and made a sharer of the nature of adopted sons;[26] the Lord of all, and the servant of many.[27] This is the Lamb who takes away the sins of the world.[28] This is the Lion who has conquered the kingdoms of the world.[29] We were inquiring as to who

---

15 John 1.1-3; 1.14.
16 Isa. 53.8; John 1.1.
17 1 Tim. 2.5; Apoc. 19.13.
18 Gal. 4.4.
19 Rom. 6.9.
20 Isa. 53.2; Ps. 14.3.
21 Isa. 53.3-4.
22 Acts 2.33; Phil. 2.8.
23 John 20.28; Rom. 9.5.
24 Rom. 8.29.
25 Matt. 12.49-50; 25.40.
26 Phil. 2.6-7; Rom. 8.15-17.
27 Matt. 20.28; Rom. 14.9.
28 John 1.29.
29 John 16.33.

He is. Let us ask ourselves: Who are they for whom He died? Perhaps he has died for those who are holy and righteous? The Apostle does not say so, for he says: 'Christ has died for the wicked.'[30] He has died for them, not in order that they should remain wicked, but in order that the wicked man may become righteous through the death of the Just One, and in order that the handwriting of sin may be blotted out through the shedding of innocent blood.[31]

---
30 Rom. 5.6.
31 Col. 2.14.

SERMON 5 (Den.)[1]

Life from Death
(John 3.16; Rom. 8.32)

(1) Paying attention to the Gospel lesson which has been read, we have heard the account of the Resurrection of our Lord Jesus Christ. Christ rose from the dead; therefore Christ had died, for a resurrection is a proof of death. The death of Christ is the destruction of fear. Hence, let us not be afraid to die, for Christ has died for us. Let us die with the hope of eternal life, for Christ has risen in order that we also may rise. In His Death and Resurrection we have our appointed task and our promised reward. Suffering is our appointed task; resurrection is our promised reward. The martyrs fulfilled that task. Let us fulfill it through piety if we cannot fulfill it through suffering. Death comes to all men, but not to all men is it given to suffer and to die for the sake of Christ. Happy are those who have done for the sake of Christ that which had to be done anyway; they could not have escaped death, but they could have refused to die for Christ. Death will come to all men, but not in every case will it be a death for Christ. As regards those whose good fortune it was to die for the sake of Christ, it may be said that in a certain manner they made repayment for the benefit that had been conferred upon them. The Lord had conferred on them the benefit of dying for them; in return, they made repayment by dying for Him. But, how could a

[1] See p. 307, n. 1.

miserable needy man repay, unless a generous master had given him wherewith to do so? So, Christ gave to the martyrs the means of making repayment to Christ for what Christ had given them. The song of the martyrs is this: 'If it had not been that the Lord was with us, perhaps they [our persecutors] had swallowed us up alive.'[2] Alive? What does that mean? Here, it means *cognizant, not unaware.* The martyrs' meaning is this: Although we would know that we would be committing a sin if we were to deny Christ, we would nevertheless have committed that sin. Hence, our persecutors would have swallowed us up while we were alive—not because we were dead, that is, while we were cognizant of the sin, not because we were unaware of it. But by what power did they resist their persecutors' efforts to force them to commit that sin? Let us put that question to the martyrs themselves; let them give us the answer. Here it is: 'If it had not been that the Lord was with us.' Hence, the Lord Himself had given them the wherewithal to make repayment to Him. Let Him be thanked. He is rich, but it is written that He became poor in order to make us rich.[3] We are enriched through His poverty; we are healed by His wounds; we are exhalted by His lowliness; we receive life through His death.

(2) 'What shall I render to the Lord, for all the things that he has rendered to me?'[4] So spoke the martyr. Hear what he says next. He reflected, and sought for some fitting repayment to make to the Lord. After reflection, what did he say? He said: 'I will take the chalice of salvation.' 'This,' says he, 'is what I will render to the Lord: the chalice of salvation, the chalice of martyrdom, the chalice of suffer-

---
2 Ps. 123.1-3.
3 2 Cor. 8.9.
4 Ps. 115.12-13.

ing, the chalice of Christ.' He means: 'I will take the chalice of salvation, for Christ is our salvation.' Hence, the martyr says: 'I will take up this chalice, and I will make recompense to Him.' It was with reference to this chalice that, on the eve of His passion, Christ said to the Father: 'Father, if it be possible, let this chalice pass from me.'[5] For this purpose had He come, namely, to suffer and to die. He had power over death. (If I am wrong on this point, then hearken to His own words when He says: 'I have power to lay down my life, and I have power to take it up again. No one takes my life from me; but I lay it down of myself, and I take it up again.')[6] You have heard the power: 'No one takes my life from me.' The Jews have no reason to glory in His death. It is a manifestation of their fault, not of their power. Christ died because He willed to die. He says in one of the Psalms: 'I have slept and have taken my rest.'[7] They cried out: 'Crucify him, crucify him.'[8] They seized Him and they crucified Him, and they were jubilant because they thought they had some power over Him. But: 'I have slept.' What else does He say? 'And I have taken my rest.' Yes, that rest lasted for three days. But what does He go on to say in that Psalm? 'And I have risen up, because the Lord has protected me.' (Of course, He is speaking in the form of a servant when He says: 'The Lord has protected me.' Also speaking in the form of a servant, He says in another Psalm: 'He that sleeps, shall he rise no more?')[9] 'The Jews,' says Christ, 'are exulting as if they had vanquished Me. But, he that sleeps, shall he rise no more? They crucified Me in order to kill Me. But I have slept, for I laid down

---
5 Matt. 26.39.
6 John 10.17-18.
7 Ps. 3.6.
8 Luke 23.21.
9 Ps. 40.9.

My life when I willed to lay it down, and I rose again when I willed to rise.'

(3) So, the chalice which He had come to drink is the very chalice which He would have pass away from Him. But what, O Lord, is the reason for Your saying: 'Father, if it be possible, let this chalice pass from me'? And when Your passion unto death was about to begin, why did You say to the disciples: 'My soul is sad, even unto death'?[10] I am trying to reconcile these words of Yours with the words You previously spoke, namely: 'I have power to lay down my life, and I have power to take it up again.' Why is it that I hear: 'My soul is sad, even unto death'? Why are You sad, since no one can take away Your life from You? Since You have power to lay down Your life, why do You say: 'Father, if it be possible, let this chalice pass from me'? If we ask Him that question, He gives us this answer: 'You are a man, but I assumed your flesh. Did I not therefore assume your voice as well? I, the Creator, am proclaiming Myself when I say: "I have power to lay down My life, and I have power to take it up again." But I, the creature, am proclaiming Myself when I say: "My soul is sad, even unto death." Rejoice that I am one with you, and acknowledge that you are one with Me. Behold Me as your refuge and strength when I say: "I have power to lay down My life." Recognize Me as a mirror in which to behold yourself when I say: "My soul is sad, even unto death." '

(4) Have you not read that Christ died? Could we deny it? Were we to deny His death, we would have to deny His resurrection also. His death was possible because He deigned to become man; His resurrection was possible because He deigned to become man—for we, being men, are

---
10 Matt. 26.38.

destined to die and to rise again. But, was it possible for the Word to die when Christ died? Could the Word undergo a change of any kind? 'In the beginning was the Word, and the Word was with God, and the Word was God.'[11] What kind of change could such a Word undergo? It was necessary that Christ should die for us.[12] So, it was necessary that Christ should die, and it was impossible that the Word should die. 'In the beginning was the Word, and the Word was with God, and the Word was God.' Where is the blood? Where is death? How could there be either death or blood in the Word? And, since there is neither death nor blood in the Word, where is our ransom, which is the blood of Christ? In other words, how could Christ pay this ransom if he continued to be nothing else than the Word? How could He pay this ransom unless He assumed flesh? How, indeed, could He pay this ransom unless He assumed a living body, animated by a human soul? This assumed body could be killed, even though the Word could not die, for this body is animated by its own soul. But the soul itself could not die, because its union with the divine nature makes it one with divinity. The union of that soul with divinity is not in the manner of our union with divinity. The precise reason of that soul's union with divinity lies in the fact that the Lord assumed it unto Himself, whereas we are united with divinity by believing in the Lord, as it is written: 'He who is joined to the Lord is one spirit.'[13] We cleaved to God by believing; for, as long as we were unbelivers, we were unworthy and we were strangers to God.[14] But the soul of Christ was created worthy of cleaving to God; for, at the very

---
11 John 1.1.
12 Luke 24.46.
13 1 Cor. 6.17.
14 Col. 1.12; Eph. 4.18; Heb. 11.6.

instant of its creation, it was assumed into the unity of the divine person. When this singular unity of the two unequal spirits was suspended, the body suffered death. But that body was forsaken for a short time only. In manner and in kind, its life was *sui generis;* for it had a marvelous twofold principle, being sustained by the unity of the two spirits.[15] And both of these—the divine spirit and the human, which is an image of the divine—are certainly immortal.

(5) Hence, our divine Lord and Savior addresses us, as it were, in the following words: 'I created man upright, but he rendered himself perverse. You withdrew from Me, and you perished in yourselves, but I am about to seek that which was lost. You have withdrawn from Me, and you have lost the life, for "the life was the light of men."[16] Behold what you forsook when you all perished in Adam! The life was the light of men. What life? "In the beginning was the Word, and the Word was with God, and the Word was God." There was life, but you were lying dead. As the Word, I had not wherein I might die; as a man, you had not whereby to live.' (Since Christ the Lord graciously allows it, I

---
15 The unity of two spirits is not to be confused with the hypostatic union of the divine and the human nature. There was never any severance of the union of the Divine Word with either the soul or the body of Christ. The life of that body was sustained by the unity of operation of the human soul and the Divine Word. When the soul departed from the body, this unity was severed, and the body died. It was forsaken by the soul, not by the Divine Word. 'Because the Word was made flesh . . . and the whole man—soul and body—was assumed by the Word, what else did the passion and death effect but the separation of the soul and the body? . . . The soul forsook the body for a short time, but the body was to rise again when the soul returned' (*In Joan. evang.* tr. 47.10). This is the teaching which is now accepted as the *'sententia communis'*. For the opinions of Doctors and ecclesiastical writers before the time of St. Leo (d.461), cf. Lebon 'Une ancienne opinion sur la condition du Christ dans la mort,' in *Revue Hist. eccles.*, 23 (1927), 5-43; 209-241.
16 John 1.4.

am appropriating His words, for, if He made my words His own, is there not all the more reason why I should make His words mine?) It is as though Christ were addressing us—not through the sound of words, but through the silent speech of deeds—and saying to us: 'I had not wherewith to die; as man, you had not wherewith to live. I partook of what is yours, so that I could die for you; partake of what is Mine, so that you may be able to live with Me. Let us engage in mutual exchange. I am giving something to you; give Me something in return. I am receiving death from you; receive life from Me. Pay attention. See what I am giving! What I am receiving! Exalted in heaven, I assumed your lowliness on earth. Your Lord, I assumed your form of a servant. Your health, I assumed your wounds. Your life, I assumed your death. Being the Word, I became flesh so that I could die for you. From the Father I had no flesh, but I assumed flesh from your flesh in order to share my riches with you.' (The Virgin Mary was of our flesh, and Christ received His flesh from her; hence, He received flesh from the human race.) 'Yes,' say He, 'I assumed flesh from you, so that I could die for you; receive the life-giving spirit from Me, so that you may be able to live with Me. Finally, I died through what I received from you; live through what you receive from Me.'

(6) Therefore, brethren, when you hear it said that Christ was born of the Virgin Mary, through the Holy Spirit[17] that He suffered, that He was scourged, that He was smitten on the face—when you hear it said that Christ suffered those things, do not imagine that the Word, who was in the beginning with the Father, could have undergone any such sufferings in His own nature and substance. Could we ever deny

---

17 A variant Latin version of the Creed.

that the Word of God, the only-begotten God, has suffered for us? He has indeed suffered, but His sufferings were according to His soul and body, for they were susceptible to suffering. Of course, He had a soul and a body, for He had come to make the whole man free, not by losing [His divine] life, but by imparting it. Let us give an illustration, so that you may more readily fix your minds on what we are saying. For instance, when Stephen or Focas[18] or any other martyr suffered and was killed and buried, it was only their bodies that were killed and buried; their souls could be neither killed nor buried. Nevertheless, it is perfectly proper for us to say that Stephen or Focas or any other martyr *died* for the name of Christ. In like manner, when the only-begotten Son of God suffered and was killed and was buried, of course it was only His flesh that was killed and buried, His soul could not be killed, and—for a greater reason—neither could His divinity. Therefore, we are safe in saying that the only Son of God— that is to say, the only-begotten Son of God—died for us and was buried. Hence, the Lord Christ Himself, who is Truth without falsehood, speaks the truth, and not falsehood, when He says: 'For God so loved the world that he gave his only-begotten Son, that those who believe in Him may not perish, but may have life everlasting.'[19] The Apostle also says of the Father: 'He who has not spared even his own Son, but has delivered Him for us all.'[20] Do you wish to know what Christ is? Do not fix your attention on His flesh alone, which lay in the tomb; do not fix your attention on His soul alone, of which He said: 'My soul is sad, even unto death'; do not fix your attention on the Word alone, for the Word was God. Bear in mind that the whole Christ is the Word, the soul and the flesh.

---

18 A martyr in Africa; Cf. *Anal. Bolland.* 30 (1911) 252-272.
19 John 3.16.
20 Rom. 8.32.

(7) Do not ascribe any defect to the soul of Christ. The Apollinarist heretics maintained that that soul had no mind. In other words, they contended that it had no understanding, but that it had the Word instead of mind and understanding. That is what Apollinaris holds, but the Arians say that Christ had no soul whatever. Brethren, hold fast to the tenet that the whole Christ is both the Word and a soul and a body. And, when you hear the words, 'My soul is sad, even unto death,' understand that it is a human soul, not the soul of a brute animal. For, a soul without an intellect is not a human soul, but the soul of a beast. If He did not come to make the mind free, He had no mind. Hence, the same Christ is both the Word and a soul and flesh. What is man? Man is both soul and body. What is Christ? He is both the Word and a man. So, the same Christ is both the Word and a soul and a body. When you strike a man with your fists, which part of him do you hit? the soul? or the body? You admit that you hit the body. Yet, the soul cries out: 'Why do you hit me? Why are you beating me?' Now, suppose you were to reply to the soul by saying: 'Who has touched you? I am not hitting you; I am hitting the body.' If you were to make that reply, would you not be laughed at? would you not be considered silly? or even insane? Neither can such a reply be given by those who scourged the flesh or slapped the face of the Word of God. They cannot say: 'We scourged His flesh and we slapped His face, but we did not scourge or slap either the Word of God or the soul of Christ.' They slapped the face and scourged the flesh of the whole Christ, who is at once the Word, the soul, and the flesh; it was not His dead body that they slapped and scourged. Although they could not inflict death by crucifixion on either His soul or His divinity—that is His very life itself—yet the delight of their hearts and the object of their evil wills was to kill the whole Christ. For, when anyone

assails a man for the purpose of killing him, that assailant wishes the man's life to become as extinct as the light of a lamp that has been smashed against the ground. And that light becomes so completely extinguished as to shine no more, because some evil-doer has seen that it was a hindrance to him. However, such complete extinction is impossible with regard to man. Total extinction cannot befall a man, for, although he has a substance which is mortal, he has also a substance which is immortal. The flesh is the only mortal substance in man. And, for a greater reason, total extinction could not befall Christ, the only-begotten Son of God, although the Jews thought that they were extinguishing Him completely. Of the three substances which He had, one is eternal and divine, and two were temporal and human. He had only one mortal substance, namely, the body; for, certainly, His soul and, above all, His divinity were immortal. He was not only a human soul and a human body, but He was also God. He was one [person], soul and body and the only-begotten Son of God. Hence it is that only He, by His death for a short time, could redeem us from eternal death. 'For he who decended into the lower parts of the earth, he it is who ascended also above all the heavens.'[21] A mere man could not do this.

(8) Dearly beloved brethren, let us confidently rejoice and be glad because He who was slain and yet triumphed over His enemies has redeemed us by His death. He slew death when He Himself was slain, and He has redeemed us from the hand of death for all eternity. Even when He was lying in the tomb, He was able to send the confessing thief into paradise. 'Ascending on high, he led captivity captive,' and, having sent the Holy Ghost, 'he gave gifts to men.'[22]

---
21 Eph. 4.9-10.
22 Eph. 4.8; Ps. 67.19.

SERMON 6 (Den.)[1]

The Holy Eucharist

(1) Dear brethren, that which you see on the Lord's table is bread and wine. But when a word is added, that bread and wine become the body and blood of the Word. Because the Lord, 'who in the beginning was the Word, and the Word was with God, and the Word was God'[2]—because that same Lord, in His mercy, did not despise that which He had created to His own image, 'the Word was made flesh and dwelt among us.'[3] As you know, that Word assumed human nature by assuming a human soul and a human body, and thus became man without ceasing to be God. In this way, He suffered for us, and He has left us His body and blood in this sacrament.[4] He has even made us His body, for we have become the body of Christ. Through His mercy, therefore, we are that which we receive.

Consider that finished product. Recall what it was at one time, when it was in the field. The earth produced it, nourished it with rain, and formed it into an ear of grain. Human labor piled it on the threshing-floor, beat it loose from the straw, winnowed it, stored it away, brought it out again, ground it into flour, moistened it, baked it, and changed it into bread.

Now consider yourselves. At one time, you did not exist. You were created; you were brought to the Lord's threshing-

---
1 See p. 307, n. 1.
2 John 1.1.
3 John 1.14.
4 'Without this bread, men may have temporal life; but by no means may they have eternal life without it' (*In Joan. evang. tr.* 26.15).

floor; by the tread of oxen (that is, by the labors of those who expound the Gospel), the grain in your midst was beaten loose from the straw; all through the period of your probation as catechumens, you were stored in the granary; when you submitted your names,[5] you began to be ground into flour through fasting and exorcisms; afterwards, when you came to the font, you were sprinkled, and kneaded into one mass; then, the fire of the Holy Ghost having been enkindled, you were baked into bread—the bread of the Lord.[6]

(2) Now consider what you have received, and, since you see that is was made into one when it was made what it is, be you also at one. Be united in love; be united in holding the same faith and the same hope; be united in undivided charity. When heretics receive this sacrament, they receive testimony against themselves, because they strive for division; whereas this bread betokens unity. And at one time, the wine also was in many grapes, but now it is one. The pleasant wine in the chalice is one, but it was not one until it had been crushed in the wine-press. In the name of Christ, you have now, as it were, reached the chalice of the Lord, but you did not reach it until you had been rendered humble and contrite through fasting and labors. You are there on the table; you are there

---

5 In classical Latin, *nomen dare* (to give one's name), meant to *enlist as a soldier*. In Christian usage it came to mean *to enlist as a soldier of Christ*, by formally asking to be enrolled for baptism. It is in this sense that Augustine uses it in this sermon, as well as in the *Confessions* (9:6:14): 'When the time arrived wherein it behooved me to give my name.'
6 In *Sermon 227*, Augustine institutes this same comparison between the production of bread and the formation of a Christian, and he quotes Saint Paul (1 Cor. 10.17): 'Because the bread is one we though many, are one body.' Augustine's figurative language was perfectly clear to his hearers, for they had just advanced from the rank of catechumen.

in the chalice. You are this body with us, for, collectively, we are this body.⁷ We drink of the same chalice because we live the same life.

(3) Today you will be told what you were told yesterday as well, but today you will receive an explanation of the things

---

In those days, when a pagan made serious inquiry about the teachings and practices of the Christian religion or expressed a desire to embrace it, his notive and sincerity had to be tested. See *Commentary* 2.2.7, n. 7). Such inquirers would be directed to assemble in a church, where authorized teachers would give them preliminary instruction and practical tests.

As soon as an inquirer was approved, he was withdrawn from that group and enrolled as a catechumen. (On the Lord's threshing-floor, evangelical laborers separated the grain from the straw.) The catechumen was not immediately admitted to the reception of baptism, but had to undergo an indefinite period of further instruction and probation. (The grain was stored in the granary.) When the catechumen had won final approval, he was still permitted to postpone his reception of baptism. It was not until he had submitted his name for baptism that he began to be known as a 'competent,' and began to receive special instructions to prepare him for baptism on the following Holy Saturday or Vigil of Pentecost. All through the season of Lent, the 'competents' spent several hours a day in a church, where the bishop or a priest gave them special instructions on the sacraments which they were about to receive and the obligations they were about to accept. For forty hours preceding the feast of Easter, an absolute fast from every kind of food was observed. The 'competents' were exorcised against the influence of demons, whose works and pomps they were to renounce in the ceremony of baptism. (The grain had been brought from the granary, and was being ground into flour through fasting and exorcism.) On the night of Holy Saturday, they were conducted to the font and, by the reception of baptism, were made members of the Church. (They were sprinkled with water, and were kneaded into one mass.)

The sacrament of confirmation was now administered to those who had just received the sacrament of baptism. (The fire of the Holy Spirit was enkindled, and they were baked into bread.) The hour was now well after midnight, and the Sunday Mass was at once begun. At this Mass, the newly baptized received Holy Communion; hence, Augustine goes on to say: 'Consider what you have received . . .' Cf. P. DePuniet, in *Dictionnaire d'archéologie chrétienne et de liturgie*, s. v. Catechumenat, col. 2579-2621.

7 1 Cor. 12.27.

that you were told and of the responses that you gave yesterday. And even if you remained silent while the responses were being given, at least you learned yesterday the responses that are to be given today. After the *Dominus vobiscum* [The Lord be with you]—a salutation which you already knew[8]—you heard the *Sursum cor* [Lift up the heart]. The whole life of true Christians is an uplifting of the heart. Of course, it is not the whole life of those who are Christians in name only, but it is the whole life of those who are Christians in reality and truth. What does an uplifted heart mean? It means trust in God, not in yourself. You are from beneath, but God is from above. If you rely on yourself, your heart is not lifted up, it is directed downwards. Accordingly, when you hear the *Sursum cor* said by the priest, you give the response, *Habemus ad Dominum* [We have it (lifted up) to the Lord]. Strive to make this response correspond with the truth, because your response is recorded at God's tribunal. Let your heart be as you say it is. Let not your conscience deny what your tongue affirms, But, this uplifting of the heart is a gift from God, not a natural endowment of your own. Therefore, when you respond that you have your hearts lifted up to God, the priest immediately says, *Domino Deo nostro gratias agamus* [Let us give thanks to the Lord our God]. Why should we give thanks? Because we have our hearts lifted up, for, if God had not lifted them up, we would be groveling on the earth. This is also the reason for the thanks expressed in the holy supplications which you will hear pronounced in order that, when the word is added, the oblation may become the

---

8 Catechumens used to be present at the Mass up to the beginning of the Offertory. At that point, the celebrant would address them with the parting salutation, *Dominus vobiscum*. Hence, that salutation was already well known to those whom Augustine is now addressing.

body and blood of Christ.⁹ Without the word, the oblation is bread and wine, but, when the word is added, the oblation is at once something else. And that something else—what is it? It is the body of Christ and the blood of Christ. Hence, without the word, it is bread and wine, but, when the word is added, it will become a sacrament. To this you respond with an *Amen*. To say *Amen* is to express assent, for *Amen* means *yes*.

Then comes the recitation of the *Lord's Prayer*, a prayer which you have already learned and recited. Why is this prayer recited before the receiving of the body and blood of Christ? It is recited because of human frailty. If, perchance, our mind has conceived any thought that was improper, if our tongue has spoken any words that were indecent, if our eye has gazed on any object that was immodest, if our ear has been rather pleased to listen to something unbecoming —if, through human frailty, we have contracted any such stains from the world's temptation, they are wiped off by the recitation of the *Lord's Prayer* when we say: 'Forgive us our trespasses.'¹⁰ Then we may come forward without fearing that we shall eat and drink judgment to ourselves¹¹ when we eat and drink what we receive. After this, the *Pax vobiscum* [Peace be to you] is said. The kiss of peace is a significant sacrament.¹² Give it and receive it in such a way that you will have charity. Be not a Judas. The traitor Judas kissed Christ with his lips, but in his heart he was plotting against

---
9 The words of Consecration express neither thanks nor supplication, but they occur at the end of the prayer, *Quam oblationem*, in which supplication is expressed and in which we are reminded that Christ gave thanks to God the Father.
10 Matt. 6.12.
11 1 Cor. 11.29.
12 Christians embrace one another in the holy kiss. It is a pledge of peace' (*Sermon* 227).

Him. Perhaps someone is hostile in his feelings toward you, and you can neither dissuade nor convince him. You must bear with him. Do not return evil for evil in your heart. Love him, even though he hates you. Cheerfully give him the kiss of peace.

You have been told only a few things, but they are of great moment. Let them not be despised for their fewness. Rather, let them be prized for their importance.

SERMON 7 (Den.)[1]

Sonship or Servitude

(1) Everybody knows that we are celebrating the feast of the Pasch during the days when we sing the *Alleluia*. But, brethren, we must try to understand the inner meaning of that which we are openly celebrating when we say that we are celebrating the Pasch. *Pasch* is a Hebrew word, and it means a passover; *paschein* is a Greek word, and it means to suffer; *pascere* is a Latin word, and it means 'to feed.'[2] For, who are they that celebrate the Pasch, except those who pass over from the death of their sins to the life of the righteous? In this sense, the Apostle says: 'We have *passed over* from death to life, because we love the brethren.'[3] Who are they that keep the Pasch, except those who believe in Him who has *suffered* on earth, in order that they may reign with Him in

---

1 See p. 307, n. 1.
2 At first sight, Augustine may seem to be inferring that the words, *Pasch, paschein,* and *pascere* are etymologically related. Elsewhere (cf. *Enarratio in ps.* 140.25), he explicitly denies that there is any such relation: 'As pronounced in Greek, *Pascha* seems to signify suffering, because *paschein* means to suffer. But, in the Hebrew tongue, *pascha* means a passover, according to the interpretation of those who know that language, and if you ask those who are proficient in Greek, they will tell you that *pascha* is not a Greek word ... The Greek word for suffering is *pathos*, not *pascha*.' In the present instance, then. Augustine disregards etymology and ingeniously avails himself of those three words—remarkably apt by reason of their similarity of sound and diversity in meaning—in order to fix in the minds of his hearers the three virtues he is inculcating, namely, repentance, patience, charity.
3 1 John 3.14.

heaven? Who are they that keep the Pasch, except those who *feed* Christ in the persons of the poor? For, with reference to the poor, Christ Himself says: 'Whosoever has done it for one of the least of mine, has done it for me.'[4] Christ is enthroned in heaven, and is needy on earth; He makes intercession for us with the Father,[5] and here He asks us for bread. So, fellow bishops, if we wish so to celebrate the Pasch that it will be profitable to us; let us pass over; let us suffer; let us give food. Let us pass over from sins to righteousness; let us suffer for Christ; let us feed Christ in the persons nes; let us suffer for Christ; let us feed Christ in the persons of the poor. Let us fittingly celebrate the Paschal feast, in order that we may enjoy the heavenly feast with Abraham in the kingdom of God. So, let us sing the *Alleluia;* that is to say, let us praise Him who is.[6] Let us praise Him in prosperity and in adversity. Let us not be elated by the prosperity of riches, and let us not be shaken by their loss. Let us say the *Alleluia* as Job has said it: 'The Lord gave, and the Lord has taken away: as it has pleased the Lord so is it done: blessed be the name of the Lord.'[7] So, let us 'bless the Lord at all times.'[8] If our members are moved to the working of righteousness in accord with the sound of our voice, if our conduct re-echoes the notes of our song, then we are always singing the *Alleluia.*

(2) Now, hear how both the rich and the poor are ordered to sing the *Alleluia.* The Apostle says: 'Charge the rich of this world not to be proud and not to trust in the uncertainty of riches, but to trust in the living God, who provides all things

---
4 Matt. 25.40.
5 Rom. 8.34; Heb. 7.25.
6 Exod. 3.14.
7 Job 1.21.
8 Ps. 33.1.

in abundance for our enjoyment. Let them be rich in good works, let them give readily, let them share with others, let them provide for themselves treasure for the time to come, in order that they may lay hold on the true life.'[9] Tobias teaches what the poor should sing: 'Fear not, my son, because we lead a poor life. Thou shalt have good things in abundance if thou dost fear the Lord thy God and dost do the things that are pleasing in His sight.'[10] Dearly beloved members of the body of Christ, let us wait in expectation of our Head, who is to come from heaven. Cohering with Him, we shall remain so inseparable from Him that we shall reign in heaven with Him whose passion we celebrate on earth. Let us maintain His discipline, in order that we may be corrected, for God deals with us as with sons. 'For what son is there,' says the Apostle, 'whom his father does not discipline? If you withdraw from God's discipline, then you are bastards, and not sons.'[11] Let us bear with scourgings from God as our Father, lest we meet with severity from Him as our Judge.

(3) God and the Devil; a Father and a slave-dealer. As a Father, God scourges, corrects, and reclaims; the slave-dealer cajoles, deceives, and betrays. The Father carries a scourge; the slave-dealer carries a net. If you take refuge in the arms of the Scourger, you shall be safe from the evil designs of the betrayer. See what determines whether you will rest in the kingdom of heaven or be consigned to the toils of hell. If you long for the kingdom of heaven, you will enjoy the reward of freedom; if you choose the net of the deceiver, you will be held in the bondage of servitude, your hands and your feet shall be bound, and it shall be said of you: 'Take him, and cast him forth into the darkness outside, where there will

---
9 1 Tim. 6.17-19.
10 Tob. 4.23.
11 Heb. 12.7-8.

be weeping and gnashing of teeth.'[12] We are strongly warned: 'He that has ears for hearing, let him hear what the Spirit says to the churches.'[13]

---
12 Matt. 22.13.
13 Apoc. 2.7.

SERMON 8 (Den.)[1]

On Baptism

(1) My words are addressed to you, newborn babes, little ones in Christ, new offspring of the Church, grace of the Father, born of the Mother, a godly seed, a new swarm, the flower of our honor and the fruit of our labor, my joy and my crown—all you who stand fast in the Lord.[2] I address you in the words of the Apostle: 'Behold, the night is far advanced; the day is at hand. Lay aside the works of darkness, and put on the armor of light. Walk becomingly as in the day, not in revelry and drunkenness, not in debauchery and wantonness, not in strife and jealousy. But put on the Lord Jesus Christ, and make no provision for the lusts of the flesh.'[3] Do this, in order that your conduct may be endued with the virtues of Him whom you have put on in the sacrament. 'For all you who have been baptized in Christ, have put on Christ. There is neither Jew nor Greek, there is neither slave nor freeman; there is neither male nor female. For you are all one in Christ.'[4] This is the inherent power of the sacrament. It is the sacrament of a new life, which begins now with the remission of all past sins, and will be brought to perfection

---
1 See p. 307, n. 1.
2 Augustine is preaching at the Mass on Easter Sunday. He is addressing those who were baptized some hours previously. For the source of the Scriptural expressions, see 1 Cor. 3.1; Phil. 1.22; 4.1; Heb. 2.7; 1 Peter 2.2; 5, 10; Judges 14.8; Mal. 2.15.
3 Rom. 13.12-14.
4 Gal. 3.27-28.

331

at the resurrection of the dead.⁵ 'For you were buried with Him by means of baptism into death, in order that, just as Christ has risen from the dead, . . . so you also may walk in the newness of life.'⁶ For now, as long as you are in this mortal body and are thus exiled from the Lord, you walk by faith.⁷ But you are hastening to Jesus Christ, who has deigned to become man for our sake, and who, in His human nature, has made Himself the fixed way for you.⁸ He has indeed laid up much sweetness for those who fear Him.⁹ He will reveal it to those who hope in Him, and He will bring it to perfection when we have received in reality what we have now received in hope. 'For we are the children of God, and it has not yet appeared what shall be. We know that, when He appears, we shall be like to Him, for we shall see Him just as He is.'¹⁰ Christ Himself has made us this promise, for He says in the Gospel: 'He who loves me, keeps my commandments. And he who loves me will be loved by my Father, and I will love him and will manifest myself to him.'¹¹ Of course, those whom He was addressing were able to see Him, but they saw Him in the form of a servant, the form in which the Father is greater than He; they did not see Him in His divine nature, in which He is one with the Father.¹² To those who fear Him, He manifested His form of a servant; for those who hope in Him, He has reserved the manifestation of His divine nature. In the form of a servant, He manifested himself to the exiles; to [the vision of] His divine nature, He called those who will abide

---

5 Acts 2.38; Luke 20.36.
6 Rom. 6.4.
7 2 Cor. 5.6-7.
8 John 14.6.
9 Ps. 30.20.
10 1 John 3.2.
11 John 14.21.
12 John 14.28; 10.30; Phil. 2.6-7.

with Him. With His human nature, He has strewn the path of the exiles on their journey, and He has promised them the vision of His divine nature when their pilgrimage is over.

(2) 'Having therefore these promises, beloved, let us cleanse ourselves from all defilement of the flesh and of the spirit, perfecting holiness in the fear of God.'[3] 'I . . . exhort you to walk in a manner worthy of the calling with which you were called, with all humility and meekness, . . . bearing with one another in love, careful to preserve the unity of the Spirit in the bond of peace.'[14] On what precise condition has such a pledge been given to us? For there are some who have put on Christ in the sacrament, but are not endued with His faith or morals. Certainly, many heretics have the sacrament of baptism, but they have neither the fruit of salvation nor the bond of peace, 'having a semblance of piety but disowning its power,'[16] as the Apostle says. On an attaintable body, they bear the seal of the true king; for either they have been enrolled by deserters or they have become deserters themselves. They say to us: 'If we are not of the household of the faith,[17] why do you not give us baptism? If we are, then why do you question us?' As though they had not read that Simon Magus also had received baptism, and that Peter nevertheless said to him: 'Thou hast no part or lot in this faith.'[18] See, then, how it can come to pass that a man may have the baptism of Christ and still not have the faith or the love of Christ; how it is that he may have the sacrament of holiness and still not be reckoned

---
13 2 Cor. 7.1.
14 Eph. 4.1-3.
15 2 Cor. 1.22.
16 2 Tim. 3.5.
17 *Fideles';* cf. *Epist.* 217.5.16.
18 Acts 8.21.

in the lot of the holy.[19] With regard to the mere sacrament itself, it makes no difference whether someone receives the baptism of Christ where the unity of Christ is not. For, in the case of desertion from the Church by someone who had been baptized in the Church, the deserter will be deprived of the holiness of the life, but he will not lose the sacramental character. From the fact that the sacrament is not readministered to a deserter when he returns, it is clear that he could not have lost it when he withdrew. A military deserter is deprived of membership in the army, but he is still marked as a soldier of the king. And, if he signs another man with the same seal as his own, he does not give him participation in the life of the army; rather, he makes him—like the deserter himself—a soldier deprived of that membership. However, if the one would return to the army and if the other would join it, then, when the king's severity is softened, the one would be forgiven and the other would be accepted. In each of them the fault would be corrected, for each of them the penalty would be remitted, to each of them peace would be restored, but in neither of them would the character be repeated which had once been sealed.

(3) On this point, let those heretics not ask us: 'What can you give us, since we already have baptism?' They are so far from understanding what they say that they will not even read the testimony of the Sacred Scripture which tells us that even within the Church (that is, within the communion of the members of Christ), many who had been baptized in Samaria had been merely baptized, but had not yet received the Holy Spirit until Apostles came to them from Jerusalem,[20] and that, on the other hand, Cornelius and those who were with

---
19 Col. 1.12.
20 Acts 8.5-17.
21 Acts 10.44.

him merited to receive the Holy Spirit before they received the sacrament of baptism.²¹ Hence, God has taught us that the sign of salvation is one thing, but that salvation itself is another; and that the form of piety is one thing, but that the virtue of piety is another. Notwithstanding all this, those men ask us: 'What will you give us, since we already have baptism?' Oh, what sacreligious vanity! To be without the Church, and to think so little of her that they think they receive nothing by acquiring membership in her communion! Let the prophet Amos say to them: 'Woe to those who regard Sion as nothing.'²² 'What would I receive?' says he, 'if I already have baptism?' You would receive the Church, which you have not; you would receive unity, which you have not; you would receive peace, which you have not. Now, deserter, if you regard all this as nothing, then fight against your supreme Head, who says: 'He who does not gather with me, scatters.'²³ Fight against His Apostle, and thereby fight against Him who speaks through the voice of the Apostle, when He says: 'Bearing with one another in love, careful to preserve the unity of the Spirit in the bond of peace.' Count the things He has mentioned: forbearance, unity of the Spirit, peace. The Spirit who is mentioned here is the Spirit who works all things;²⁴ and you have him not. Have you exercised forbearance? You have withdrawn from the Church. Whom have you loved? You have deserted the members of Christ. What kind of unity have you in a sacrilegious schism? What kind of peace have you in nefarious dissension? Far be it from us to regard these things as nothing. On the contrary, you are nothing without them. If you disdainfully refuse to receive these things in the Church, then you may indeed have bap-

---
22 Amos 6.1. Differs from the Vulgate.
23 Luke 11.23.
24 1 Cor. 12.11.

tism, but, as long as you have not these things, then whatever else you have will be but a greater mark of your mutilation. For, if you had these things, the baptism of Christ would be the prop of your salvation. But, as long as you have them not, it only testifies to your hostility.

(4) And now, devout children, Catholic members, you have not received a different kind of baptism; you have received the same baptism, but you have received it for a different effect. Because you have at the same time received also the unity of the Spirit in the bond of peace, you have therefore received baptism into life, not into penalty; you have received it into salvation, not into destruction; you have received it into honor, not into condemnation. My wish and my hope, my exhortation and my prayer for you is that you will preserve inviolate what you have received, and that you will progessively advance to greater heights. Today is the octave of your nativity, and the seal of faith is completed in you today.[25] In the Old Law, the seal used to be effected through the circumcision of the flesh on the eighth day after birth, because the divesting of mortality used to be figuratively represented in that bodily member through which man is born to die. Even the Lord himself divested Himself of the mortality of the flesh by rising again, for He did not raise up another body; He raised up the same body, which nevertheless will die no more. By His resurrection He has therefore put the seal of *Lord's Day* on the day which is the third from the day of His passion, and which is at once the eighth and the first day after the Sabbath. Hence, you have received also the pledge of the Spirit. For, while you have

---

25 By baptism on Easter Sunday, they were born again. (Cf. John 3.3-5.) On the following Sunday, they put off the distinctive robes of neophytes. (Cf *Commentary* 1.4.12, n. 8.)

not actually received that pledge in its fulfillment, you have received it in a hope that is certain, because you have received the sacrament of that which is pledged. 'If you have risen with Christ, mind the things that are above, where Christ is seated at the right hand of God. Seek the things that are above, not the things that are on earth. For you have died and your life is hidden with Christ in God. When Christ, your life, shall appear, then you, too, will appear with him in glory.'[26]

---
26 Col. 3.1-4.

SERMON 13 (Den.)[1]

Christ: The Glory of Martyrs

(1) Because of the weariness of our audience, this discourse ought to be omitted, but for the sake of honoring the martyr it must be delivered. With the help of the Lord, therefore, it will be so modified as to be neither burdensome to our hearers nor insufficient for our purpose. A day of great solemnity has dawned in Rome, for vast crowds are assembling there to celebrate this feast. Although we are not among them in the flesh, we are nevertheless joined with them; for in spirit we are one with them, our brethren in one body under one Head. The commemoration of a martyr's merit is not confined to the place where his body lies entombed. In all places devotion is his due; for, although his body is laid to rest in a certain place, his soul is living in triumph with Him who is present everywhere. We are told that the blessed Lawrence had the physical appearance of a youth but the character of a mature and serious man, and that his youthful vigor, like an unfading garland, made him very attractive. He was a deacon, and therefore of lower rank than a bishop; but the crown of martyrdom has made him the equal of an apostle. This annual commemoration of all the glorious martyrs has been instituted in the Church in order that those who have not witnessed their

---

[1] See p. 307, n. 1. This sermon was delivered in the basilica at Carthage, on the feast of St. Lawrence, August 10.

sufferings may be reminded of them by this commemoration and may be led to imitate the constancy of the martyrs,[2] for if a deed is not presented anew by a yearly commemoration, it may lose its hold on the hearts of men. But in all places there are some martyrs whose fervent commemoration cannot be held, because there would then be no day without such a commemoration, since you can find no day in which somewhere or other no martyr received the crown. If solemn feasts were being celebrated continuously they would occasion distaste, whereas intervening periods reenkindle desire. Let us follow what has been prescribed, let us look forward to what has been promised. On the occasion of the feast of any martyr, let us so prepare our hearts for the festival that we may not exclude ourselves from following his example.

(2) The martyr was human; we, also, are human. By whom he was made, by that same Being we also were made. We have been redeemed by the same price with which he also was redeemed. So, it behooves no Christian to say: 'Why should I follow his example?' And of course no Christian ought to say: 'I will not follow his example.' You have heard the words of the blessed Cyprian, the trumpet and the exemplar of martyrs: 'In presecution, warfare receives the crown; in peace, constancy is rewarded.'[3] Then let no man think that he lacks opportunity. The occasion for suffering is sometimes absent, but the opportunity for devotion

---
2 In the early days of Christianity a special yearly celebration was held for each martyr at the place where he or she suffered martyrdom. When the number of martyrs had become so great that a separate day could not be assigned for each, the Church instituted a common feast day for all the martyrs. This commom feast has evolved into the present-day Feast of All Saints.
3 The concluding words of the *De exhortatione*. St. Cyprian had been bishop of Carthage and had suffered martyrdom in that city.

is always present. And let no man think himself weak when God affords him strength, lest he not only fear for his own weakness but even lose trust in Him who works in him.[4] In fact, God has willed that both sexes and all ages be included as examples of martyrs. Aged men receive the crown; young men, adolescents, and children have also received it. And not men only, but women also have received the crown; and women of every age have received it. The woman did not say that because of her sex she was unequal to the task of overcoming the Devil. Rather, she became all the more determined to overthrow the enemy by whom she had been overcome, and to combat with faith the seducer to whose wiles she had consented. But, did women therefore presumptuously rely on their own strength? To every human being it has been said: 'What hast thou that thou hast not received?'[5] So, the glory of the martyrs is Christ. He leads the martyrs, gives strength to the martyrs, and awards them the crown. And even though peace reigns at one time and persecution rages at another, is there any time when there is not a hidden persecution? The hidden persecution is always with us; for, although that dragon, lion-and-serpent, is neither always raging nor always lurking, he is always in hostile pursuit. When his rage is manifest, his ambush is not hidden; when his ambush is hidden, his rage is not manifest. In a word, when he rages like a lion he does not crawl like a serpent, and when he crawls like a serpent he does not rage like a lion; but, because he is either lion or serpent, he is always in hostile pursuit. When his roar is not heard, beware of his ambush; when his ambush is revealed, keep away from his roar. You will avoid both

---
4 Phil. 2.13.
5 1 Cor. 4.7.

the lion and the serpent if you keep your heart constant in Christ. Transient, indeed, are the terrors of this life. But in the next life, what we ought to love does not pass away, and neither does that which we ought to fear.

(3) In the Gospel which has just now been read, the Lord addressed the Jews and said to them: 'Woe to you, Scribes and Pharisees! For you build the sepulchres of the prophets, and say, "If we had lived in the days of our fathers, we would not have consented with them in the murder of the prophets." For you give testimony that you are the children of those who killed the prophets. You also will fill up the measure of your fathers.'[6] By saying: 'If we had lived in the days of our fathers, we would not have consented with them in the murder of the prophets,' they affirmed that they were the children of those who killed the Prophets. As for us, however, if we direct our course aright, we do not say that our fathers are those who killed the Prophets; rather, we say that our fathers are those who were killed by the fathers of those whom the Lord was addressing. Just as a man degenerates by reason of his morals, so also does a man gain sonship by reason of morals; for, brethren, we certainly have been called the children of Abraham, although we have neither seen the face of Abraham nor derived our lineage from his racial stock. In what way are we the children of Abraham? Not in the flesh, but in faith; for 'Abraham believed God and it was credited to him as justice.'[7] So, if Abraham is righteous because he believed, all subsequent imitators of the faith of Abraham have been made the children of Abraham. The Jews, although born of his

---

6 Matt. 23.29-32. The sentence, *You also will fill* . . .. varies from the Vulgate.
7 Gen. 15.5; Rom. 4.3.

flesh, have lost the sonship; but we, although born of strangers, have acquired by imitation what they have lost by degeneration. Although they descend from the flesh of Abraham, they are far from having Abraham as their father. Their fathers are those whom they acknowledged when they said: 'If we had lived in the days of our fathers, we would not have consented with them in the murder of the prophets.' It is as though the Lord were saying to them: How can you say that you would not have consented with those whom you call your fathers; for if they were your fathers you are their children, and if you are their children you would have consented with them? On the other hand, if you would not have consented with them you are not their chilrden, and if you are not their children they are not your fathers. So, from the very fact that they called the killers of the Prophets their fathers, the Lord pointed out to them that they would have done what the killers of the Prophets had done, for he said to them: 'You give testimony against yourselves that you are the children of those who killed the prophets, because you call them your fathers; and you will fill up the measure of your fathers.'

(4) Let us now consider who are the children of the slain and who are the children of the slayers. You see many hastening to the tombs of martyrs, you see them blessing their chalices at the tombs of martyrs, and you see them returning in a maudlin state from the tombs of martyrs. Examine them closely, and you will find that some of them are persecutors of martyrs. Because of them we have tumults, quarrels, dancings, and every kind of debauchery that is hateful to God. Since the martyrs have already received their reward, these persecutors cannot now assault them with stones, but they assail them with goblets. Who are those whose dancing

was prohibited at the grave of the blessed martyr, Cyprian, during the recent celebration which is almost of yesterday? Who are they? and whose children are they? They were dancing there, and they were hilarious.[8] They had been eagerly looking forward to that celebration. Anticipating the pleasure it would afford them, they were always eager to attend that celebration. But in what category are they to be reckoned? Are they to be classed among the persecutors of the martyrs? or among the children of martyrs? When they were forbidden to dance, they revealed their character; they showed their arrogance by starting a riot. The children of martyrs render praise, the persecutors of martyrs engage in dancing: the children sing hymns, the others indulge in revelry. Their

---

8 Profane amusement on religious feast days had been permitted for the purpose of removing the danger of idolatrous practices from the converts from paganism; for, if such amusements were not offered at the Christian festival, many of those converts would undoubtedly attend a pagan festival on the same day, and would thus be exposed to the danger of participating in idolatrous worship. The practice was, originally, not peculiar to Africa or to the fifth century. In Asia Minor, St. Gregory Thaumaturgus fostered it in Neo-Caesarea about the middle of the third century; and the Pope, St. Gregory I (590-604), advised Mellitus to permit it in England. St. Augustine did not condemn the action or impugn the motives of those who introduced the practice or allowed it to continue; but he maintained that in his day it no longer served the original purpose, that it had been discontinued in Italy and elsewhere, while throughout Africa it had become a vicious and scandalous practice of revelry and drunkenness. Less than two years after his ordination to the priesthood, he pleaded for concerted action on the part of all the bishops in Africa toward the abolishing of the practice (*Epist* 23). The following year, the bishops assembled at Hippo and adopted a measure forbidding the attendance of priests or bishops at such profane amusements, and urged that the laity be dissuaded from engaging in them. A few years later, this measure was formulated and adopted as a canon of the Council at Carthage. Not only in the present sermon, but in others also, St. Augustine strongly condemned the practice as sinful and scandalous. (Cf. *Sermons* 254, 311.) In one of his letters (*Epist.* 29.11.), he speaks of at least partial success in his efforts to abolish the abuse, and an observation is *Sermon* 311.5 would indicate a still greater measure of success.

seeming rendering of praise is a matter of no importance. When such as those render praise they are of the same character as those who said: 'If we had lived in those days, we would not have consented with our fathers in the murder of the prophets.' Let them be in accord with the faith of the martyrs; then we shall believe that they would not have been in accord with the murderers of martyrs. What is the reason why the martyrs received the crown? I believe that they received it because they kept to the godly path and patiently endured their sufferings, because they loved their enemies and prayed for them. This is what constitutes both the martyr's merit and the martyr's crown. If you love the martyrs, if you imitate and praise them, then you are the children of the martyrs. But if your conduct is in opposition with theirs, you will receive an opposite recompense.

(5) Dearly beloved, as I have already said, the Devil is always either raging or lying in ambush. So, it behooves us to be always prepared by keeping our hearts fixed on the Lord. It behooves us to exert ourselves to the utmost in beseeching the Lord for fortitude in the midst of those harassing trails and tribulations, for of ourselves we are nothing but little children. What should we say with regard to ourselves? You have heard the answer from the Apostle Paul during the reading of the Epistle, wherein he says: 'For as the sufferings of Christ abound in us, so also through Christ does our comfort abound.'[9] In the psalm, it is expressed in this way: 'According to the multitude of my sorrows in my heart, thy encouragements have given joy to my soul.'[10] The Psalmist expresses it one way, the Apostle expresses it in another, but each of them tells us that if the Comforter were

---
9 2 Cor. 1.5.
10 Ps. 93.19.

not with us we would yield to the persecutor. Listen also to what the Apostle says with regard to an occasion when—because of the calls for his ministry—he was bereft either of the very power of endurance, or at least of a certain facility over and above that power. He says: 'I make known to you, brethren, the tribulation which came upon us in Asia, because we were crushed beyond measure and beyond our strength.'[11] This tribulation exceeded human power of endurance. But was it more powerful than the help of God? 'We were crushed,' says he, 'beyond measure and beyond *our* strength.' How far beyond his strength? Hear what he says about his strength of mind: 'So that we were weary even of life.' How depressed he must have been by the multitude of his afflictions when weariness was holding him back and charity was goading him on! And how was charity goading him on? Elsewhere, he says with regard to that charity: 'But to stay on in the flesh is necessary for your sake.'[12] And yet, persecution and tribulation had become so great that he was weary of life itself. Fear and trembling had come upon him and darkness had enveloped him, as you have heard when it was read in the psalm. That is the voice of the body of Christ, the voice of the members of Christ. Would you like to recognize it as your own voice? Then, be one of Christ's members, and hear what the psalm says: 'Fear and trembling are come upon me, and darkness has covered me. And I said, Who will give me wings like a dove, and I will fly and be at rest.'[13] Is not this like to the cry of the Apostle when he says: 'So that we were weary even of life'? It is as though he were suffering weariness from the slime of the body, for he was longing to fly to

---

11 2 Cor. 1.8.
12 Phil. 1.24.
13 Ps. 54.6-7.

Christ while the abundance of tribulations was impeding his flight without rendering it impossible. Yes, he was weary of life, weary of this life; for weariness is not to be found in the everlasting life, to which he refers when he says: 'For to me to live is Christ and to die is gain.'[14] Charity was forcing him to stay on in this life. What was the result of this constraint? 'But if to live in the flesh is my lot, it is a fruitful labor here for me. But I know not which to choose; for, having the desire to be dissolved and to be with Christ, I am hard pressed from both sides.'[15] 'Who will give me wings like a dove?' 'But to stay on in the flesh is necessary for your sake.' He would yield for the sake of his chirping nestlings. He would shield and cherish them under his extended wings. His own expression is: 'I have become as a child in your midst, like a nurse cherishing her children.'[16]

(6) Now, brethren, consider the passage of the Gospel which was read to you a moment ago: 'How often would I have gathered thy children together, as a hen gathers her chickens, but thou wouldst not.'[17] Consider the hen, and then consider the other birds which build nests that we can see. These birds hatch their eggs and nourish their young, but you will not see them becoming weak with their offspring. In contrast, note the condition of the hen while she is nourishing her chickens. Notice how her cackle changes into a somewhat raucous cluck. Even her wings are not contracted and lively; they are disheveled and drooping. If you were to see another bird while you knew nothing about her nest, you could not tell whether she had eggs or younglings in her nest. But the hen is so unique in this regard

---
14 Phil. 1.21.
15 Phil. 1.22-23.
16 1 Thess. 2.7.
17 Matt. 23.37.

that even though you do not see either her eggs or her chickens, yet from her cluck and the condition of her body, you would know that she is a mother. What, then, has our mother, Wisdom, done?[18] Wisdom became weak in the flesh, in order to gather chickens, in order to generate and nourish them. But the weakness of God is stronger than men.[19] Under the wings of the weakness of His flesh and under the hidden power of His divinity, the Lord would have gathered the children of Jerusalem. He had taught His Apostle to do this, for it was He that was doing it in the person of the Apostle, as the latter tells us when he says: 'Do you seek a proof of the Christ who speaks in us?'[20] He also says that the sufferings of Christ abound in him—not his own sufferings, but the sufferings of Christ. For he was a member of Christ in the body of Christ; and whatever was being effected in him with regard to the nurturing of little ones was being effected by the Head through His member. And hence it is that, although the Apostle ardently desired to fly like a dove, yet, through love for his nestlings, he would stay with them like a hen. Again, he says: 'Yes, we have been carrying within our very selves our death sentence, in order that we may not trust in ourselves, but in God who raises the dead. He it is who delivered us, and will deliver us, from such great deaths. In him we have hope to be delivered yet again.'[21] What does he mean when he says:

---

18 Cf. 1 Cor. 1.24. Elsewhere, Augustine says: 'Not without reason has the hen been compared with the very Wisdom of God. . . . No other bird is thus weakened with her nestlings. . . . We recognize her in the weakness of her voice and in the drooping of her wings. . . . Likewise, the Wisdom of God made Himself weak because we were weak' (*Enarr. in ps.* 90.1.5).
19 1 Cor. 1.25.
20 2 Cor. 13.3.
21 2 Cor. 1.9-10.

'He has delivered us and will deliver us'? He means to tell the Corinthians that Christ is preserving his present life for their sake; for He delivered him from many kinds of death, lest he should be so overcome by persecutors that he would receive the crown before his nestlings had ceased to need him. This is also what he means when he says: 'But to stay on in the flesh is necessary for your sake. And with this conviction I know that I shall stay on and continue with you for your progress and joy in the faith.'[22] His ardent longing was driving him in one direction, but his nestlings' need was holding him still. 'Desiring to depart and to be with Christ, a lot by far the best.'[23] He does not say that this is necessary; he says that it is best. That which is best is sought for its own sake; that which is necessary is accepted through necessity, and that is why it is said to be necessary.

(7) Necessity has imposed the added need of the thing that is necessary. For instance, the food that we consume is a *necessary* food for us now, because we need it in order to sustain this temporal life. But there is another food, the food of virtue and wisdom, the living bread, the ever-refreshing and never-failing bread. This is the food that is *best*. Yes, this food is best; the other food is necessary. Consequently, that food will be no longer necessary when the demands of hunger and the necessity of sustaining this mortal body will have passed away. Hear what the Apostle says: 'Food for the belly and the belly for foods, but God will destroy both it and them.'[24] When will God destroy them? He will destroy them when, in the resurrection, this animal body becomes a spiritual body; for there will then be

---

22 Phil. 1.24-25.
23 Phil. 1.23.
24 1 Cor. 6.13.

no want and there will be no works of necessity. The works which are now called good works, and even the works which we are admonished to perform every day—all those works, brethren, are works of necessity. To share your food with one who is hungry, to share your home with one who is needy and shelterless, to furnish care and clothing to one who is naked, to concern yourself with the burial of the dead, to seek to effect an agreement between litigants, to visit a sick man or to provide for his care—what other work could be so good, so praiseworthy, so characteristically Christian? All these works are praiseworthy. But if you reflect upon them, you will see that necessity is the mother of them all. For instance, you share your food with one who is hungry. But if no one were hungry, with whom could you share your food? Take away the necessity induced by another's misery, and there will be no need for your mercy. Nevertheless, even though it is necessity that has given rise to these works, it is through them that we reach the life in which there is no necessity. These works may be compared with a ship which is bearing us to our homeland, for a man has no need of the ship if he is never to depart from his homeland, but is to remain there always. And yet, the ship bears passengers to the homeland, even though it is not needed in the land itself. So, we can no longer perform those works when our life's journey will have ended; but, unless we have performed them during the course of this life, we cannot reach the other life. Therefore, brethren, busy yourselves now with those works of necessity, in order that you may be happy in the enjoyment of that eternity where necessity will not be. It will not be there, because death itself, the mother of all necessities, will have died. 'For this corruptible body must put on incorruption, and this mortal body must put on immortality.'²⁵ When death will be asked the question: 'O death, where is thy victory? O death, where is thy sting?'²⁶ that question will be addressed to a death which is already vanquished and destroyed; for 'the last enemy to be destroyed will be death.'²⁷

(8) In this life a war with death is being waged through all the works of necessity; for every want is exerting a pull toward a death, while every remedy is helping us to retreat from a death. The body is so unstable that some kinds of deaths are, as it were, repelled by other kinds of deaths. One might say that whatever remedy may be applied against a death becomes the remote beginning of another kind of death as soon as its application cannot be continued any longer. See how that is verified in our present life. Every remedy against a death is itself the remote beginning of a death if you would suffer a death by continuing to apply it. For instance, take the case of one who applies the remedy of fasting. He is refreshed if he eats food and digests it; but when he fasts he is applying the remedy of fasting in order to repel the death which intemperance would bring upon him, and he will not repel that death unless he applies the remedy of fast and abstinence. Nevertheless, he will have reason to fear death from hunger if he continues to apply the remedy of fasting, although he began to apply that remedy in order to repel the death which intemperance would bring upon him. So, just as he applied fasting as a remedy against the death which intemperance would bring upon him, he must also apply food as a remedy in order to escape the death which fasting would bring on. There-

---
25 1 Cor. 15.53.
26 1 Cor. 15.55.
27 1 Cor. 15.26.

fore, whichever of these two remedies you apply, you will die if you continue with it. Has walking fatigued you? You will grow faint and die of fatigue if you continue to walk without ceasing. Then you sit down to rest, in order to avoid growing faint. But, if you continue seated at rest, you will die of it. Did a heavy sleep press its weight upon you? You had to awake, or you would die of it. But you will die of sleeplessness unless you sleep again. For repelling any evil which oppresses you, can you name any remedy which you could adopt with so much security that you would be willing to continue it indefinitely? Whatever remedy you may adopt will itself become a threat. So, throughout this inconstant succession of needs and remedies, a war is being waged with death. But when this corruptible body will have put on incorruption, and this mortal body will have put on immortality, then death itself will be asked: 'O death, where is thy strife? O death, where is thy sting?'[28] Then we shall see, then we shall give praise, then we shall abide. No aid will then be needed, for there will be no want. In that life you find no beggar with whom to share your bread, no stranger with whom to share your home. You find no one thirsting to partake of your drink, no one naked for you to clothe, no sick one for you to visit, no litigants for you to reconcile, no dead for you to bury. In that life all are fed with the food of righteousness and with the drink of wisdom, all are clothed with immortality, all are living in their everlasting home. Eternity itself is the health of all; their peace and well-being are everlasting. In that life there is no litigation; for no one asks for judgment or for settlement of claims, and no one seeks punishment for offenses. In that life there is no sickness, no death.

---

28 1 Cor. 15.55. Varies from the Vulgate.

(9) We can enumerate those things, things which will *not* be there. But who could describe what will be there? 'Eye has not seen nor ear heard, nor has it entered into the heart of man.'[29] Aptly indeed does the Apostle say: 'The sufferings of the present time are not worthy to be compared with the glory to come that will be revealed in us.'[30] Remember then, O Christian, that, no matter what sufferings you may have to undergo, they are as nothing in comparison with the reward you are to receive. By our faith we hold fast to that tenet. Let it not lose hold on your affection. You cannot thereby grasp and see what you shall be. But how great must that be which cannot now be grasped by him who is destined to receive it! Yes, we shall be what we shall be, but we cannot now see what we shall be; for it is beyond the reach of our weakness, beyond all our powers of thought, beyond the utmost limit of our intellect. But at any rate, as St. John says: 'Beloved, we are the children of God.' Of course, in this life we are His children by adoption, by faith, by promise. For, brethren, we have received the Holy Spirit as a pledge; and how could he default who has given such a pledge? 'We are', says the Evangelist, 'the children of God, and it has not yet appeared what we shall be. We know that, when he appears, we shall be like to him, for we shall see him just as he is.'[31] The Evangelist says: 'It has not yet appeared,' but he does not describe that which has not yet appeared. He says: 'It has not yet appeared what we shall be.' Would that he had said: We shall be this or that, and such as this shall we be. But to whom could he give the description of what he might des-

---

29 Isa. 64.4; 1 Cor. 2.9.
30 Rom. 8.18.
31 1 John 3.2.

cribe? I ask: To whom could he describe it? I would not dare to ask: Who could describe it? Perhaps the Evangelist himself was one who could describe it; for it was he who reclined on the bosom of Christ and imbided wisdom from that bosom at the Last Supper.[32] Enlarged with that wisdom, he thundered forth the sentence: 'In the beginning was the Word.'[33] He it is that has told us: 'We know that, when what we shall be is made manifest, we shall be like to him, for we shall see him just as he is.' To whom shall we be like? To him, of course, whose children we are. The Evangelist says: 'Beloved, we are the children of God, and it has not yet appeared what we shall be. We know that, when he appears, we shall be like to him (whose children we are), for we shall see him just as he is.' Now, if you wish to be what you will be like, if you wish to know Him to whom you will be like, fix your gaze upon Him if you can. But you cannot fix your gaze upon Him. Hence, you do not know Him to whom you will be like. Therefore, you do not know how like to Him you will be. Because you do not know what *He* is,[34] you do not know what you yourself will be.

(10) With this in mind, dearly beloved, let us always look forward with longing toward our everlasting joy; let us always pray for fortitude in our temporal labors and trials; let us offer prayers for one another; let my prayers be offered for you, and yours for me. And, brethren, do not think

---

[32] John 13.23. 'John the Evangelist, who reclined on the Lord's bosom for no other reason than to imbibe the secrets of His sublime wisdom . . .' (*In Joan. evang.* tr. 20.1).
[33] John 1.1.
[34] 'God is ineffable. We can more easily say what He is not than we can say what He is' (*Enarr. in ps.* 85.12). 'There is indeed no small beginning of a knowledge of God if we begin to know what He is not before we can know what He is' (*Epist.* 120.3.13; cf. *De Trinit.* 8.2.3; *In Joan. evang.* tr 23.9).

that you need my prayers, but that I have no need of yours. We have mutual need of one another's prayers, for those reciprocal prayers are enkindled by charity and—like a sacrifice offered on the altar of piety—are fragrant, and pleasing to the Lord. If the Apostles used to ask for prayers on their own behalf,[35] how much the more does it behoove me to do so? For I am far from being their equal, although I long to follow their footsteps as closely as possible; but I have neither the wisdom to know nor the rashness to say what progress I have made. Those men, with all their greatness, were anxious to have prayers offered by the Church in their behalf. They used to say: 'We are your glory, as you also will be ours, in the day of the Lord Jesus Christ.'[36] They used to pray mutually for one another in anticipation of the day of our Lord Jesus Christ; for *on* that day there will be glory, but *until* that day there will be weakness. Let us pray in weakness, that we may rejoice in glory. At different times, and yet at the same time, we are all to reach that day. Various, indeed, are the respective times for our departure from this life, but the time for receiving the reward is the same for all; for we shall all be assembled at the same time and place to receive the reward which at various times we had hopefully desired. This is illustrated by the case of the workers in the vineyard. They were hired at different hours, some at the first hour, some at the third, some at the sixth, some at the ninth, and some at the tenth;[37] but the reward was given to all at the same time.

---

35 Rom. 15.30; 2 Cor. 1.11; Phil. 1.19; Col. 4.3; 1 Thess. 5.25; 2 Thess. 3.1; Heb. 13.18.
36 2 Cor. 1.14.
37 Matt. 20.1-6. In the Gospel, the eleventh—not the tenth—hour is mentioned.

SERMON 11 (Morin)[1]

On the Beatitudes

(Matt. 5.3-10)

(1) Dearly beloved, you have joined with us in listening to the reading of the Holy Gospel. May the Lord assist us while we address you on the portion that has been read, in order that our words may be appropriate to your needs and may bear spiritual fruit in your daily lives. Everyone who hears the word of God ought to bear in mind that his life ought to be conformed to what he hears. Therefore, let him not disregard that word in his conduct while he seeks to praise it with his lips. If the word of God is sweet to hear, how much sweeter must it be to do? I, indeed, may be likened to those who sow the seed; you are the fields in which the word of God is sown. May the seed perish not; may the harvest be plentiful. You have joined with us in listening to the words which Christ our Lord spoke to his disciples when they had drawn near to Him: 'And opening his mouth he taught them, saying: *"Blessed are the poor in spirit, for theirs is the kingdom of heaven,"*'[2] and so forth. Thus the one true Master, saying those things which we have briefly summarized for you,[3] taught His disciples as they were drawing close to Him. You

---
1 See p. 307, n. 1.
2 Matt. 5.3.
3 At this point, Augustine had undoubtedly summarized all the beatitudes, but either then or later a scribe substituted the expression, 'and so forth.'

have now drawn close to us, in order that we, with the help of that same Master, may address you and teach you. And, while we are expounding the truths which so great a Master has pronounced, what could be more helpful for us than to do what He has told us? Therefore, be poor in spirit, so that the kingdom of heaven may be yours.

(2) Why should you be afraid to be poor? Consider the riches of the kingdom of heaven. Yes, men fear poverty. But they ought to have a greater fear of iniquity. For, when poverty will have passed away, then will come the great happiness of the righteous, because they will then be free from all anxiety. In this present life, fear is all the more increased and covetousness is all the more unloosed according as there is an increase of those things which are called riches, for those things are not true riches. Were I to ask you, you could mention many a rich man. But, could you name one of them who is free from anxiety? The rich man is in a frenzy to increase his riches, and he is in trepidation lest he lose them. How could such a servant be free? A slave, indeed, is the servant of any mistress. Can the servant of avarice then be free? Hence: *'Blessed are the poor in spirit.'* What does it mean to be poor in spirit? The poor in spirit need not be poor in worldly possessions, but they must be moderate in their desires. The man who is poor in spirit is an humble man. God gives ear to the sighs of the humble, and does not despise their petitions. So, when the Lord delivered his Discourse,[4] he based its very beginning on humility, which means poverty. You could find a godly man who has an abundance of worldly wealth, but such a man is not puffed up with pride. You could also find a man so poverty-stricken that he has neither ownership nor possession of any worldly goods. There is no more as-

---
4 The Sermon on the Mount.

surance for the latter than for the former. The one is poor in spirit, because he is humble; the other is poor, indeed, but not poor in spirit. Thus it is that, when Christ the Lord said: *'Blessed are the poor,'* He added the clause, 'in spirit.' Therefore, I urge all of you who are poor and have heard those words not to seek become rich.

(3) Hear the words that were spoken, not by me, but by the Apostle. Hear what he has said: 'And godliness with contentment is indeed great gain. For we brought nothing into this world, and certainly we can take nothing out. Having food and clothing, with that let us be content. For those who seek to become rich fall into temptation and a snare.' He did not say: Those who *are* rich. He said: Those who *seek to become* rich. So he said: 'Those who seek to become rich fall into temptation and a snare and into many vain and harmful desires, which plunge men into destruction and perdition. For covetousness is the root of all evils; and some, pursuing it, have strayed from the faith and have involved themselves in many troubles.'[5] The name of riches is, as it were, sweet-sounding to the ear. But, 'many vain and harmful desires'—does that sound sweet? 'Destruction and perdition' —does that sound sweet? To be 'involved in many troubles' —does that sound sweet? Be not so misled by one false good that you will thereby cling to so many real evils. The holy Apostle was not addressing the rich when he used those words; he was addressing the poor, lest they should seek to become what they were not. So, let us see what words he used in his charge to those whom he found rich. We have told you what you ought to be told, and you who are poor have heard us. Now, if any one of you is rich, then listen to the selfsame holy Apostle.

(4) Among the other admonitions which he gave in writing

---
5 1 Tim. 6.6-10.

to his disciple Timothy, he included the following: 'Charge the rich of this world.' (The word of God had found them rich, for, if it had found them poor, he would have used the words we have already quoted.) Hence, he says: 'Charge the rich of this world not to be proud and not to trust in the uncertainty of riches, but to trust in the living God, who provides all things in abundance for our enjoyment. Let them be rich in good works, let them give freely, let them share with others, let them provide for themselves a good foundation against the time to come, in order that they may lay hold on the true life.'[6] Let us now devote a little time to the consideration of those few words. First of all, he says: 'Charge the rich not to be proud.' For riches, more than anything else, engender pride. Of course, if the rich man is not proud, he has already spurned his riches and has fixed his hopes in God. On the other hand, if he is proud, he does not possess his riches; he is possessed by them. Such a man may be compared with the Devil. What, indeed, does he have, since he has not God? The Apostle also admonished the rich 'not to trust in the uncertainty of riches.' A man's regard for his riches ought to be so moderated that he will bear in mind that what he has can perish. Let him lay hold, therefore, on that which he cannot lose. So, when the Apostle had told the rich 'not to trust in the uncertainty of riches,' he then told them 'to trust in the living God.' Yes, riches can be lost; and may they be lost in such a way that you will not be lost with them. The Psalm addresses the rich man, and mocks him if he puts his trust in riches. It says: 'Although man walks according to the image of God.'[7] (Man has indeed been created to the

---

[6] 1 Tim. 6.17-19.
[7] Ps. 38.7. A translation from the Vulgate would read: 'But man passes as an image.' A translation from the latest Latin version would read. 'Man passes only as a shadow.' (Cf. Commentary 1.21.72, n. 12.)

image of God. Let him therefore acknowledge himself to be what he has been created. Let him lose what he himself has made, and let him remain what God has made him.) So the Psalm says: 'Although man walks in the image of God, yet shall he be disquieted in vain.' How shall he be disquieted in vain? 'He is storing up treasures, and he knows not for whom he has gathered them.' The living notice this with regard to the dead. They see that in many cases the children do not possess the property of their deceased parents, but that they either squander their inheritance by dissipation or lose it through chicanery. Worse still, others are contending for a man's possessions while the man himself is dying. In fact, many are murdered for the sake of their riches. All that they possessed in this life, they have left behind. And with what dejection of spirit have they made their exit hence to stand before Him whose commands from heaven they had not obeyed? As for you, therefore, let your true riches be God Himself, 'who provides all things in abundance for our enjoyment.'

(5) 'Let them be rich in good works,' says the holy Apostle. In the field of good works, let riches be their servant in the sowing of the seed. For, it is this kind of well-doing that the same Apostle was speaking of when he said: 'And in doing good let us not grow tired: in due time we shall reap.'[8] Let them sow the seed. In sowing this kind of seed, a man does not already see the reward of his labors. But then, does the tiller of the soil already see the gathered harvest while he is sowing the seed? Yet, how laboriously he toils in bringing out and scattering the grain which has been gathered with so much care. He entrusts that seed to the earth. Will you not entrust your good works to Him who has made both heaven and earth? Yes, let them be rich, but

---
8 Gal. 6.9.

rich in good works. 'Let them give freely, let them share with others.' What does that mean? Let them not keep to themselves the enjoyment of their riches—that is the meaning of 'Let them share with others.' You, O Apostle, have addressed the rich and have instructed them to sow. Show them also what the harvest will be. But he has shown you what the harvest will be. Avaricious man, be not loath to sow your garnered treasure. Listen, and hear what the harvest will be. The Apostle did not stop speaking when he had said: 'Let them be rich in good works, let them give freely, let them share with others.' His one purpose is saying this was to induce the rich to scatter wide their riches. So, it was fitting that he should also tell them what harvest they would gather. Accordingly, he went on to say: 'Let them provide for themselves a good foundation against the time to come, in order that they may lay hold on the true life.' A false and fleeting life is the life in which riches afford delight. And, when a man has finished with that life, then he must pass on to the true life. Do you love your possessions? Then establish them in that safer place, lest you lose them. For any of you who loves riches, all his worry arises from the fear of losing them. Hearken, then, to the counsel of the Lord; transfer your riches to heaven, for there is no safe place on the earth. To none but a most faithful servant would you be willing to entrust the care of the treasure you have stored up. Entrust it to your faithful Master. No matter how faithful your servant may be to you, he could unwittingly lose what you entrust to him. Your God cannot lose anything. Whatever you entrust to God you will have with God when you will have God Himself.

(6) Now, let no material notions creep into your mind because I have told you to transfer your riches and to place them in heaven. Do not begin to ask yourself how you can

dig or raise your riches from the earth and place them in heaven, how you can ascend to heaven, or with what mechanical contrivance you can lift your riches up to heaven. Help the hungry, the naked, and the needy; help strangers and those in bondage. They will be the porters to convey your riches to heaven. Perhaps you are now wondering and asking yourself how those can be such porters. Just as you could find no answer when you were wondering how you yourself could lift your riches up to heaven, so, perhaps, you can find no answer now while you are wondering how those to whom you consign your riches can lift them up to heaven. Then hearken to what Christ tells you. He says: 'Construct a catapult; at your post consign your riches to Me, and I will repay you at My abode.' In other words, He says: 'On earth, where you have possessions, give them to Me and I will repay you here.' Perhaps you are wondering how you could give anything to Christ, since He is in heaven and sits at the right hand of the Father. You may be reasoning in this fashion: When Christ was here in the flesh, he deigned to be hungry for our sake, and also to be thirsty and in need of hospitality. But all his needs were then supplied to Him by devout persons who were found worthy to receive their Lord into their homes. However, he needs nothing now for he has placed His incorruptible flesh at the right hand of the Father. So, since He needs nothing here, how can I give Him anything? When you reason in that wise, you are forgetting that He says: 'What you did for one of the least of mine, you did it for me.'[9] As our Head, He is in heaven, but He has members on earth. Then, let a member of Christ give to a member of Christ. Let a member who has give to a member who needs. You are a member of Christ and you have the where-

---

[9] Matt. 25.40.

withal to give; the other is a member of Christ and he needs your gift. Both of you are traveling the same road; you are companions on the journey. Lightly laden are the poor man's shoulders, but yours are burdened with heavy luggage. Give away some of the load that is weighing you down; give some of your luggage to the needy man—and you will thus afford relief both to yourself and to your companion. The Scripture says: 'The rich and the poor have met one another; but the Lord has made them both.'[10] Where have they met, except in this life? The one is now arrayed in costly garments, while the other is clad in rags. When did they meet? Both were born naked, and even the rich man was born poor. Let him disregard what he found when he had come; let him consider what he brought with him. Miserable at his birth, what did he bring with him but tears and nakedness? Hence, the Apostle says: 'We brought nothing with us into this world, and certainly we can take nothing out.' Let the rich man, therefore, send out beforehand that which he will find when he himself goes out. Yes, one man is poor and another is rich, but the Lord has made them both. He has made the one man rich in order that he, in turn, may come to the aid of the poor man. He has left the other man poor in order to test the rich man. In either case, *'Blessed are the poor in spirit, for theirs is the kingdom of heaven.'* Whether they have riches or have them not, if they are poor in spirit *'theirs is the kingdom of heaven.'*

(7) *'Blessed are the meek, for by inheritance they shall possess the land.'*[11] The meek are those who do not resist the will of God. How do they practice meekness? When things are going well with them, they give praise to God; when things

---
10 Prov. 22.2.
11 Matt. 5.4.

are going badly, they do not blaspheme Him. For their good works, they give glory to God; for their sins, they blame themselves. *They shall inherit the land.* What land shall they inherit, but the land of which the Psalmist says: 'Thou art my hope, my portion in the land of the living'?[12]

(8) *'Blessed are they who mourn, for they shall be comforted.'*[13] My brethren, mourning is a sorrowful thing, for it is the sob of one who is sorry. Does anyone mourn, except for one who is dead? But, every sinner ought to mourn for himself, since there is nothing else so dead as a man in sin. Yet, how marvelous! If he mourns for himself, he comes to life again. Let him mourn through repentance, and he shall be comforted through forgiveness.

(9) *'Blessed are they who hunger and thirst for justice, for they shall be satisfied.'*[14] This means that in this land of ours they are hungry for justice. Elsewhere, where no one will sin, they shall have such a fullness of justice as the holy angels enjoy. But, while we are hungry and thirsty for justice here, let us continue to say to God: 'Thy will be done on earth, as it is in heaven.'[15]

(10) *'Blessed are the merciful, for they shall obtain mercy.'*[16] Having said: *'Blessed are they who hunger and thirst for justice, for they shall be satisfied,'* it was most timely for Him to add: *'Blessed are the merciful, for God will show mercy to them.'* You are hungry and thirsty for justice, and, being hungry and thirsty, you are God's beggar. Now, while you stand as a beggar before the door of God, another man stands as a beggar before your door. Howsoever you deal with your beggar, in that same way will God deal with His.

---
12 Ps. 141.6.
13 Matt. 5.5.
14 Matt. 5.6.
15 Matt. 6.10.
16 Matt. 5.7.

(11) *'Blessed are the pure of heart, for they shall see God.'*[17] If any man has put into practice all that has been already said [in expounding the beatitudes already discussed], his heart is now being purified. Such a man has a pure heart, for he is not displaying a false friendship while harboring enmity in his heart. Where the eye of God beholds, there the hand of God bestows a crown. In your heart, let there be neither approval nor praise for anything which delights you there. If evil concupiscence occasions a pleasant sensation, let no consent be given; if it flames into passion, let God be implored against it that the heart may be inwardly aroused and cleansed, for it is within the heart that petition is made to God Himself. Be sure to make the chamber clean if you wish to invite God to enter it, and clean it from within, in order that God may vouchsafe to hear you. At times, the tongue is silent while the soul is sighing, for within the chamber of the heart supplication is being made to God. Let there be nothing in it to offend the eyes of God, nothing to displease Him. If you are earnestly striving to make your heart pure, call upon Him who will not disdain to make it a clean abode for Himself, and who will deign to abide with you. Can it be that you are afraid to provide hospitality within your home for such a mighty potentate? Are you perturbed about it? Are you like certain stolid or stingy men who are wont to be afraid that they will be constrained to furnish the hospitality of their homes to some important personages who may be passing by? Of course, there is nothing greater than God. But be not perturbed about the narrowness of your chamber, for He will enlarge its capacity. You have nothing good enough to set before Him? Receive Him, and He will provide the feast for you. Yes—and what is still more pleasant

---

17 Matt. 5.8.

for your ears to hear—He will give you Himself to eat. He will be your nourishment, for He has said: 'I am the bread that has come down from heaven.'[18] Such bread as this will always refresh and never fail. Hence: *'Blessed are the pure of heart, for they shall see God.'*

(12) *'Blessed are the peacemakers, for they shall be called the children of God.'*[19] Who are the peacemakers? They are those who make peace. Do you see two persons at odds with each other? Try to restore peace between them. To one of them, speak well of the other; to the latter, speak well of the former. After the manner of an angry man, one of them may have told you something bad about the other. Do not reveal it. Bury within your bosom any disparaging remarks you have heard from the man in anger. Let harmony be the constant aim of your advice. If you would be a peacemaker between two of your friends who are at odds, begin by making peace with yourself. You must first have peace within yourself, whereas you may now be striving and contending with yourself every day. Take the case of the man who said: 'The flesh lusts against the spirit, and the spirit against the flesh; for these are opposed to each other, so that you do not do what you would.'[20] These are the words of the same holy Apostle who also says: 'For according to the inner man, I am delighted with the law of God; but I see another law in my members, warring against the law of my mind and making me prisoner to the law of sin that is in my members.'[21] Did not this man have strife within himself? Now, if there is a daily strife within a man, and if it is occasioned by a constant praiseworthy effort to prevent his lower appetite from gaining

---

18 John 6.41.
19 Matt. 5.9.
20 Gal. 5.17.
21 Rom. 7.22-23.

ascendancy over his higher faculty, to prevent lust from overcoming the mind, to prevent concupiscence from prevailing over wisdom, then there is a righteous peace which you ought to attain within yourself. This kind of peace consists in keeping all your lower desires in subjection to that higher faculty which is within you and in which the image of God is. This faculty is called mind; it is also called intelligence. In this faculty, faith is enlivened, hope is strengthened, and charity is inflamed. Now, do you wish to have your mind prepared and ready to control your carnal desires? Then, let the mind itself be obedient to a higher power. In that way, it will control your lower desires, and you will have peace with yourself—the peace which is genuine, well established, and orderly in the highest degree. What is the orderly arrangement of this peace? There is no arrangement more orderly; the mind obeys God and commands the flesh. Of course, the flesh still has its infirmities, but this was not the case in paradise. It is through sin that the flesh has been reduced to this condition; because of sin, it makes the bond [of union with the soul] an occasion of discord against us. In order to bring our flesh into harmony with our soul, One who is without sin has come and has deigned to give us 'the pledge of the Spirit.'[22] 'For whoever are led by the Spirit of God, they are the children of God.'[23] *'Blessed are the peacemakers, for they shall be called the children of God.'* As yet we are not free from all this warfare, which saps our strength because of our weakness. For, as long as we do not consent to our carnal desires, we are, as it were, engaged in battle against them. But there will be no contention whatever when death will have been swallowed up in victory. Hear how it is that there

---

22 2 Cor.. 5.5.
23 Rom. 8.14.

will be no contention then. This is what the Apostle says: 'For this corruptible body must put on incorruption, and this mortal body must put on immortality. But when this mortal body puts on immortality, then shall come to pass the word that is written, "Death is swallowed up in victory." '[24] The war is over; it is concluded in peace. Listen to the shout of the victors: 'O death, where is thy contention? O death, where is thy sting?' The meaning of that cry of the victors is this: No enemy of any kind will be left; there will be no strife within, and no attack from without. Hence, *'Blessed are the peacemakers, for they shall be called the children of God.'*

(13) *'Blessed are they who suffer persecution for justice' sake.'*[25] The added clause, *'for justice' sake,'* marks the difference between the martyr and the thief. Even the thief suffers persecution, but he suffers it for his evil deeds; he is not seeking to gain a crown, he is suffering a just penalty. It is the cause for which he suffers, and not the punishment inflicted, that makes a man a martyr. First, he must willingly embrace the cause; then he can tranquilly suffer the punishment. There were three crosses in the same place when Christ endured His passion. Hanging on the middle cross, He had a thief hanging beside Him on the right hand side and another on the left. If you consider merely the sufferings they were undergoing, you will find no cases more alike. Yet, one of the thieves gained paradise through the cross, for Christ, acting as judge while hanging on the middle cross, condemned the proud thief and came to the aid of the thief who was humble. The Cross of Christ became Christ's tribunal. Since He had this power while under judgment, what will be His power

---
24 1 Cor. 15.53-55.
25 Matt. 5.10.

when He comes to render judgment? To the thief who had confessed his sins, Christ said: 'Amen I say to thee, this day thou shalt be with me in paradise.'[26] That thief was his own accuser. But of what did he accuse himself when he said: 'Lord, remember me when thou comest into thy kingdom?' This is what he meant: I acknowledge the evil I have done; so, let me be crucified until Thou comest [into Thy kingdom]. Then, because everyone that humbles himself shall be exalted,[27] Christ at once pronounced the sentence, and granted forgiveness. He said: 'This day thou shalt be with me in paradise.' But was not the Lord wholly buried in the tomb that day? At any rate, His body was to be in the tomb Yes, and his soul was to be in hell—not that He was to be confined in hell, but that He was to release those who were confined there. Now, since His soul was to be in hell that very day and since His body was to be in the tomb, how could Christ say: 'This day thou shalt be with me in paradise'? In the person of Christ, is there nothing more than body and soul? Does it escape you that 'In the beginning was the Word, and the Word was with God, and the Word was God'?[28] Does it escape you that Christ is 'the power of God and the wisdom of God'?[29] And where is it that the wisdom of God is not? Of that wisdom, is it not written: 'She reaches from end to end mightily, and orders all things sweetly'?[30] Therefore, the Lord was speaking of the person of the Word when He said: 'This day thou shalt be with me in paradise.' That is to say: With regard to My soul, I descend into hell, but as regards My divinity, I depart not from paradise.

(14) Dearly beloved, to the best of my ability I have ex-

---

26 Luke 23.43.
27 Matt. 23.12.
28 John 1.1.
29 1 Cor. 1.24.
30 Wisd. 8.1.

pounded all the beatitudes enunciated by Christ; yet I see that you are eager to hear more. Our love toward you has induced us to speak at length. Perhaps we could say more, but it is better that you should carefully ponder and profitably digest what has been said.

INDEX

INDEX

Abraham, 342, 343
Acts of St. Thomas, 93 n.
Acyndinus, 71-73
Adam, 54, 251, 260, 316
Adultery, 52-56, 58-73, 205-206
Alexander, the coppersmith, 100, 101, 104
Almsgiving, 113-118, 165-168, 191, 249, 259-273, 275-286, 287-292
Ambrose, St., 6, 27 n., 133 n.
Anger, 40-44, 204, 233-238, 367
Apollinarists, 318-319
Arians, 319
Astrologers, 250
Athanasius, St., 207 n.
Augustine, St., as bishop, 12, 13; Commentary on the Lord's Sermon on the Mount, purpose of, 3, 9; his knowledge of Greek, 7-9; of Hebrew, 7-9; of Latin, 5-10; of Punic, 6-8; of Scripture, 4-11; his preaching, 4, 11-15; *Sermons*, 11-15, 211-371; works cited:

Comment. in quattuor S. Evang., 97 n.
Confessiones, 5 n., 6 n., 7 n., 54 n., 78 n., 322 n.
Contra adversarium legis et prophetarum, 188 n.
Contra Faustum, 71 n., 93 n.
Contra Julianum, 50 n., 188 n.
Contra Adimantum, 71 n., 93 n., 205 n.
De bono conjugali, 67 n., 70 n., 205 n.
De catechizandis rudibus, 13 n., 71 n.
De civitate Dei, 5 n., 7 n., 9 n., 86 n., 87 n., 203 n.
De conjugiis adulterinis, 205 n.
De consensu evangeliorum, 182 n.
De correptione et gratia, 102 n.
De cura pro mortuis gerenda, 125 n.
De diversis quaestionibus, 205 n.
De doctrina Christiana, 3 n., 7 n., 9 n., 10 n., 30 n., 250 n.

375

De dono perseverantiae, 92 n., 138 n.
De fide et operibus, 203 n.
De Genesi ad litteram, 11, 54 n., 91 n.
De Genesi contra Manich., 54 n., 71 n., 92 n., 187 n., 204 n.
De gratia et libero arbitrio, 176 n.
De libero arbitrio, 185 n.
De moribus ecclesiae Cath. et de moribus Manich., 86 n., 192 n.
De Trinitate, 11, 354 n.
De utilitate credendi, 10 n., 92 n.
De vera religione, 189 n.
Ennarationes in psalmos, 5 n., 31 n., 40 n., 54 n., 82 n., 83 n., 86 n., 87 n., 132 n., 145 n., 171 n., 172 n., 188 n., 198 n., 203 n., 265 n., 337 n., 348 n., 354 n.
Epistola, 7 n., 13 n., 30 n., 87 n., 92 n., 102 n., 120 n., 125 n., 164 n., 175 n., 205 n., 221 n., 276 n., 333 n., 344 n., 354 n.
In Joannis evangelium, 7 n., 87 n., 116 n., 203 n., 208 n., 316 n., 321 n., 354 n.
Locutiones in Heptateuchum, 7 n., 83 n., 86 n.
Retractationes, 3 n., 28 n., 29 n., 35 n., 38 n., 40 n., 46 n., 62 n., 63 n., 100 n., 128 n., 156 n., 165 n., 176 n., 182 n., 201-208.
Sermones, 30 n., 55 n., 70 n., 75 n., 82 n., 83 n., 86 n., 87 n., 92 n., 102 n., 132 n., 139 n., 215 n., 265 n., 293 n., 322 n., 325 n., 344 n.

Baptism, 30 n., 239 n., 251-252, 321-326, 331-337
Barry, Sister M. Inviolata, 11 n.
Beatitudes:
Blessed are the meek, 23, 27, 29, 52, 147, 188, 212, 215, 217, 364
Blessed are the merciful, 23, 26, 28, 29, 108, 147, 213, 215, 217, 218, 271, 365
Blessed are the peacemakers, 23, 24, 26, 28, 29, 148, 197, 201, 366-368
Blessed are the poor in spirit, 21, 22, 25-28, 46, 146, 211, 215, 217, 357, 358, 364
Blessed are the pure of heart, 23, 28, 29, 148, 187, 213, 214, 217, 218, 226, 305, 366
Blessed are they that mourn, 22, 23, 28, 29, 56, 147, 213, 215, 217, 365
Blessed are they who hunger, 23, 28, 29, 147, 168, 213, 215, 217, 280, 365
Blessed are they who suffer persecution, 24-26, 29, 31, 369

INDEX   377

Bede, Venerable, 30 n.
Benevolence, 46-52; see Charity
Bishop, 294

Capelle, P., 9 n.
Cassamassa, A., 3 n., 4 n.
Charity, 20, 21, 85-88, 94, 245, 347, 366; see Love
Chastity, 58-73
Christ, 20, *passim*; Counsellor and Corrector, 259; Glory of Martyrs, 339-355; heirs with, 105, 106, 123; Lamb and Lion, 308-310; Redeemer, 311-320; see Redemption; Resurrection
Christian life, perfect standard of, 19
Cleansing of heart, 109-110, 118, 149ff.
Clement of Alexandria, 125 n.
Constantius, 71
Cornelius, 334
Counsel, 27-29, 147
Covetousness, 52-54, 68, 154, 269, 298; see Greed
Creed, 241, 317 n.
Cyprian, St., 129 n., 138 n., 340, 344

DeBruyne, E., 7 n., 118 n.
Death, 259-268, 296, 311-320, 327, 350-352, 361, 368, 369, *passim*
Denis, M., 307 n.

Devil, 49, 102, 140-144, 156, 241, 244, 296-299, 329, 345, 360
Discipline of the Secret, 4, 116 n.
Donatists, 30, 31

Easter, 331 n., 336 n.
Elias, 202
Eliseus, 202
Elpidius, 5
Epiphanius, 207 n.
Eunoon, 49
Eusebius, 173 n.

Faith, 31, 45, 193, 296, *passim*; and hope and charity, 220-221, 368
Farthing, last, 47-52, 136
Fasting, 149-152, 191
Feast of All Saints, 340 n.
Fidelity, 58
Flavius Josephus, 9
Florus, 211 n.
Focas, 318
Forgiveness of sins, 135-138, 148, 203, 248-256, 276 n.
Fornication, 58-73, 154, 205-206
Fortitude, 25-28, 147

Gehenna, 40 n., 41-43, 56, 233
Gentiles, 8, 96, 98, 99, 159, 239, 240, 264
God, as Chastiser, 236, 237, 292, 329; as Creator, 20; as Father, 122-124, 242-243;

378 INDEX

Name of, 127, 146, 147, 229, 240; vision of, 215-226; will of, 128-132, 244-246
Good works, 36, 37, 185, 224-225, 227, 277, 290-291, 329, 361-364
Grabmann, M., 7 n.
Greed, 152-153, 212, 359-360
Gregory I, Pope, 344 n.
Gregory of Nyssa, St., 126 n.
Gregory Thaumaturgus, St., 344 n.

Heaven, 32, 33, 38-40, 124-132, 145, 153, 222-223, 242-246, 269, 299, 301-305
Holy Eucharist, 132-135, 145-146, 213, 246-248, 253, 257, 271, 321-326, 349
Holy Spirit, 8, 23, 27, 30, 31, 100, 102, 103, 321; sin against, 102
Hypocrisy, 113-122, 149-152, 174, 191, 227, 232

Idolatry, 68, 69, 250
Incarnation, 317, 321
Irenaeus, 30 n., 172 n.
Itala, 8, 9

Jerome, St., 4, 7, 9, 97 n.
Jews, 20, 96 n., 98, 102, 175, 231, 239, 253, 274, 303, 304, 313, 342, *passim*
John Chrysostom, St., 97 n., 133 n.

John the Baptist, St., 295
Joseph, 140
Joy, 193, 195
Judas, 97, 101, 166, 241, 325
Judgment, 169-176; *see* Charity
Judgment, Last, 127-128, 206-207
Justice, 23, 31, 32, 34, 365

Knowledge, 27, 147
Kunzemann, A., 11 n.

Law and Prophets, 37-40, 52, 77, 81, 96, 97, 153, 175, 184-186, 288, 289, 336
Lawrence, St., 339 n.
Lawsuits, 86-87, 93
Light, 34-37, 153-155, 227-232
Lord's Prayer, 122-148, 239-257, 325
Love of enemies, 95-108, 204-205, 241, 248-256
Love of God, 24-28, *passim*
Love of neighbor, 80-108
Lust, 24, 25, 52-56, 236-237, 245, 367, *see* Adultery

Mammon, 155
Manichaeism, 4-6, 50 n., 91 n., 189 n.
Marriage, 58-73, 205-206
Martyrs, 104-105, 312-313, 318, 339-355
Measure, 34, 35, 202
Meekness, 23, 25, 27, 79-84, 147, 197; *see* Beatitudes

Mercy, 79, 82, 109, 156; see Beatitudes
Messe, 7
Messias, 7
Morin, G., 14, 307 n.
Moses, 58, 81

Neo-Platonists, 7

Oaths, 73-77
Origen, 4, 126 n., 173 n.

Pasch, 327-328
Pauline privilege, 67 n.
Pearls before swine, 176-182
Pelagians, 276 n.
Pentecost, 30
Perfection, grades of, 25-29, 202
Persecution, 30-33, 100, 105; see Martyrs; Tribulation
Perseverance, 92, 138, 183-184
Peter, St., 97, 172, 220, 333
Piety, 27, 147
Pontet, M., 11 n.
Possidius, St., 12 n., 286 n.
Prayer, 118-148, 191, 192, 239-257, 278-280, 354-355; see Lord's Prayer
Preaching, 11, 12
Presumption, 21
Pride, 21, 22, 50, 110-122, 149-152, 157-163, 192, 260, 261; see Beatitudes
Prophets, false, 188-193
Providence, 158-163, 208
Pseudo-Aristeas, 9

Punic, 6, 7 n., 155

Raca, 40-46, 57
Redemption, 225, 295-296, 308, 311, 336, 369-370
Regan, R. E., 11 n.
Repentance, 50, 51; 156, 272-273, 365
Resurrection, 29, 55, 61, 180, 308, 311-320, 332
Retaliation, 80-95

Salt of the earth, 33-34
Scandal, 56-57
Scribes and Pharisees, 39-44, 78, 80, 198, n., 203, 204, 342
Scripture, Holy. Quotations from or references to Biblical writers or books:
  Acts, 84 n., 91 n., 98 n., 100 n., 104 n., 109 n., 114 n., 161 n., 167 n., 219 n., 220 n., 255 n., 309 n., 332-335 nn.
  Amos, 235 n., 335 n.
  Apocalypse, 62 n., 104 n., 255 n., 307-309 nn., 330 n.
  Canticle of Canticles, 176 n.
  Colossians, 31 n., 55 n., 60 n., 62 n., 154 n., 194 n., 208 n., 223 n., 288 n., 297 n., 303 n., 310 n., 315 n., 334 n., 337 n., 355 n.
  1 Corinthians, 21 n., 28 n., 33 n., 35 n., 45 n., 48 n., 50 n., 54 n., 59 n., 61 n., 63-67 nn., 69 n., 71 n., 74 n., 77

380 INDEX

n., 92 n., 100 n., 105 n., 111 n., 115 n., 125 n., 129-131 nn., 135 n., 143 n., 151 n., 160 n., 161 n., 163 n., 166 n., 167 n., 169 n., 170 n., 175-177 nn., 194-197 nn., 202 n., 205 n., 215-217 nn., 223 n., 225 n., 226 n., 228 n., 231 n., 236 n., 264 n., 303 n., 307 n., 315 n., 322 n., 323 n., 325 n., 331 n., 335 n., 341 n., 348 n., 349 n., 351 n., 352 n., 369 n., 370 n.
2 Corinthians, 35 n., 49 n., 62 n., 74 n., 78 n., 83 n., 94 n., 109 n., 151 n., 160 n., 161 n., 168 n., 215 n., 221 n., 228 n., 231 n., 301-305 nn., 312 n., 332 n., 333 n., 345 n., 346 n., 348 n., 355 n., 368 n.
Daniel, 140 n., 270 n.
Deuteronomy, 80 n., 97 n., 139 n.
Ecclesiastes, 21 n., 276 n., 284 n.
Ecclesiasticus, 22 n., 27 n., 28 n,. 50 n., 138 n., 140 n., 156 n., 249 n., 270 n., 273 n.
Ephesians, 44 n., 45 n., 55 n., 62 n., 151 n., 154 n., 167 n., 171 n., 176 n., 208 n., 214 n., 215 n., 224 n., 240 n., 289 n., 294 n., 303 n., 315 n., 320 n., 333 n.
Exodus, 80 n., 84 n., 97 n.,
196 n., 288 n., 297 n., 328 n.
Ezechiel, 55 n.
Galatians, 36 n., 37 n., 44 n., 60 n., 62 n., 74 n., 106 n., 111 n., 123 n., 138 n., 148 n., 175 n., 192 n., 220 n., 228 n., 239 n., 242 n., 245 n., 309 n., 331 n., 361 n., 367 n.
Genesis, 33 n., 48 n., 53 n., 70 n., 77 n., 107 n., 125 n., 140 n., 187 n., 260 n., 265 n., 308 n., 342 n.
Habacuc, 31 n.
Hebrews, 90 n., 135 n., 196 n., 226 n., 236 n., 308 n., 315 n., 328 n., 329 n., 331 n., 355 n.
Isaias, 27, 28 n., 107 n., 123 n., 128 n., 140 n., 145 n., 151 n., 193 n., 199 n., 222 n., 249 n., 307 n., 309 n., 353 n.
James, 50 n., 219 n., 233 n., 234 n., 271 n., 308 n.
Jeremias, 128 n., 145 n., 191 n., 276 n.
Job, 140 n., 328 n.
Joel, 239 n.
John, 23 n., 32 n., 35 n., 47 n., 51 n., 55 n., 63 n., 64 n., 85 n., 91 n., 123 n., 128 n., 129 n., 132 n., 134 n., 139 n., 145 n., 155 n., 158 n., 166 n., 172 n., 177 n., 181 n., 206 n., 213 n., 216 n., 217 n., 271 n., 287 n., 301 n., 303 n.,

INDEX 381

309 n., 313 n., 315 n., 316 n., 318 n., 321 n., 332 n., 336 n., 354 n., 367 n., 370 n.
1 John, 62 n., 99 n., 105 n., 203 n., 248 n., 303 n., 327 n., 332 n., 353 n.
Judges, 331 n.
1 Kings, 217 n.
3 Kings, 91 n.
4 Kings, 91 n., 202 n.
Leviticus, 81 n., 97 n.
Luke, 24 n., 50 n., 55 n., 60 n., 68 n., 90 n., 91 n., 98 n., 100 n., 101 n., 109 n., 125 n., 129 n., 136 n., 142 n., 159 n., 173 n., 196 n., 220 n., 242 n., 243 n., 245 n., 254 n., 273 n., 275 n., 278 n., 279 n., 288 n., 292 n., 293 n., 295-297 nn., 313 n., 315 n., 332 n., 335 n., 370 n.
Malachy, 106 n., 123 n., 331 n.
Mark, 40 n., 55 n., 125 n., 257 n.
Matthew, 20 n., 24 n., 26 n., 35 n., 36 n., 46 n., 47 n., 50 n., 52 n., 56 n., 58 n., 60-63 nn., 75 n., 79 n., 89 n., 96-98 nn., 101-103 nn., 108 n., 109 n., 111 n., 113 n., 114 n., 120 n., 128-130 nn., 132-134 nn., 136 n., 137 n., 140 n., 146 n., 147 n., 149 n., 150 n., 153 n., 158 n., 165-167 nn., 169 n., 171 n., 172 n., 180 n., 181 n., 185-188 nn., 190 n., 191 n., 197 n., 199 n., 203 n., 204 n., 212-257 *passim*, 265 n., 266 n., 268 n., 271 n., 272 n., 275 n., 280 n., 287 n., 288 n., 293-299 nn., 301 n., 302 n., 305 n., 309 n., 313 n., 314 n., 325 n., 328 n., 330 n., 342 n., 347 n., 355 n., 357 n., 363-367 nn., 369 n., 370 n.
Numbers, 76 n., 97 n.
Osee, 108 n., 308 n.
Paralipomenon, 225 n.
1 Peter, 62 n., 103 n., 331 n.
Philippians, 33 n., 112 n., 145 n., 223 n., 229 n., 231 n., 309 n., 331 n., 332 n., 341 n., 346 n., 347 n., 349 n., 355 n.
Proverbs, 28 n., 50 n., 90 n., 115 n., 206 n., 364 n.
Psalms, 21 n., 22 n., 28 n., 31 n., 36 n., 48 n., 50 n., 51 n., 85 n., 97-99 nn., 110 n., 119 n., 123 n., 125 n., 127 n., 135 n., 146 n., 147 n., 152 n., 153 n., 184 n., 197 n., 205 n., 207 n., 213 n., 216 n., 223-226 nn., 234 n., 237 n., 240 n., 241 n., 260 n., 261 n., 269 n., 272 n., 277 n., 288 n., 291 n., 307 n., 309 n., 312 n., 313 n., 320 n., 328 n., 332 n., 345 n., 346 n., 360 n., 368 n.
Romans, 22 n., 26 n., 27 n., 31 n., 49 n., 50 n., 56 n., 59 n., 69 n., 74 n., 83 n., 98 n., 103 n., 104 n., 106 n.,

111 n., 115 n., 123 n., 130 n., 131 n., 141 n., 144 n., 147-149 nn., 153 n., 156 n., 168 n., 170 n., 201 n., 216 n., 225 n., 228 n., 231 n., 240 n., 276 n., 283 n., 287 n., 307 n., 309 n., 310 n., 318 n., 328 n., 331 n., 332 n., 342 n., 353 n., 355 n., 367 n., 368 n.
1 Thessalonians, 129 n., 167 n., 347 n., 355 n.
2 Thessalonians, 83 n., 145 n., 147 n., 167 n., 355 n.
1 Timothy, 101 n., 152 n., 170 n., 207 n., 241 n., 281-283 nn., 289 n., 329 n., 359 n., 360 n.
2 Timothy, 98 n., 136 n., 180 n., 197 n., 302 n., 308 n., 333 n.
Titus, 249 n., 294 n.
Tobias, 329 n.
Wisdom, 23 n., 106 n., 107 n., 156 n., 216 n., 271 n., 370 n.

Septuagint, 8, 9, 99
Simplicity of heart, 23, 109, 176; *see* Beatitudes
Simon, R., 11 n.

Simon Magus, 333
Sloth, 293-294
Soul, 63, 157-158, 182 n.
Stephen St., 100, 105, 293 n., 318
Susanna, 140
Syriac, 7

Temptation, 138-144, 148, 193, 256-257, 276 n.
Tertullian, 126 n., 172 n., 173 n.
Thomas Aquinas, St., 126 n.
Tichonius, 30 n.
Tribulation (misery, grief), 22, 23, 25, 26, 29-31, 147, 168, 312, 346, 353.; *see* Beatitudes; Martyrs; Persecution

Understanding, 27, 28, 148

Valerius, Bishop, 12, 13
Van Lierde, 30 n.
Virgin Mary, 317
Vogels, H. J., 7 n.
Vulgate, 8, 9, 139 n., 167 n., 335 n., 342 n., 352 n.

Will, 185 n., 193
Wisdom, 24, 27, 28, 148, 197

www.ingramcontent.com/pod-product-compliance
Lightning Source LLC
Chambersburg PA
CBHW030527010526
44110CB00048B/661